Intervening With Drug-Involved Youth

Intervening With Drug-Involved Youth

Clyde B. McCoy
Lisa R. Metsch
James A. Inciardi
editors

 SAGE Publications
International Educational and Professional Publisher
Thousand Oaks   London   New Delhi

For information address:

SAGE Publications, Inc.
2455 Teller Road
Thousand Oaks, California 91320
E-mail: order@sagepub.com

SAGE Publications Ltd.
6 Bonhill Street
London EC2A 4PU
United Kingdom

SAGE Publications India Pvt. Ltd.
M-32 Market
Greater Kailash I
New Delhi 110 048 India

Printed in the United States of America

Library of Congress Cataloging-in-Publication Data

Main entry under title:

Intervening with drug-involved youth / editors: Clyde B. McCoy, Lisa R. Metsch, James A. Inciardi.
    p.   cm.
   Includes bibliographical references and index.
   ISBN 0-8039-7371-3 (cloth).—ISBN 0-8039-7372-1 (pbk).
    1. Youth—Drug use—United States. 2. Drug abuse—United
States—Prevention. 3. Youth—Drug use. 4. Drug abuse—Prevention.
I. McCoy, Clyde B., 1941- .II. Metsch, Lisa R. III. Inciardi, James A.
HV5824.Y68I56 1996
362.29′17′0835—dc20   96-10052

This book is printed on acid-free paper.

96 97 98 99 10 9 8 7 6 5 4 3 2 1

Sage Production Editor: Vicki Baker   Sage Typesetter: Marion Warren

Contents

Part 4: International Perspectives

Preface

The roots of drug abuse are obscure and are probably buried in antiquity. The use of opium dates back at least to the ancient Greeks, and references to marijuana appear in early Persian, Hindu, Greek, Arab, and Chinese writings. Similarly, when the Spanish conquistador Francisco Pizarro stumbled on the Inca empire in 1531, the chewing of coca had already been in local mythology for centuries. Even in the United States, a nation with a relatively short history, the beginnings of drug abuse, particularly among youthful populations, remain somewhat mysterious.

The use of drugs (other than alcohol) in this country for the enhancement of pleasure and performance probably began sometime in the early 18th century. During those years, medicinal opium was introduced and quickly became popular because of its euphoric and anesthetic properties. The first preparation, imported from England in 1709 and sold under the name of Dover's Powder, was a patent medicine containing opium (Cook & Martin, 1951). The introduction of Dover's Powder apparently started a trend. By the latter part of the 18th century, the so-called "patent" medicines (which were actually unpatented to keep their contents secret) containing opium were readily available throughout urban and rural America. They were sold in pharmacies, groceries, and general stores, at traveling medicine shows, and through the mail. As "home remedies," they were seductively advertised as "painkillers," "cough mixtures," "soothing syrups," "consumption cures," and "women's friends." Others were promoted for the treatment of such varied ailments as diarrhea, dysentery, colds, fever, teething, cholera, rheumatism, pelvic disorders, athlete's foot, and even baldness and cancer.

In 1803, the chief alkaloid of opium was isolated (Jaffe & Martin, 1970, p. 245), and named *morphine*. Its discovery had profound effects on medicine, for morphine was, and still is, the greatest single pain reliever the world has ever known. Then the hypodermic syringe was invented, and the use of morphine by injection in military medicine during the Civil War and Franco-Prussian War granted the procedure legitimacy and familiarity to both physicians and the public (Bartholow, 1891). Furthermore, hypodermic medication had its pragmatic aspects: It brought quick local relief, its dosage could be regulated, and it was effective when oral medication was impractical. The regimen, however, was used promiscuously, for many physicians were anxious to illustrate their ability to quell the pain suffered by their patients, who, in turn, expected instant relief from discomfort (Kane, 1880, p. 5).

There is virtually no historical evidence of the abuse of patent medicines and morphine by needle among juveniles during this era. By contrast, however, chloroform and ether went through a cycle of nonmedical appeal beginning in the 1850s (Morgan, 1981, p. 13). Numerous press and scientific reports indicated that both drugs were attractive to youths, particularly to those in high society bent on getting intoxicated without suffering a hangover (see Browning, 1885; Clark, 1884; Hubbard, 1881, p. 257).

As the uncontrolled use of opium in patent medicines and morphine by injection increased in adult populations, the practice of opium smoking also became prevalent. It was introduced by the Chinese laborers who had been imported to build the railroads and work the mines in the trans-Mississippi West. It was estimated that by 1875 opium smoking had become extremely widespread, particularly among prostitutes, gamblers, and other denizens of the underworld, but also among more "respectable" men and women of the middle and upper classes (Terry & Pellens, 1928, p. 73). Interestingly, opium smoking appeared to be the first drug abuse situation in the United States in which critics of the practice used the welfare of youth as a major reason for regulation (Morgan, 1981, p. 37). However, it is unclear in the literature whether the smoking of opium was actually widespread or a real problem among 19th-century youth.

Beyond opium and morphine, the patent medicine industry branched out even further in the 1880s and 1890s, introducing new potentially abusable drugs. In 1883, for example, some two decades after cocaine in its pure form was isolated from the coca leaf, a German military physician secured a supply of the drug and issued it to Bavarian soldiers during maneuvers. He noted the beneficial effects of cocaine, particularly its ability to suppress fatigue. Among those who read about the Bavarian experience was a struggling young Viennese neurologist, Sigmund Freud. Suffering from chronic fatigue, depression, and various neurotic symptoms, Freud obtained a measure of cocaine and tried it himself. Finding the initial results to be quite favorable, Freud decided that cocaine was a "magical drug" (Jones, 1953, p. 81). By the close of the 1880s, however, Freud and the others who had praised cocaine as an all-purpose drug began to withdraw their support for it in light of an increasing number of reports of compulsive use and undesirable side effects. Yet by 1890, the patent medicine industry in the United States had also discovered the benefits of the unregulated use of cocaine. The industry quickly added the drug to its reservoir of home remedies, touting it as helpful not only for everything from alcoholism to venereal disease but also as a cure for addiction to other patent medicines.

A final 19th-century entry into the pharmacopoeia of abusable drugs first appeared in 1874 with the development of diacetylmorphine (Wright, 1874, p. 1031). Some 24 years later, in 1898, the pharmacologist Heinrich Dreser reported on a series of experiments he had conducted with diacetylmorphine for Friedrich Bayer and Company of Elberfeld, Germany, noting that the drug was highly effective in the treatment of coughs, chest pains, and the discomforts associated with pneumonia and tuberculosis. Dreser's commentary received immediate notice, for it had come at a time when antibiotics were still unknown and pneumonia and tuberculosis were among the leading causes of death. He claimed that diacetylmorphine had a stronger sedative effect on respiration than morphine, that therapeutic relief came quickly, and that the potential for a fatal overdose was almost nil. In response to such favorable reports, Bayer and Company began marketing diacetylmorphine, under the trade name of Heroin (Berridge & Edwards, 1987, pp. xix-xx).

Estimates as to the number of individuals actually addicted to drugs at the close of the 19th century tended to be compiled rather loosely and ranged as high as 3 million (Morgan, 1974; Terry & Pellens, 1928, pp. 1-20). Interestingly, discussions of addiction among youth during these emerging years of America's drug problem were quite rare. What the literature suggests is that narcotic addiction and drug abuse were concentrated in adult populations of middle- and working-class self-medicators and in the underworld predator populations of professional thieves, gamblers, and prostitutes (see Trebach & Inciardi, 1993, p. 185). At the same time, however, a few small-scale, retrospective studies documented that drug abuse among youth was not unknown. For example, in a study of 100 inmates at California's San Quentin Prison early in the 20th century, 51% of those reporting drug abuse as a factor contributing to their criminal careers indicated that they had started drug use as minors. Most had initiated drug use during late adolescence, and the drug of choice was typically smokable opium (Stanley, 1918).

Drug abuse and addiction began to decline dramatically after the turn of the 20th century for a variety of reasons. First, both the medical and the religious communities agitated against the haphazard use of narcotics, defining much of it as a moral disease. For many, the sheer force of social stigma and pressure served to alter their use of drugs (Morgan, 1974). Second, the passage of the Pure Food and Drug Act in 1906 initiated a decline of the patent medicine industry, further reducing the number of narcotics and cocaine users. Third, by 1912 most state governments had enacted legislative controls over the dispensing and sale of narcotics, and the federal government followed suit in 1914 (Inciardi, 1992, pp. 11-18). For the better part of the early 1920s through the late 1940s, drug abuse remained hidden in the submerged regions of vice and crime, the netherworlds of the jazz scene, and the bohemias of the avant-garde.

Within a few years after the close of World War II, addiction to heroin was noticed in a number of America's inner cities, primarily in New York. By the opening years of the 1950s, the prevailing image of drug use was one of heroin addiction on the streets of the urban ghetto.

In the popular media of the time, a rather curious image of the heroin scene was offered. *Time, Life, Newsweek,* and other major periodicals spoke of how teenagers jaded with marijuana had found greater thrills in heroin. For most, the pattern of initiation had been the same. They had begun with marijuana, the use of which had become a fad in the slums. Then, enticed in schoolyards by brazen Mafia pushers dressed in dark suits, white ties, and wide-brimmed hats, they received their first dose of heroin for free. By then, however, it was too late: Their fate had been sealed, and they were already addicted (see Anslinger, 1951; "Children in Peril," 1951; "Heroin and Adolescents," 1951;

"High and Light," 1951; "Narcotics: An Ever-Growing Problem," 1951; "Narcotics and Youth," 1950; "Narcotics: Degradation in New York" 1951; "New York Wakes Up," 1951; Salisbury, 1951; "The White Stuff," 1951). Or as a saying of the 1950s went, "It's so good, don't even try it once!"

Within the scientific community, the literature and research presented a dramatically different view. Like the mass media reports, most explanations of drug addiction focused on heroin in the inner city. Yet by contrast, young addicts were believed to be either psychotic or neurotic casualties for whom drugs provided relief from anxiety and a means for withdrawing from the stress of daily struggle in the slums. Among the more celebrated studies of the period was *The Road to H,* by the psychologist Isador Chein and colleagues (Chein, Gerard, Lee, & Rosenfeld, 1964). Concerning youthful addiction in New York City, Chein et al. concluded:

> The evidence indicated that all addicts suffer from deep-rooted personality disorders. Although psychiatric diagnoses are apt to vary, a particular set of symptoms seems to be common to most juvenile addicts. They are not able to enter into prolonged, close, friendly relations with either peers or adults; they have difficulties in assuming a masculine role; they are frequently overcome by a sense of futility, expectations of failure, and general depression; they are easily frustrated and made anxious, and they find frustrations and anxiety intolerable. (p. 14)

By focusing on such problems as "weak ego functioning," "defective superego," and "inadequate masculine identification," Chein et al. were suggesting the notion of a psychological predisposition to drug use—in other words, an "addiction-prone personality." They went on to imply that the series of predispositions could be traced to the addict's family experiences. If the youth received too much love or not enough, or if the parents were overwhelming in terms of their affection or indulgence, then the child would develop inadequately. As a result, the youth would probably be unable to withstand pain and discomfort, to cope with the complexities of life in the neighborhood and community, to assess reality correctly, and to feel competent around others of more varied social experiences. Although this has certainly been the case over the years with a number of addicts, it does not explain all addiction. Chein et al. concluded, however, that this type of youth would be more prone to trying drugs than others of more conventional family backgrounds.

The prevailing portrait of addiction in the scientific community, then, was one of passive adaptation to stress. Drugs allowed the user to experience fulfillment and the satiation of physical and emotional needs. This general view was also supported by sociological attempts to explain the broader concepts of deviance and delinquency. Given this predisposition, consider what became known in the literature as the "double-failure" hypothesis. According to sociologists Richard A. Cloward and Lloyd E. Ohlin (1960, pp. 178-186), double failures were inner-city youths who were unable to succeed in either the gang subculture or the wider legitimate culture. They embraced drugs, in turn, as a way of finding a place for themselves in society.

For those who lived in the ghetto, worked in the ghetto, took drugs in the ghetto, policed the ghetto, or in some other fashion actively observed or participated in ghetto life, the "addiction-prone personality," "double failure," and other escapist theories of addiction were found absurd. The conduct of most addicts at the time appeared to be anything but an escape from life. Much of their time was spent in drug-seeking behaviors, in meaningful activities and relationships on the street corners surrounding the economic institutions of heroin distribution. As the late urban anthropologist Edward Preble once put it, they were "taking care of business":

> The brief moments of euphoria after each administration of a small amount of heroin constitute a small fraction of their daily lives. The rest of the time they are aggressively pursuing a career that is exciting, challenging, adventurous, and rewarding. They are always on the move and must be alert, flexible, and resourceful. The surest way to identify heroin users in a slum neighborhood is to observe the way people walk. The heroin user walks with a fast, purposeful stride, as if he is late for an important appointment—indeed, he is. He is *hustling* [robbing or stealing], trying to sell stolen goods, avoiding the police, looking for a heroin dealer with a good *bag* [the street retail unit of heroin], coming back from *copping* [buying heroin], looking for a safe place to take the drug, or looking for someone who *beat* [cheated] him—among other things. (Preble & Casey, 1969, p. 2)

Although one could argue with the interpretations of the causes of heroin use offered by Chein et al. in *The Road to H,* their work was nevertheless groundbreaking. It was the first large-scale, systematic study of juvenile drug use in the United States and represented the starting point for much of the subsequent research. Furthermore, it went a long way to debunk the Mafia-man/schoolyard theory of heroin initiation:

> Contrary to popular belief, the great majority of juvenile regular users are not initiated into drug use by an adult pusher; even those who are, are not necessarily

persuaded by the adult pusher. Some boys seek out even their initial dose on their own. Most take their first dose of heroin, free, in the company of one or more boys of their own age—in the home of one of the boys, on the street, on a roof, or in a cellar—rarely on school property. Frequently, the first occasion arises just before a dance or party, probably for the same reason that some of their peers brace themselves with one or more shots of alcohol, as a source of poise and courage. (Chein et al., 1964, p. 12)

As America moved through the 1960s and into the 1970s, the juvenile drug scene changed dramatically from one of heroin in the inner city to one of a wide variety of drugs that seemed to be everywhere. Among white middle-class students, there was extensive marijuana use, as well as involvement with such non-narcotic drugs as barbiturates, tranquilizers, and amphetamines. There also was use of LSD and other hallucinogenic drugs, first in the "hippie" counterculture and then elsewhere.

The explanations of youthful drug use were almost as abundant as the number of users. One interpretation suggested that drug use was a form of purposive dissent and protest characteristic of a new breed of young people who conformed to a unique "hang-loose" ethic:

One of the fundamental characteristics of the "hang-loose" ethic is that it is irreverent. It repudiates or at least questions such cornerstones of conventional society as Christianity, "my country right or wrong," the sanctity of marriage and premarital chastity, the accumulation of wealth, and the right or even competence of parents, the schools, and the government to head and make decisions for everyone—in sum, the Establishment. (Simmons & Winograd, 1966, p. 12)

An alternative explanation maintained that there were two subgroups of youthful drug users, "heads" and "seekers" (Keniston, 1968). "Heads" were those who genuinely felt alienated from society, whereas "seekers" were better-than-average students who were determined to find some meaning to life. Still another explanation was simply that ours was "the addicted society," that through drugs, millions were searching for "instant enlightenment," and that drug taking and drug seeking would persist as continuing facts of American social life (Farber, 1966; Fort, 1969; Geller & Boas, 1969).

Since the 1970s, although the drugs of choice have often changed and the numbers using drugs have varied from year to year, a few broad populations of users have tended to dominate the youthful drug scene. First, there is a fairly large population of juveniles from all levels of society, the great majority of whom are not psychologically disturbed and who tend to avoid such "hard" drugs as heroin and cocaine (including crack). Much of their drug use is a response to their environment, a part of adolescent peer group activity, and an affirmation of their own values. There are many subtypes in this group as well, including numerous experimenters and social recreational users for whom drug use is but an incidental part of their lives. At the same time, there are smaller populations of street users, from the inner cities and elsewhere, many of whom are addicted to drugs and are members of drug subcultures. And finally, there are many others among whom alcohol use is pervasive and often debilitating or among whom drinking and drug use occur concomitantly.

The 10 chapters that follow, distributed among four broad sections, discuss the youthful drug scene in the 1990s in detail, focusing on etiology and epidemiology combined with prevention and intervention issues. Part 1, composed of three chapters, addresses etiological and epidemiologic issues. In the opening essay, "The Epidemiology of Drug Use Among American Youth," Lana D. Harrison and Anne E. Pottieger present an historical and empirical overview of drug use among youth from the 1970s through the 1990s, providing readers with basic knowledge about patterns, correlates, and consequences of adolescent drug abuse. In "Risk and Protective Factors for Drug Use," Judith S. Brook and David W. Brook explore how some youths become involved with drugs, whereas others manage to avoid them. The authors focus on the many causes of drug abuse, particularly the influences of peers, family, social environments, and economic opportunities and necessities, as well as biological factors and the interrelationships among all of these dimensions. The final chapter in this section, "Modeling Adolescent Health Behavior" by Lilly M. Langer, reviews both classical and contemporary theories on how adolescents make decisions about drugs and health and how these influence their behaviors about drugs.

Part 2 examines drug abuse prevention initiatives in the United States that target youth populations. Mario A. Orlandi's "Prevention Technologies for Drug-Involved Youth" reviews a number of strategies designed to prevent and/or reduce drug use, with a specific focus on both school- and community-based programs. "DARE," by Richard R. Clayton, Carl G. Leukefeld, Nancy Grant Harrington, and Anne Cattarello, discusses what is perhaps the most popular and widely established drug prevention program in the world: Drug Abuse Resistance Education (DARE). The authors review the reasons for DARE's popularity and present research on its effectiveness. The final prevention chapter, "Religious Belief and the Initiation and Prevention of Drug Use Among Youth," by Duane C. McBride, Patricia B. Mutch, and Dale D. Chitwood, offers some important insights into how religion affects the lives of many young people. The chapter examines religious perspectives from the world's three major monotheistic religions (Judaism, Christianity, and Islam), reviews selected research findings on religiosity and drug use, and examines data on reasons for alcohol and drug abstinence among students.

Part 3 addresses treatment initiatives. Historically, drug treatment programs have been aimed toward adult, particularly male, drug users. The particular needs of adolescents are often unrecognized and unaddressed in treatment services. The two chapters in this section examine alternative approaches to the range of problems facing drug-involved youth. "Juvenile Health Service Centers: An Exciting Opportunity to Intervene With Drug-Involved and Other High-Risk Youth," by Richard Dembo and James E. Rivers, describes the experience of implementing and evaluating the Hillsborough County (Tampa, Florida) Juvenile Assessment Center, which serves as a national model for intervening with high-risk youth who are both drug involved and criminally involved. "Issues and Intervention: Substance Abuse Treatment for Adolescents Using a Modified Therapeutic Community Model," by Sally J. Stevens, Naya Arbiter, Rod Mullen, and Bridget Murphy, describes the components of an Arizona-based adolescent therapeutic community.

Part 4 examines drug-involved youth in two international settings. "Drug Use, HIV Risks, and Prevention/Intervention Strategies Among Street Youths in Rio de Janeiro, Brazil," by Hilary L. Surratt and James A. Inciardi, describes the problems of street children living in Rio de Janeiro. The problems include poverty, violence, drug use, and involvement in high-risk behaviors, including prostitution. Finally, in "Drug Use and HIV Among Youth in Manipur, India," by Swarup Sarkar, Anindya Chatterjee, Clyde B. McCoy, Abu S. Abdul-Quader, Lisa R. Metsch, and Robert S. Anwyl, details how Manipur, India, known for centuries as a world cultural center, has been facing a major emergence of drug use, particularly heroin, among its youth.

Special thanks go to Heather McAnany of the University of Miami for all her work in helping us prepare this book.

Clyde B. McCoy
Lisa R. Metsch
James A. Inciardi

References

Anslinger, H. J. (1951, October). The facts about our teenage drug addicts. *Reader's Digest,* pp. 137-140.

Bartholow, R. (1891). *A manual of hypodermatic medication.* Philadelphia: J. B. Lippincott.

Berridge, V., & Edwards, G. (1987). *Opium and the people: Opiate use in nineteenth-century England.* New Haven, CT: Yale University Press.

Browning, A. G. (1885). A new habit. *Medical Record, 27,* 452-545.

Chein, I., Gerard, D. L., Lee, R. S., & Rosenfeld, E. (1964). *The road to H: Narcotics, juvenile delinquency, and social policy.* New York: Basic Books.

Children in peril. (1951, June 11). *Life,* pp. 116, 119-122.

Clark, J. E. (1884). The chloroform habit. *Detroit Lancet, 9,* 254-256.

Cloward, R. A., & Ohlin, L. E. (1960). *Delinquency and opportunity.* New York: Free Press.

Cook, E. F., & Martin, E. W. (1951). *Remington's practice of pharmacy.* Easton, PA: Mack.

Farber, L. (1966, December 11). Ours is the addicted society. *New York Times Magazine,* p. 43.

Fort, J. (1969). *The pleasure seekers: The drug crisis, youth, and society.* New York: Grove.

Geller, A., & Boas, M. (1969). *The drug beat.* New York: McGraw-Hill.

Heroin and adolescents. (1951, August 13). *Newsweek,* p. 50.

High and light. (1951, February 26). *Time,* p. 24.

Hubbard, F. H. (1881). *The opium habit and alcoholism.* New York: A. S. Barnes.

Inciardi, J. A. (1992). *The war on drugs II: The continuing epic of heroin, cocaine, crack, crime, AIDS, and public policy.* Mountain View, CA: Mayfield.

Jaffe, J. H., & Martin, W. R. (1970). Opioid analgesics and antagonists. In L. S. Goodman, A. Gilman, T. W. Rall, & P. Taylor (Eds.), *The pharmacological basis of therapeutics* (8th ed., pp. 485-521). New York: Pergamon.

Jones, E. (1953). *The life and work of Sigmund Freud* (Vol. 1). New York: Basic Books.

Kane, H. H. (1880). *The hypodermic injection of morphia.* New York: C. L. Bermingham.

Keniston, K. (1968). Heads and seekers: Drugs on campus, countercultures, and American society. In J. N. McGrath & F. R. Scarpitti (Eds.), *Youth and drugs* (pp. 118-136). Skokie, IL: Scott, Foresman.

Morgan, H. W. (1974). *Yesterday's addicts: American society and drug abuse, 1865-1920.* Norman: University of Oklahoma Press.

Morgan, H. W. (1981). *Drugs in America: A social history, 1800-1980.* Syracuse, NY: Syracuse University Press.

Narcotics: An ever-growing problem. (1951, June 11). *Newsweek,* pp. 26-27.

Narcotics and youth. (1950, November 20). *Newsweek,* pp. 57-58.

Narcotics: Degradation in New York. (1951, June 25). *Newsweek,* pp. 19-29.

New York wakes up to find 15,000 teen-age dope addicts. (1951, January 29). *Newsweek,* pp. 23-24.

Preble, E., & Casey, J. J. (1969). Taking care of business: The heroin user's life on the street. *International Journal of the Addictions, 4,* 1-24.

Salisbury, K. (1951, September 17). The junk war. *Newsweek,* p. 60.

Simmons, J. L., & Winograd, B. (1966). *It's happening: A portrait of the youth scene today.* Santa Barbara, CA: Marc-Laid.

Stanley, L. L. (1918). Morphinism and crime. *Journal of the American Institute of Criminal Law and Criminology, 8,* 749-756.

Terry, C. E., & Pellens, M. (1928). *The opium problem.* New York: Bureau of Social Hygiene.

Trebach, A. S., & Inciardi, J. A. (1993). *Legalize it? Debating American drug policy.* Washington, DC: American University Press.

The white stuff. (1951, May 7). *Time,* pp. 82, 85.

Wright, C. R. A. (1874). On the action of organic acids and their anhydrides on the natural alkaloids. *Journal of the Chemical Society, 12.*

PART 1

The Scope of the Problem

1

The Epidemiology of Drug Use Among American Youth

Lana D. Harrison
Anne E. Pottieger

Epidemiology is the study of the distribution and determinants of health-related states or events in a specified population and the application of this study to the control and prevention of health problems (Last, 1988). Having its roots in ancient Greece, epidemiology emerged as the method to identify the source of illness by characterizing its occurrence in terms of person, place, and time. The application of epidemiology to the study of drug use and drug problems is relatively recent, becoming prominent with the dramatic upsurge in illicit drug use among youth in the late 1960s and early 1970s (Greene, 1974; Hughes, Senay, & Parker, 1972; Musto, 1973). Medical epidemiologists have studied drug use as a public health problem, and similar investigations have been conducted by social scientists viewing drug use as a psychiatric and behavioral problem (de Alarcon, 1985; Robins, 1985).

Epidemiological methods are designed to detect causal associations between a disease, or a problematic health condition or event, and the characteristics of individuals and their environment that contributed to the problem. These personal and environmental characteristics are studied for two major reasons. First, a particular segment of the population may be at greater risk for contracting a particular health problem. Second, etiological or causal evidence may be detected and preventive measures developed. Epidemiology does not produce an explanation for the problem being studied, although sometimes it points to potential explanations. The contributions of epidemiology to our understanding of drug problems in particular are measurement and analysis of (a) drug use levels and patterns, (b) correlates of drug use such as attitudes about drugs, and (c) the health-related consequences of drug use or abuse. When such data are collected at regular intervals over a long enough period, it is possible to examine trends in the way drug use behaviors, correlates, and consequences change over time. The purpose of this chapter is to examine drug use among youth in the United States, using descriptive epidemiological prevalence and trend data from national surveys, and to explore some of the possible reasons for the increases and decreases in drug use among youth.

History of Illicit Drug Use Among Youth

The first national surveys on illicit drug use were telephone polls of college students conducted by the Gallup Organization.[1] In 1967, 5% of college students reported some marijuana use, and 1% indicated that they had tried LSD. By 1969, these numbers had quadrupled to 22% and 4%, respectively. And by 1971, fully half (51%) of all college students reported using marijuana sometime in their lifetime, 41% had used in the past year, and 30% had used in the past 30 days. Some experience with hallucinogens was reported by 18%, 22% had tried amphetamines, 15% had tried barbiturates, 7% had tried cocaine, and 2% had tried heroin. These large, rapid increases in drug usage indicated that American youth were in the throes of an epidemic.

The first national survey of drug use in the "general population" was conducted under the auspices of the National Commission on Marihuana and Drug Abuse in 1971. The commission determined that "marihuana became a common form of recreation for many middle and upper class college youth in the mid-1960s. The trend spread across the country, into the colleges and high schools and into the affluent suburbs as well" (National Commission, 1972, p. 7). In the commission's 1971 survey, 14% of youth (ages 12 to 17) reported trying marijuana, as did 15% of adults (ages 18 and older). About 5% of both youth and adults indicated some lifetime use of a hallucinogen.

The general classes of sedatives, stimulants, and tranquilizers had been used (for other than medical reasons) by 6% of youth and 7% of adults. Some experience with cocaine was reported by 1.5% of youth and 3% of adults, and 0.6% of youth and 1.3% of the adults reported heroin use. About half (53%) the adults and an astounding quarter (24%) of youth reported consuming alcohol in the week prior to the survey. This led the commission to conclude that the most widely used mood altering substance in American was alcohol. Perhaps the major contribution of this first national study of drug use was to dispel some of the hysteria in the nation that all kids were "on drugs." However, illicit drug use had obviously grown from a deviant, isolated behavior practiced by marginalized members of society to a behavior that was much more mainstream, particularly with regard to youth, and particularly with regard to marijuana. Marijuana was and continues to be the most widely used of the illicit drugs in the United States.

Although the National Commission stated that it did not understand the causal connections between historical changes and the growth in marijuana use among youth, it did propose to illuminate some of the societal changes that might have contributed to the increase. First, it noted that American institutions had declined in their capacity to "help the individual find his place in society" (p. 19). Work had dwindled in importance, leisure time had increased, and individuals were unable to find meaning in either work or recreational pursuits. Further, advances were occurring so quickly in society that people could not envision the future. The commission concluded that this led to living in the present and looking for immediate gratification. Another historical force identified by the commission was the loss of a sense of community—a sense of belonging. The push toward urbanization and the mobility of the American family resulted in a more insular orientation without the protection of home and family. Increasing affluence maximized individual choice, developing simultaneously with the previously mentioned social trends to undermine traditional value systems. "All of these social trends have their most potent impact on young people who are just beginning to develop their values, beliefs and commitments" (p. 21). For youth, without a "sense of direction, the result is restlessness, boredom and an increase in the likelihood of present-oriented choices. Self-destructive drug-taking is one form such behavior may take" (p. 22).

An analysis by McGlothlin (1975) provided another historical assessment. McGlothlin dated the upsurge in marijuana use back to the 1950s and pointed out that even in the 1950s avant-garde young adults were experimenting with LSD and other hallucinogens to expand their consciousness and heighten self-understanding. McGlothlin asserted that by about 1967, LSD "trips" were adopted as a unifying principle by hippie communities. Marijuana was also embraced by the hippies, but it was viewed as little more than a mood modifier. McGlothlin felt it was used as a symbol of protest and an expression of rebellion, especially against the Vietnam war.

The rise of the "counterculture" is also often linked to the youthful drug epidemic. Johnston (1973) defined the counterculture as

> a class of young people who are "turned off" by many American institutions: the current system of government, the educational establishment, the organization-man style of life, etc. Those in the counter-culture are said to be repulsed by American outer-directedness and to turn inward for their satisfactions. Drugs, it is alleged, provide some of the vehicles for that journey. (pp. 181-182)

Johnston identified two attitudinal measures indicative of the counterculture movement and their relationship to drug use: alienation from government and anti-Vietnam War sentiment. He found a dramatic and parallel relationship between the two measures and levels of drug use, with those most alienated and professing the greatest amount of disagreement with U.S. policy in Vietnam much more likely to use illicit drugs. He also found a strong relationship between delinquency and all forms of drug use, both licit and illicit. There was virtually no relationship between alienation and the use of either heroin or the licit drugs, alcohol and tobacco.

Perhaps the largest structural change propelling the epidemic, however, was the maturing of the baby boom generation (Harrison, 1988). The baby boom encompasses those born between 1946 and 1964, years when the U.S. birthrate was dramatically larger than usual; the peak year of the boom was 1957. The baby boomers were the youth who experienced the initiation and spread of the drug epidemic. These youths were subjected to a tremendous amount of political turmoil throughout the 1960s—the civil rights movement, the Vietnam war, and the assassination of key political leaders. The country had experienced political turmoil before, but never in an age when virtually the entire population could get almost instantaneous news reports of protests, riots, battles, and other evidence that the country was falling apart at the seams (Harrison, 1988). However, perhaps more important than the coverage and speed of news was that the boomers were the largest generation ever and were reaching adulthood during this period. Youth have always been the harbingers of change. "Because youth is the messenger, any increase in the number of youth in society carries with it the potential for activating those forces [of social change]" (Jones, 1980, p. 115).

It is not obvious why this generation of youth embraced marijuana rather than alcohol or a different illicit drug. One likely attraction of marijuana was its bohemian historical legacy and the symbolism attached to its use. It symbolized dissatisfaction with the current social order, from dissent against the Vietnam War to a more general rebellion/alienation factor manifested in defiance of the law. Another reason that marijuana in particular rose to epidemic levels is the nature of the drug itself. Compared to other available drugs, marijuana is a relatively benign euphoriant. It entails a low risk for physical or psychological dependence, the euphoria it produces is mild, the high is relatively short-lived, and youth were able to integrate its use into a wide variety of settings (Harrison, 1988). Most other drugs were not reasonable substitutes because their effects are longer term and/or more intense, with consequently greater risk of physical incapacitation and/or addiction. Also, marijuana was most commonly used in a group situation, so it helped to solidify youths' identity and camaraderie with other youth. Although alcohol also can be used in a group setting, it did not have the historical symbolism of societal rejection attached to it. The increasing level of affluence in the country allowed many youth to extend their adolescence by attending college. And in colleges and universities across the country, youth were finding solidarity in questioning the social order and lighting up in protest.

Current Use Patterns

The National Commission's small 1971 study and its somewhat larger 1972 follow-up were the start of what is now referred to as the National Household Survey on Drug Abuse (NHSDA). Since 1974, the NHSDA has been conducted at 1- to 3-year intervals on a representative sample of the household population aged 12 and older; it thus excludes persons in institutions, including colleges, prisons, the armed forces, hospitals, and residential drug treatment programs. The 1994 survey (Substance Abuse Mental Health Service Administration [SAMHSA], 1995) included 17,809 individuals, 4,698 of whom were 12 to 17 years old. In 1994, just over a third (37.6%) of the population aged 12 and older reported at least one occasion of illicit drug use in their lifetimes, 12.4% reported some use in the past year, and 5.8% reported use in the past month. The most frequently used illicit drug was marijuana, with 34.1% lifetime prevalence, 9.2% past-year prevalence, and 4.7% past-month prevalence. The lifetime prevalence rate for cocaine was 9.7%, with annual prevalence at 1.9% and past-month prevalence at 0.6%. As Figure 1.1 shows, alcohol and tobacco were used at much higher rates than any of the illicit drugs. Five out of six people (84.2%) reported drinking alcohol in their lifetimes, 66.9% drank in the past year, and 52.6% drank in the past month. Some 71.2% of the population had smoked cigarettes in their lifetimes, with 28.1% reporting smoking in the past year and 23.4% in the past month. (See SAMHSA, 1995, for a more complete description of the NHSDA and 1994 survey results.)

The NHSDA found a strong linear relationship between age and drug use up to about age 21. Figure 1.2 shows the 1994 past-month prevalence rates for alcohol, cigarettes, any illicit drug, marijuana, cocaine, and inhalants among 12- to 13-year-olds, 14- to 15-year-olds, 16- to 17-year-olds, 18- to 21-year-olds, 22- to 25-year-olds, 26- to 34-year-olds, and those aged 35 and older. Figure 1.2 shows that the prevalence rates generally increase by age to a high point among 18- to 21-year-olds. Prevalence rates generally start to decline after age 21. The one exception to the overall pattern is found for inhalants, with the highest rates among 16- to 17-year-olds. Notice that the second highest prevalence rates for past-month inhalant use are found among 12- to 13-year-olds. The prevalence of inhalants starts to decrease after age 17, with the highest prevalence rates evident among the youngest age groups. The odd age distribution for inhalant use probably has two causes. First, compared to older youth, younger children have more difficulty in acquiring either illicit drugs or alcohol and tobacco. They are therefore more attracted to inhalants, given that most of these substances are legal products found around the home, such as glues, aerosols, solvents, and butane. Second, unlike most other drug types, inhalants are often replaced in a user's drug use pattern rather than being kept as part of the total. Thus inhalants are more likely than any other drug to be a substance that an adolescent once used but has discontinued.

Another major source of information about drug use by American youth is an ongoing national research study entitled Monitoring the Future (MTF). The MTF study has been conducted by a team of researchers from the University of Michigan, with funding from the National Institute on Drug Abuse (NIDA). Since 1975, they have administered annual questionnaires

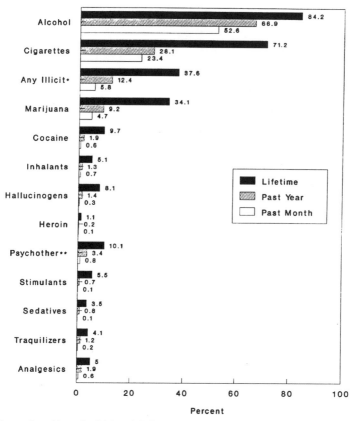

Figure 1.1. Prevalence of Licit and Illicit Drug Use Among the U.S. Population, 1994

SOURCE: 1994 National Household Survey on Drug Abuse (SAMHSA, 1995).

on drug use and a variety of related attitudes and behaviors to a representative sample of 12th-grade students in public and private high schools in the coterminous United States. High school seniors were chosen as the focus of study because high school marks the transition from youth to adulthood. The study also includes follow-up questionnaires mailed to a subsample of young adults, including college students, from previous high school graduating classes. Sample sizes have ranged between 15,000 and 19,000. The seniors

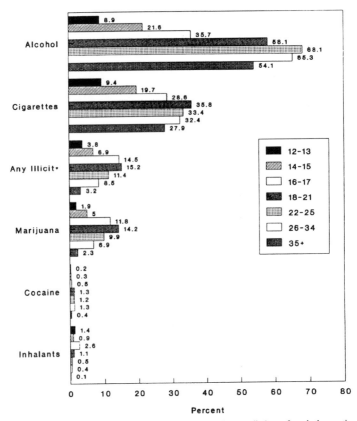

*Includes use of cannabis, cocaine, inhalants, hallucinogens, heroin, and non-medical use of psychotherapeutics.

Figure 1.2. Past-Month Prevalence of Selected Drugs Among Adolescents and Young Adults, 1994
SOURCE: 1994 National Household Survey on Drug Abuse (SAMHSA, 1995).

fill out self-administered questionnaires given to them in their classrooms by University of Michigan personnel. The findings from 1975 to 1994 are published in Johnston, O'Malley, and Bachman (1995), and findings for 1995 are given in a press release from the University of Michigan News and Information Services (1995).

In 1991, a similar but not identical questionnaire was first used with a nationally representative sample of 8th- and 10th-grade students; this is also an annual survey. In 1993, follow-ups were begun with subsamples of the 8th and 10th graders initially surveyed 2 years earlier. Equivalent numbers of 8th- and 10th-grade students are included in the study, so that the total 1995 sample (University of Michigan, 1995) included approximately 50,000 students in about 420 public and private secondary schools. There are a few differences in drug use prevalence rates generated by the MTF and NHSDA surveys for comparable age groups, with slightly higher prevalence rates reported from the MTF survey. The setting of the interview may make a difference, with adolescents more willing to disclose sensitive information on drug use in a school setting than at home. Both questionnaires employ self-administration procedures for the questions on drug use.

In 1995, nearly half (48.4%) of the high school seniors in the United States reported some experience with an illicit drug prior to graduating from high school (University of Michigan, 1995). One in four (28.1%) had tried an illicit drug other than marijuana. As seen in the NHSDA, the mostly widely used illicit drug was marijuana. The 1995 MTF study found that 41.7% of high school seniors had tried marijuana, 34.7% had used it in the last year, 21.2% reported past-month use, and 4.6% were daily marijuana smokers. The next most frequently used class of illicit drugs among high school seniors was the inhalants (17.4% lifetime use), followed by stimulants (15.3%) and hallucinogens (12.7%). Six percent of the seniors had tried cocaine, and 3.0% had tried crack cocaine specifically. Less than 10% of high school seniors reported any use of the remaining classes of illegal drugs. Table 1.1 shows annual and past-month prevalence rates from the MTF survey for several drugs by school grade. As would be expected from the NHSDA results shown in Figure 1.2, the general tendency seen in Table 1.1 is one of more drug use among older students for almost all drug types. And in the MTF study as in the NHSDA, inhalants are the exception. Eighth, 10th, and 12th graders had roughly equal lifetime prevalence rates, but inhalant use in the last year or the last month was most likely among 8th graders and least likely among 12th graders. This suggests that many 8th-grade inhalant users drop inhalant use by the time they are seniors.

Perhaps the most striking aspect of the 1995 MTF findings shown in Table 1.1 is the strong prevalence of alcohol and cigarette use at all three grade levels. Drinking, even drinking to the point of getting drunk, was common. Over half of the seniors had been drunk at least once in the last year (52.5%), as had 38.5% of 10th graders and 18.4% of 8th graders. Episodes of binge drinking were also common: Drinking five or more drinks

Table 1.1 1994 Youth Drug Use by School Grade (Percentages)

Drug Use Type	Last 12 Months			Last 30 Days		
	8th	10th	12th	8th	10th	12th
Alcohol	46.8	63.9	73.0	25.5	39.2	50.1
Got drunk	18.2	38.0	51.7	8.7	20.3	30.8
Cigarettes	x	x	x	18.6	25.4	31.2
Half pack+ per day	x	x	x	3.6	7.6	11.2
Marijuana	13.0	25.2	30.7	7.8	15.8	19.0
Inhalants	11.7	9.1	7.7	5.6	3.6	2.7
Hallucinogens	2.7	5.8	7.6	1.3	2.4	3.1
Stimulants	7.9	10.2	9.4	3.6	4.5	4.0
Tranquilizers	2.4	3.3	3.7	1.1	1.5	1.4
Barbiturates	—	—	4.1	—	—	1.7
Cocaine	2.1	2.8	3.6	1.0	1.2	1.5
Heroin	1.2	0.9	0.6	0.6	0.4	0.3

SOURCE: Monitoring the Future Study, 1995 (University of Michigan, 1995).
NOTE: x = Annual use not measured. — = Data not available for 8th and 10th graders.

in a row at least once in the past 2 weeks was reported by 14.5% of 8th graders, 24.0% of 10th graders, and 29.8% of 12th graders. Smoking tobacco in the past month was reported by 19.1% of 8th graders, 27.9% of 10th graders, and 33.5% of seniors. Smokeless tobacco was also popular among some students, especially males. The 1994 Monitoring the Future study indicates such use in the last 30 days by under 3% of female students but 12.8% of 8th-grade boys and about 20% of 10th-and 12th-grade boys.

Retrospective reports from the MTF study indicate that the peak ages for first use of cigarettes were in the sixth and seventh grades and that daily smoking appeared to develop primarily in Grades 8 through 11 (Johnston et al. 1995, p. 141). The same data source indicates that for alcohol, peak initiation ages were in the seventh through ninth grades, with the first occurrence of drunkenness most likely in Grades 7 through 10. The young initiation ages and widespread prevalence of drinking and smoking among high school students are all the more surprising when one remembers that it is illegal for virtually all of these students to buy either alcoholic beverages or cigarettes. Further, use of alcohol and tobacco by youth is a concern because these drugs cause organ damage even in adults if used heavily or often. Chances of regular use are increased by another problematic feature of these drugs, namely that alcohol is moderately addicting and tobacco is highly addicting.

But in addition to these direct problems with alcohol and cigarettes, their use by youth is also problematic in that these substances serve as "gateway drugs." Doubtless because of their status as licit drugs, their use almost always precedes use of any other drug. They are an introduction to drug use, and their use provides experiences that make use of other drugs easier or of more potential interest. Specifically, alcohol usually provides a youth's first experiences with being "high," or intoxicated, and cigarette use entails most of the skills needed to get high smoking marijuana. Alcohol and cigarettes are, in particular, gateways to other drug use in that relatively few youth begin using other drugs without first using alcohol and cigarettes. This is not the same as saying that all or even most youth who use either of these drugs will proceed to use other drugs as well. On the contrary, comparison of the drug use prevalence rates in Table 1.1 shows that even if every single marijuana user were also an alcohol user, most alcohol users would nonetheless not have used marijuana. The same contrast appears even if one considers lifetime prevalence rates for the oldest students: In 1994, 80.4% of 12th graders had tried alcohol at some time in their lives, and 62.0% had smoked a cigarette, but only 38.2% had ever tried marijuana.

Youth choices as to which drug to use or to try next are not random. Rather, the first drugs used tend to be those that are perceived as least risky, deviant, or illegal; most commonly, these are alcohol and tobacco. The next drug types used are more risky or deviant, and if they are continued beyond experimentation, they tend to be additions to, not replacements for, the first drugs used. The most common drug in this second stage is marijuana, although sometimes it is an inhalant. The progression is similar at the next stage, which most commonly entails pills or hallucinogens. Finally, the most problematic stage involves the most risky, deviant, and illegal drugs: cocaine and heroin. At this stage, as in prior stages, the new drugs are still most typically added to the drug use patterns initiated previously. The additive nature of these progression patterns implies lower drug use prevalence for the drug types that are more risky and illegal. That is, adding more drug types rather than replacing the earlier types means that the more dangerous and illegal a drug, the fewer youth are using it. The differences in prevalence between drug types can be extreme, as displayed in Table 1.1. For 12th graders, for example, prevalence in the 30 days prior to interview goes from 51.3% for alcohol all the way down to 1.8% for cocaine. This means that for high school seniors, current alcohol use is some 30 times more likely than current cocaine use.

Twenty-Year Trends in Youth Drug Use

Trend data are available from the repeated cross-sectional surveys of high school seniors in the MTF study and from the NHSDA. Both surveys show that overall rates of illicit drug use peaked in the late 1970s. In 1979, 65% of the nation's high school seniors reported some experience with an illicit drug; about half had used only marijuana. One in 10 used marijuana on a daily or near-daily basis. Nearly all had used alcohol (93%), 73% in the past month, and 7% reported drinking daily or near daily. Two in five seniors (41%) reported that on at least one occasion in the past 2 weeks, they had five or more drinks in a row. One in four were daily cigarette smokers, and 17% smoked one-half pack or more a day (Johnston, Bachman, & O'Malley, 1979). Figure 1.3 shows the trends in alcohol and cigarette use and Figure 1.4 the trends in use of several illicit drugs among high school seniors from 1975 through 1995.

Both the MTF and NHSDA studies show that marijuana use peaked in 1979 and that use of most pills peaked in the early 1980s. Both surveys also show that cigarette smoking among youth leveled around 1979, not changing much after that, although it has continually decreased since 1979 among adults (18 years and older). Alcohol use also peaked among all age groups around 1979, although the decreases thereafter are very small among adults and substantial only among youth—and then only at the more frequent levels of use.[2] Cocaine use peaked a few years earlier in the NHSDA among youth than among high school seniors in the MTF study. In the MTF study, past-year prevalence rates plateaued between 1979 and 1985 before finally starting to decrease.

Figure 1.4 illustrates a recent change in youth drug use prevalence that concerns many people. The 1993 MTF survey results showed a reversal in the long-term downward trend for marijuana. Marijuana prevalence increased in 1993 for the first time since beginning its downward trend and then increased again in 1994 and again in 1995. In 1995, the proportion of students reporting any marijuana use in the year prior to the survey was 15.8% for 8th graders, 28.7% for 10th graders, and 34.7% for seniors. Each of these rates represents an increase of 8 to 13 percentage points in only 3 years. A second apparent trend accompanying the dramatic increase in marijuana use is smaller and more gradual increases in the prevalence of other drug use among youth. Between 1992 and 1995, the MTF survey found increasing prevalence for student use of hallucinogens, inhalants, ampheta-

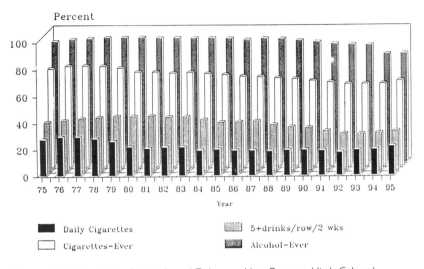

Figure 1.3. Trends in Alcohol and Tobacco Use Among High School Seniors
SOURCE: Monitoring the Future Study (University of Michigan, 1995).

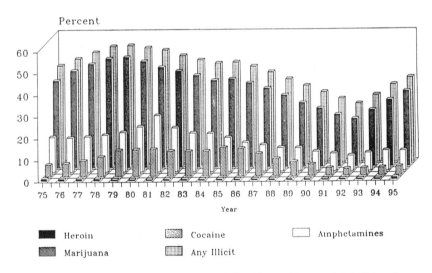

Figure 1.4. Trends in Past-Year Use of Illicit Drugs Among High School Seniors
SOURCE: Monitoring the Future Study (University of Michigan, 1995).

mines (speed pills), and barbiturates (a type of sedative, or "sleeping pill"). There was also a significant increase in cocaine and crack use between 1992 and 1995, although only among 8th and 10th graders—not among seniors. The likely connection of these increases to the rising marijuana use prevalence is that as the number of students using marijuana increases, so does the number of youth willing to try drugs that are even more dangerous or illegal (University of Michigan, 1994). However, it should be pointed out that drug use prevalence rates among adult age groups are not increasing: They are stable to decreasing. The unprecedented rise in marijuana use in particular appears to be occurring primarily among youth, with small increases also noted among young adults.

In summary, trend data show that the youth drug epidemic peaked in the late 1970s and then steadily receded over the decade of the 1980s and on into the early 1990s. Today, many drug prevalence rates are lower than they were in the early 1970s. Although this is good news, illicit drug use is still more prevalent than it was before the initiation of the epidemic, and rates of marijuana use in particular remain at epidemic levels among American youth. The use of the licit drugs—alcohol and tobacco—is also at disturbing high levels, and we have made little progress in reducing it, especially cigarette smoking, since the height of the drug epidemic. Reason for concern is also provided by recent increases in marijuana use as well as smaller increases in several other classes of illicit drugs among students.

Explaining the Trends in Youth Drug Use

What led to the decreases in illicit drug use among youth (and the general population) starting in the late 1970s? The MTF survey has shown strong links between illicit drug use and a number of factors: truancy, poor grades, more evenings spent away from home (for fun and recreation), and lack of religious commitment. However, none of these factors has changed over time in a pattern that could account for the decreases in illicit drug use. Another suspected explanation is the availability of illicit drugs, but over the same time period that youth drug use was consistently decreasing, there was virtually no change in youths' reports of how easy or difficult it was for them to obtain drugs.

However, the MTF survey has documented that shifts in attitudes about the perceived risks associated with the use of marijuana preceded the downward trend in marijuana use (Bachman, Johnston, O'Malley, & Humphrey, 1988). Increases in the perceived risks associated with cocaine use, as well as increasing disapproval of cocaine use, also preceded the decrease in cocaine prevalence rates (Bachman, Johnston, & O'Malley, 1990). Figure 1.5 shows the trends in perceived availability, perceived risks, and prevalence of use for marijuana. The MTF researchers attribute the increased perception of risks over the decade of the 1980s to increasing health consciousness in general and to improved drug education that provided factual information about drugs and turned away from the propaganda and scare tactics used in the 1960s. It appears that a large proportion of youth pay attention to new information about drugs, especially risks and consequences and that such information, presented in a factual and credible fashion, plays a vital role in reducing the demand for drugs (Bachman et al., 1990). Good scientific evidence has accrued slowly, as is generally the nature of good scientific evidence, and has been disseminated widely for the most part in an objective manner. That young people today are more concerned about their health is also evident in the MTF findings that physical and psychological effects are among the reasons most frequently cited by high school students for quitting drug use.

Figure 1.5 shows not only decreased use with more perceived risk but also the reverse—more use with less perceived risk—during both the late 1970s peaking of the epidemic and the recent changes in marijuana use discussed above. The 1995 continuation of changes in attitudes about marijuana in a direction more favorable to use is part of the reason for increasing concern about youth drug use. Fewer students are perceiving any level of marijuana use, even regular use, as dangerous. The MTF surveys found that perceived risks of use and personal disapproval of use declined between 1992 and 1995 for nearly all illicit drugs; further, this change was larger for students in 8th and 10th grades than for high school seniors. The MTF research team has observed over time that when attitudes of personal disapproval and perceived risks soften, increases in use can be expected in future surveys.

The United States has concentrated most of its monetary resources in the "war on drugs" on curtailing the supply of drugs, but the MTF survey shows that the perceived availability of drugs has not changed much in the last 20 years. Changes in drug use prevalence appear, rather, to be linked to changes in attitudes about the risks and harm associated with drugs. This is surely a topic that can be addressed effectively with youth. Most young people have seen deleterious effects of drug use among people they know personally.

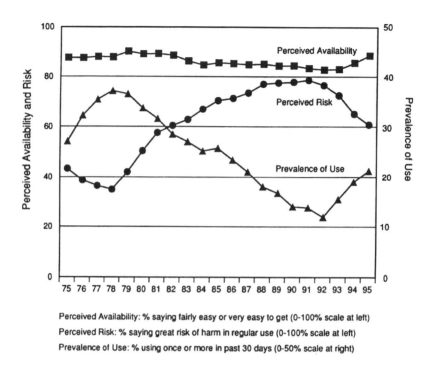

Figure 1.5. Marijuana Trends for High School Seniors: Perceived Availability, Perceived Risk of Regular Use, and Prevalence of Use in Past 30 Days
SOURCE: Monitoring the Future Study (University of Michigan, 1995).

Further, celebrities who became unfortunate symbols of the hazards of drug use include youthful heroes such as Len Bias, River Phoenix, and Kurt Cobain. Consequently efforts directed toward changing attitudes about the potential harmfulness of drug use hold great promise in further reducing drug use among youth. This type of strategy is generally termed a "demand reduction strategy": changing individuals and their attitudes, beliefs, and values associated with drug use. It appears more likely than a "supply reduction strategy" to be effective in decreasing youth drug use.

The increases in adolescent marijuana use found in recent national surveys are reason for concern, but they do not mean that conditions are ripe for another major resurgence in illicit drug use such as occurred in the late 1960s and throughout the 1970s. The increases in prevalence rates over the past few years are not as large as the overall decreases that occurred throughout the 1980s and into the early 1990s. Prevalence rates in 1995 remain much lower than in the peak years of the late 1970s and are still lower than those recorded at the beginning of the MTF and NHSDA in the early to mid-1970s. There are indications that U.S. youth have become somewhat more alienated in recent years, but not enough to predict large increases in drug use. It seems more likely that the prevalence rates for most types of drug use will remain stable for the next few years, with the exception of marijuana. Many American youths appear to regard this illicit drug as quite innocuous—a finding that suggests that there may continue to be significant increases in marijuana use among youth for several years to come.

Summary and Conclusions

Data are now available documenting over 20 years of epidemiological trends in adolescent drug use. The earliest national drug surveys were conducted in the late 1960s. Since then, two surveys have provided long-term trend data: the MTF study and the NHSDA. The data show that overall rates of adolescent drug use climbed quickly in the late 1960s and early 1970s to reach epidemic proportions. The epidemic peaked in the late 1970s, after which prevalence rates dropped slowly but steadily for most drugs. Disturbing increases have been noted since 1993 for several drugs, especially marijuana.

The bottom line for the U.S. problem with youth drug use is that even though the drug epidemic has receded, we still have a long way to go to return to pre-epidemic levels. Three decades ago, illicit drug use was an uncommon, infrequent behavior seen primarily among adults in deviant subcultures on the fringes of society. Today, some use of an illicit drug is reported by over half of high school students before they graduate from high school. Among youth who do not graduate, both lifetime and current rates of drug involvement are even higher (Mensch & Kandel, 1988). Drug experimentation is still close to normative among the nation's youth.

Further, the problem is more than just the illicit drugs. Alcohol abuse costs the United States nearly twice as much as illicit drug abuse does (Rice, Kelman, Miller, & Dunmeyer, 1990), yet because alcohol is a legal drug, its use is generally viewed as acceptable by both adolescents and adults. Many believe that alcohol is much less dangerous than illicit drugs, and parents are often pleased that their child is "only using alcohol, not drugs." But alcohol *is* a drug, alcohol abuse is the most common form of drug abuse in the United States, and current rates of problematic alcohol use by youth in particular are substantial. In 1995, one in four high school seniors reported having five or more drinks in a row at least once in the past 2 weeks. Worse, this level of drinking was reported by almost as many 10th graders (generally, 15- and 16-year-olds) and one in seven 8th-grade students (ages 13 and 14). Alcohol is especially dangerous because it relaxes inhibitions so that youth participate in risky behavior while under its influence. Considering that accidents are the leading cause of death among adolescents and that approximately 33% of traffic fatalities among 16- to 24-year-olds in 1990 were alcohol related, it is apparent that alcohol is not such an innocuous drug (Zobeck, Grant, Stinson, & Bertolocci, 1991). Much more effort must be devoted to raising the awareness of youth about the hazards of alcohol use.

Tobacco is also often neglected in this schema because it is not considered a mind-altering drug. However, tobacco users suffer severe health consequences from prolonged use and subject others to those consequences as well. In fact, a recent analysis attempting to identify and quantify the major factors contributing to death in the United States found that tobacco contributed to 400,000 deaths annually, compared to 100,000 for alcohol and 20,000 for all illicit drugs combined (McGinnis & Foege, 1993). Tobacco and alcohol cannot be separated from the illicit drugs without giving youth a mixed message about drug problems. It seems logical that if youth are concerned about the risks associated with alcohol and tobacco use, this will translate into concern about the illicit drugs as well.

However, the epidemiological evidence also suggests that intervention is possible by means of straightforward, factual drug education. To the extent that young people understand and perceive the dangers associated with drug use, their drug use prevalence rates do in fact decline. Ages 12 to 17 are clearly a critical period for the establishment of drug-using behavior. Consequently we need to educate children before they reach this age group, making sure that they know about the hazards of drug use, especially use of tobacco and alcohol. Drug education can then be continued as a part of ongoing health education for all students. But this educational campaign must be based on more than good intentions. It must begin with the existing wealth of research knowledge about drug effects and consequences and about accurate and effective drug education. Then this expanded effort to prevent youth drug problems must itself be subjected to evaluation so that pertinent research knowledge can continue to grow. We need to know more than we do now about how youth get their information and form their attitudes about drugs, about how to conduct successful drug education for students of all ages and in neighborhoods with both high and low drug use prevalence, and about how to do successful drug treatment when drug problems do arise. Drug problems will continue in this country until we focus our efforts on where the problem began and where it continues to fester: among the nation's youth. Prevention is key.

Notes

1. Polls on illicit drug use among college students for the years 1967, 1969, and 1971 can be obtained from Gallup Polls, 244 Wall St., Princeton, NJ 08540.

2. Lifetime experience with alcohol was reported by about 90% of high school seniors between 1975 and 1993. The question pertaining to lifetime alcohol use in the MTF study was changed in 1994, so the 1994 and 1995 data are not comparable with the data generated from earlier surveys. Overall, the data reveal great stability in the lifetime prevalence of alcohol use among high school seniors over the period 1975 to 1995.

References

Bachman, J. G., Johnston, L. D., & O'Malley, P. M. (1990). Explaining the recent decline in cocaine use among young adults: Further evidence that perceived risks and disapproval lead to reduced drug use. *Journal of Health and Social Behavior, 3,* 173-184.

Bachman, J. G., Johnston, L. D., O'Malley, P. M., & Humphrey, R. H. (1988). Explaining the recent decline in marijuana use: Differentiating the effects of perceived risks, disapproval, and general lifestyle factors. *Journal of Health and Social Behavior, 29,* 92-112.

de Alarcon, R. (1985). The uses of clinical epidemiology. In L. N. Robins (Ed.), *Studying drug abuse* (pp. 25-45). New Brunswick, NJ: Rutgers University Press.

Greene, M. H. (1974). An epidemiologic assessment of heroin use. *American Journal of Public Health, 64*(Suppl.), 1-10.

Harrison, L. D. (1988). *The marijuana movement: A study of a cohort on the cutting edge.* Ann Arbor, MI: University Microfilms.

Hughes, P. H., Senay, E. C., & Parker, R. (1972). The medical management of a heroin epidemic. *Archives of General Psychiatry, 27,* 585-591.

Johnston, L. D. (1973). *Drugs and American youth.* Ann Arbor, MI: Institute for Social Research.

Johnston, L. D., Bachman, J. G., & O'Malley, P. M. (1979). *1979 highlights: Drugs and the nation's high school students* (DHEW Pub. No. ADM 80-930). Rockville, MD: National Institute on Drug Abuse.

Johnston, L. D., O'Malley, P. M., & Bachman, J. G. (1995). *National survey results on drug use from the Monitoring the Future study, 1975-1994* (NIH Publication No. 95-4026). Rockville, MD: National Institute on Drug Abuse.

Jones, L. Y. (1980). *Great expectations: America and the baby boom generation.* New York: Ballantine.

Last, J. M. (Ed.). (1988). *A dictionary of epidemiology.* New York: Oxford University Press.

McGinnis, J. M., & Foege, W. H. (1993). Actual causes of death in the United States. *Journal of the American Medical Association, 270,* 2207-2212.

McGlothlin, W. H. (1975). Sociocultural factors in marihuana use in the United States. In V. Rubin (Ed.), *Cannabis and culture* (pp. 531-547). The Hague: Mouton.

Mensch, B., & Kandel, D. (1988). Underreporting of substance use in a national longitudinal youth cohort: Individual and interviewer effects. *Public Opinion Quarterly, 52,* 100-124.

Musto, D. F. (1973). *The American disease.* New York: Oxford University Press.

National Commission on Marihuana and Drug Abuse. (1972). *Marihuana, a signal of misunderstanding.* New York: New American Library.

Rice, D. P., Kelman, S., Miller, L. S., & Dunmeyer, S. (1990). *The economic costs of alcohol and drug abuse and mental illness: 1985.* San Francisco: University of California, Institute for Health and Aging.

Robins, L. N. (1985). The epidemiology of drug use and abuse: Where are we now? In L. N. Robins (Ed.), *Studying drug abuse* (pp. 1-23). New Brunswick, NJ: Rutgers University Press.

Substance Abuse Mental Health Service Administration, Office of Applied Studies. (1995). *Preliminary estimates from the 1994 National Household Survey on Drug Abuse.* Washington, DC: U.S. Dept. of Health and Human Services.

University of Michigan News and Information Services. (1994, December 8). *Drug study* (Press Release No. 7).

University of Michigan News and Information Services. (1995, December 11). *Drug use rises again in 1995 among American teens* (Press Release No. 13).

Zobeck, T. S., Grant, B. F., Stinson, F. S., & Bertolocci, D. (1991). Alcohol involvement in fatal traffic crashes in the United States: 1979-90. *Addictions, 89,* 227-231.

2

Risk and Protective Factors for Drug Use

Etiological Considerations

Judith S. Brook
David W. Brook

He says one of the two things that men who have lasted for a hundred years always say—either that they have drunk whiskey and smoked all their lives, or that neither tobacco nor spirits ever made the faintest appeal to them. — Edward Verral Lucas, *Secrets* (1926)

Numerous psychosocial studies conducted since the 1970s have produced significant findings that have contributed to our understanding of the etiology (cause) of drug use (Bachman, O'Malley, & Johnston, 1985; Hawkins, Catalano, & Miller, 1992; Newcomb & Bentler, 1986). The psychosocial factors that have been found to be associated with drug use and abuse can be classified into the following domains (i.e., sets of related factors): (a) cultural/societal, (b) family, (c) peer, and (d) personality/attitudes. As will become evident in this chapter, these social and personal factors have received both theoretical and empirical attention in the recent past (e.g.,

AUTHORS' NOTE: This study is supported by a grant from the National Institute on Drug Abuse (DA 03188), entitled "Childhood Etiologic Determinants of Adolescent Drug Use," and by a Research Scientist Award (DA 0244) to Judith S. Brook. We thank Coryl Jones for her evaluation of this research and Linda Capobianco for her preparation of the manuscript.

Glantz & Pickens, 1992). Biological (genetic) factors may also predispose individuals to drug use. In general, there is broad agreement in the field about the risks involved in the pathways leading to drug use. This chapter does not exhaustively review all of the research on the etiology of drug use but looks at studies that illustrate some of the major causes of drug use.

Specific Psychosocial Risk Factors Related to Drug Use

Cultural/Societal Domain

The cultural/societal domain consists of the social and cultural influences in a particular neighborhood that have an impact on the use or abuse of drugs. Adverse economic conditions and neighborhood disorganization have been found to be related to increased drug use; so have noxious physical and social environments, especially as perceived by young residents. To some extent, the environment can reinforce either a sense of self-worth, identity, safety, and mastery, or feelings of hopelessness and anger that lead to violent behavior. The neighborhood environment includes such measurable factors as geographic identity, quality of housing, services, employment, educational opportunity, crimes committed against individuals, community disorganization, and domestic violence. Ethnographic studies have explored the impact of community disorganization on drug use and abuse, as well as the impact of drug abuse on the community. Drug use in special populations, such as Hispanics, African Americans, and Native Americans, should be seen within the context of their cultures and neighborhoods. Finally, the degree of acculturation and assimilation of individuals and their families has been found to be of some importance in influencing drug abuse.

The use of a longitudinal study allows for the study of changes in social and environmental variables over time. For example, the introduction of gangs to many cities and the simultaneous proliferation of the use of crack cocaine and guns have caused dramatic changes in drug use in some neighborhoods in a very short period of time.

Cross-cultural studies provide a critical understanding of how the environment may affect a youth's drug use. At the present time, such cross-cultural research is relatively rare. However, several investigators have researched drug risks in other cultures outside the United States. For example, Boyle et al. (1992) reported that conduct disorders in Canadian children were highly related to marijuana use later in life. Early problem behaviors were found to distinguish heroin addicts from nonusers of heroin in Pakistan (Gillis, Tareen, Chaudhry, & Haiden, 1994). Japanese investigators have found that solvent abusers have an increased association with criminals after their first use (Wada & Fukui, 1994). In Japan, amphetamine abuse often follows solvent abuse (Fukui, Wada, & Iyo, 1994). Cross-cultural studies also raise questions about identifying protective factors. For example, in some countries where drugs are readily available, such as Colombia, it has been noted that drug use by the adolescents is not common.

Also important are the frequency and nature of representation of licit and illicit drugs in the media and of advertisements for tobacco and alcohol. The assumption is that repeated, intense presentation of substance use in a positive manner affects initiation, continued use, and increased use.

Family Domains

Parental Marital Relationship Domain

Understanding a child's development is complicated by the fact that in most cases the family consists of the husband-wife relationship in addition to parent-child relationships, at least for a period of time. Parental marital relationship variables are not as important in their direct impact on drug use as the parent-child relationship, although they do interact with other risk factors to affect drug use. However, some investigators have noted that family conflict is associated with the child's delinquency and drug use (Robins, 1980). Simcha-Fagan, Gersten, and Langner (1986) reported that youths whose parents are not emotionally supportive are at higher risk for drug use. Indeed, parental conflict may be a greater risk factor than structural variables, such as parental absence (Farrington, Gallagher, Morley, Ledger, & West, 1985).

Parental Drug Use and Personality Domains

Parental drug use is related to the child's drug use. Such transmission may be genetic and/or may reflect parental drug modeling. Not only is parental drug use of importance, but parental attitudes toward drug use also play a role. Parents who are tolerant of drug use are more likely to have children who use drugs (Barnes & Welte, 1986).

Parental personality factors are also significant in terms of the child's drug use, but their effects are mostly mediated through the action of other influences. For both parents, there are important variables that reflect the parents' identification with traditional values and behaviors. In the case of mothers, but not fathers, a lack of psychological adjustment is also important in determining the child's drug use, perhaps because mothers traditionally spend more time with their children.

Parent-Adolescent Relationship Domain

Mutual Attachment. Mutual attachment is very important in terms of adolescent drug use, both directly and indirectly (Jessor & Jessor, 1977). Parents of nonusers, in contrast to parents of users, report greater warmth (more child centeredness, affection, and communication) and less conflict in their relationships with their children. This finding reflects strong mutual attachment and a tendency for children to identify with their parents (Brook, Whiteman, Gordon, & Brook, 1986). Other similar and promising findings add to our confidence in highlighting the crucial role of attachment (e.g., Hirschi, 1969). These suggest that an affectionate and nonconflictual parent-child attachment relationship helps shape the child's behavior in ways that lead to less drug use.

The effectiveness of the attachment relationship in reducing drug use may be explained by the following factors: (a) parental warmth, which may make the parent important to the child and may obviate the use of severe forms of discipline; (b) parental models of controlled behavior for the child; (c) a conflict-free relationship, which results in less frustration, less aggression, and a decrease in the need to rebel; and (d) the child's greater identification with the parent, resulting in the incorporation of parental values and behavior (Brook, Brook, Whiteman, Gordon, & Cohen, 1990). Hawkins et al. (1992) suggested that parent-adolescent mutual attachment may inhibit drug use in a manner parallel to the way in which parental bonding inhibits delinquency. Indeed, Brook and Cohen (1992) found common family bonding variables that inhibit both drug use and delinquency.

Nonshared environmental factors may play a significant role in determining the mutual attachment relationships, and which children in a family are more at risk for drug use. One cannot assume that all children in a single family will experience the same environment, including their interactions with siblings, parents, and significant others. The significance of nonshared environmental influences has been demonstrated by research in behavioral genetics (Plomin, 1986).

Parental Control Variables. Another way in which parents may help shape the behavior of the youngster is through imposing discipline. This control includes not only physical forms of discipline but psychological methods as well. There is a growing body of research examining parental control in general in terms of the children's drug use, although the findings are far from consistent. For example, structured discipline serves as a barrier to adolescent drug use (Kandel & Andrews, 1987), and appropriate parental monitoring is effective in reducing drug use and delinquency (Patterson, Chamberlain, & Reid, 1982). In general, whereas authoritative structure and consistency appear to be beneficial regarding drug use, authoritarian or power-assertive techniques may be detrimental, and permissiveness seems to have no effect.

Sibling Domain

Investigators have examined and clarified the influence of parental variables on adolescent drug use. A still more complete understanding of family influences should include attention to how siblings affect one another. Several investigators have found that an adolescent with a sibling who uses drugs has an increased probability of drug use. An older brother's personality attributes have also been found to have an influence on a younger brother's personality through identification and modeling. Such sibling identification is likely to lead to common values, attitudes, and behavioral orientation. The link between older and younger brothers' personalities may also reflect the influences of genetic factors or similar upbringing or both. This may explain the close similarities in structure and behavior in siblings (Scarr & Grajek, 1982).

According to Brook, Whiteman, Brook, and Gordon (1991), a sibling relationship characterized by more conflict (i.e., jealousy and less nurturing, less admiration, less satisfaction, and less sibling identification) is related to (a) more inner tension and intrapsychic distress, (b) less conventional attitudes and behavior in the sibling, and ultimately (c) more drug use. The sibling relationship also interacts with parental factors. For instance, if the adolescent has a conflictual relationship with the parents, a close relationship with the sibling can buffer and mitigate the adverse effects of those negative parental influences.

Peer Domain

Relations to one's peers contribute greatly to variations in drug use (Barnes & Welte, 1986; Oetting & Beauvais, 1987; Oetting & Lynch, in press). Newcomb and Bentler (1986) found among older adolescents that peers had a greater effect than parents on drug use for several groups, including whites, African Americans, Asian Americans, and Hispanics. According to Oetting and Beauvais (1987), adolescent drug use takes place within the context of peer clusters, which consist of best friends or very close friends. Their empirical data are consistent with their developmental model, which suggests that family and school factors influence the formation of peer clusters, which in turn affect drug use.

This direct connection reported by some investigators (e.g., Kandel & Andrews, 1987) may also be a function of object choice, peer pressure, imitation, identification, or a combination thereof. The focus in this discussion has been on the powerful direct effects of peer drug use, but it should be remembered that peer warmth, conventionality, values, and academic achievement can also be important in protecting against drug use.

Finally, a word should be said about the possibility of reciprocal causality and the likelihood that "feedback loops" are operating between peer drug use and self-drug use. Adolescents who are using drugs are more likely to associate with drug-using peers, and this association, in turn, increases the chance that they will maintain or increase their drug involvement. Drug availability and advocacy from peers and others are both related to greater drug use.

The influence of peers may change as the adolescent matures. We do not know whether friends' use is equally important in middle school and in high school. Is peer influence of continuing importance in adulthood when the social group changes to family, coworkers, or drinking buddies?

Adolescent and Childhood Personality Domains

An adolescent's personality characteristics have a very strong impact on his or her drug use. There are at least four distinct aspects of the adolescent personality domain: (a) conventionality versus unconventionality, (b) emotional control, (c) personal functioning, and (d) social relatedness. Of these, the most powerful predictors of more frequent drug use are the unconventionality variables, namely sensation seeking, rebelliousness, tolerance of deviance, and low school achievement (Brook, Whiteman, Gordon, & Cohen, 1986).

Adolescents with an orientation toward sensation-seeking probably need greater stimulation from outside sources and may use drugs as external or new stimulation. Adolescents who are rebellious and have fewer internalized personal controls and rules may seek out that which is forbidden (marijuana or other illegal substances or activities). Adolescents who have not incorporated mainstream middle-class attitudes and ethical values may lack the requisite moral conviction to avoid using illegal and socially unacceptable drugs. Adolescents who expect to attend college are less likely to use hallucinogens, cocaine, heroin, stimulants, or other illicit drugs than those who do not expect to attend (Johnston, O'Malley, & Bachman, 1985).

Less important in terms of drug use than unconventionality are the remaining three personality dimensions—emotional control, personal functioning, and social relatedness—although aspects of each are significantly related to drug use (Jessor & Jessor, 1977).

Social scientists (Hawkins, Von Cleve, & Catalano, 1991; Loeber, 1991) can point with confidence to several childhood risk factors associated with deviance. Robins (1978) reported that the more serious the childhood antisocial behavior, the more likely it is to continue into adulthood. Several other investigators have also found childhood aggression to be a powerful predictor of adolescent and adult drug use (Block, Block, & Keyes, 1988; McCord, 1981).

Recent findings indicate that individual personality traits, family experiences, and ecological factors during childhood strongly affect adolescent drug-using behavior. A child who is irritable and easily distracted, throws temper tantrums, fights often with siblings, and engages in predelinquent behavior is more likely to use drugs in adolescence (Brook, Whiteman, Gordon, & Cohen, 1986). These factors may continue into adolescence, and the physiological or psychological effects of the use of illicit drugs may then actually serve to exacerbate the adolescent's feelings of irritability and aggressiveness, as evidenced by continuing temper tantrums, aggression toward siblings, and predelinquent behavior.

Not only do childhood personality traits predict future drug use, but family experiences also serve as predictors. In a longitudinal study dealing with the early childhood precursors of adolescent drug use, Block et al. (1988) found that greater involvement of the mother with the child protected against later drug use. Childhood ecological factors, such as relatively low socioeconomic status, are also related to greater adolescent drug use.

Several findings about childhood personality are noteworthy. First, certain personality dispositions that are related to later drug use appear to be moderately consistent from childhood through adolescence. Early childhood signs of social inhibition, anger, and low aspirations are related to similar characteristics years later. Some of these stable characteristics are part of a general category of unconventionality, which is highly related to drug use. Other adolescent (e.g., adjustment) characteristics that seem to appear during childhood reflect a lack of emotional control and the experience of personal distress. These personality predispositions reflect two different emphases in adjustment. One, unconventionality, is directed outwardly to societal values and norms. The other, personal distress, points to internal instability or distress. It would appear that the findings indicate that at least for certain types of unconventional behavior, such as antisocial behavior and aggression, there is consistency from childhood to adulthood (Cohen & Brook, 1987; Olweus, 1980). Prenatal and perinatal factors have also been found to be related to drug use (Brook, Nomura, & Cohen, 1989).

Physiological and Genetic Factors Implicated in Drug Abuse

It is likely, on the basis of recent and ongoing research, that the etiology of drug abuse is not to be found solely in the psychosocial factors discussed previously.

Psychosocial factors refer to both psychological and social influences on the individual, such as personal, peer, and family factors. Physiological and genetic factors are also likely to influence drug abuse. Such factors may include malfunctioning of the brain's neurotransmitters, which carry impulses from one neuron to the next. Most likely it is the interaction between psychosocial and biological/genetic factors that determines the presence of drug abuse. The inherited genotype is acted on by environmental psychosocial factors, and this interaction results in the phenotypic presence of drug abuse. This is known as the risk-diathesis or stress-diathesis model of drug abuse. There may be a number of different genotypes for different types of drug abuse. Many investigators are currently exploring the exact genetic/biological inherited factors that predispose someone to drug abuse.

Although not the focus of this chapter, these findings should be mentioned here because of their role in drug abuse.

First, the high occurrence of substance abuse and alcoholism among offspring of parents with substance abuse demonstrates that a family history is a potent predictor of vulnerability to substance abuse, which results to some extent from the effects of genetic factors (Merikangas & Gelernter, 1990; Pickens et al., 1991). However, the mechanism through which the family confers an increased risk is unknown.

Also, studies of twins and adopted children have revealed an increased likelihood for monozygotic twins to be concordant for alcoholism, compared to dizygotic twins. Goodwin (1985) and other investigators have found higher rates of alcoholism in adopted biological sons of alcoholics than in adopted sons without an alcoholic biological parent. It does seem likely, however, that genetic factors by themselves cannot cause alcoholism, as half of hospitalized alcoholics do not have a family history of alcoholism (Goodwin, 1985).

It is likely that a disturbance in serotonin metabolism or functioning is important in many cases of alcoholism. Low serotonin levels have been found to be associated with antisocial personality traits, social inhibition, and aggression, as well as with alcoholism. Some research also indicates a disturbance in brain dopamine metabolism among drug abusers. The biological roots of sensation seeking and other risk and protective factors for drug abuse have been investigated by a number of people, including Cloninger, Bohman, Sigvardsen, and von Knorring (1985). Sensation seeking has been found to be related to monamine oxidase (MAO) activity by Zuckerman (1983). Platelet MAO activity has also been found to be increased in connection with the early onset of alcoholism (Cloninger et al., 1985). At least in some cases, neurological or neurotransmitter malfunctioning may play a role in susceptibility to drug abuse.

Although genetic and biological factors contribute to substance abuse, family influences and other environmental factors may also influence the development of substance abuse (Pickens et al., 1991). It is therefore critical to identify the joint role of environmental and genetic causes in the etiology of substance abuse. The genetic epidemiologic approach, which focuses on the joint effects of host, agent, and environment, provides a powerful model for understanding the complex pathways to substance abuse. Subjects who should be studied to examine pathways to drug abuse include identical twins raised apart, or half-siblings, to identify nongenetic causes of underlying vulnerability; fraternal twins, to obtain clues to the environmental risk and protective factors for drug abuse; and migrants, to discover the role of cultural factors. Rutter et al. (1990) showed that environmental risks tend to operate most strongly in children with genetic vulnerability. Identification of such risk factors is critical to the effective prevention of substance abuse and its consequences.

The Mediational Linkages Among Domains of Risk Factors

Numerous theories and research studies have focused on the linkages among the domains just discussed (e.g., Brook et al., 1990). These connections can be briefly summarized again as follows:

1. Parental identification with and use of traditional values and behavior and psychological adjustments are associated with the development of a strong mutual attachment between parent and child and subsequent identification of the child with the parent.
2. This strong parent-child relationship, in turn, is associated with the child's internalization of parental traditional norms, values, and behavior.
3. These personality traits of the child lead him or her to associate with non-drug-using peers, which then leads to nonuse of drugs. Since drug use or nonuse is a major factor in the choice of peers among adolescents and preadolescents, the final path (from peer nonuse to self-nonuse of marijuana) is the most powerful linkage in the model. In effect, parental drug use is associated with the child's choosing of peers who use drugs, which, in turn, is related to the child's drug use.

The mediational linkages among the domains of risk/protective factors are presented in Figure 2.1.

Parental Personality and the Parent-Adolescent Relationship

Parents' identification with traditional societal values is associated with a strong mutual attachment relationship between parent and child and a subsequent identification of the child with the parents. Perhaps one reason that traditionality in the parent is linked to a strong mutual attachment with the child is that the traditional parent, in contrast to the nontraditional, may be more interested in the family in general and specifically in his or her

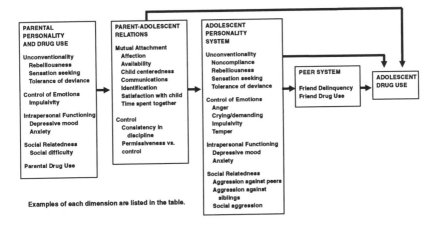

Figure 2.1. Linkages Among Domains of Risk/Protective Factors for Adolescent Drug Use

relationship to the child. Parents who are traditional, more responsible, and less rebellious are more likely to take their parenting role seriously and to spend time and energy in fulfilling it. At the same time, assuming that the adolescent is aware of parental maturity and commitment, one might expect that the adolescent would feel more secure. This greater security is likely to facilitate the growth of trust and greater adolescent identification with the parents.

The Parent-Adolescent Relationship and the Adolescent's Personality

A mutually affectionate, relatively conflict-free attachment and the consequent processes of identification with the parents and internalization of the parents' values and behavior are instrumental in forming the child's own values and behavior. Mutual attachment and identification with parents who are relatively "traditional" result in a more conventional and more well-adjusted child (Brook, Whiteman, Gordon, & Brook, 1986).

There are several possible avenues by which mutual attachment and the subsequent process of identification may lead to the adolescent's greater traditionality and psychological adjustment. First, the parent, as a restraining and socializing force in development, may prepare the child to accept the socializing and restraining forces of the broader society. Early attachment to the parents and to what they signify is perceived as an attachment to broader social conventions and structures.

Second, according to social learning theory, a strong parent-child attachment has an impact on the child's feelings about and perceptions of his or her parents and strengthens the parents' reinforcements and prohibitions; it also makes the child more receptive to instructions provided by the parents. Third, from a social learning point of view, the linkage occurs through the direct modeling effects of the parents' presumed responsibility, empathy in caring for the child, and psychological adjustment. A fourth possibility is that a child's positive feelings about him- or herself (influenced by a strong parental attachment) facilitate responsiveness and sensitivity to others.

Parental control also affects the child's personality. Numerous studies have reported that the use of authoritarian, power-assertive techniques of discipline is associated with deviant and antisocial behavior in the child (e.g., Patterson et al., 1982).

Adolescent Personality Traits and Peer Group Factors

An outstanding research finding is that unconventional youngsters are likely to have friends who use drugs. This may be explained to some extent by assortative pairing, that is, the selection of friends who are similar to oneself. This occurs specifically in terms of similarity of drug use, but, by inference, it could also include similarity in attitudes and values (Brook et al., 1990). Thus unconventional behavior in adolescents may have led them to seek out deviant friends because of the reinforcement values of mutual respect and reciprocity or because of the feeling of comfort derived from being with those who are similar to themselves. The final pathway is, of course, the direct linkage between peer drug use and the adolescent's own use of drugs.

Intergenerational Effects

The frequently observed association between the drug use of one generation and that of the next can be interpreted to some degree as a reflection of a genetic predisposition genotype (Dinwiddie & Cloninger, 1991). Among the psychosocial influences affecting adolescent drug users are the modeling of parental drug use behaviors, stressful life circumstances, the use of drugs as an adaptive device or for self-medication, the weakening of social controls, and association with drug-using peers. Through social learning, youths internalize the values and expectations and possibly acquire the maladaptive coping techniques of their parents. This has been found to be the case with adolescent cigarette smoking and initiation of marijuana use among adolescents (Bailey & Hubbard, 1990).

Parental drug use or other deviant behavior may affect the child's health, as well as resulting in other outcomes widely regarded as precursors of drug use. Drug use during pregnancy has been associated with a variety of adverse physical and psychological consequences for the newborn child, including developmental retardation (Chasnoff, 1988). Fetal alcohol syndrome is a characteristic group of malformations and retardation caused by maternal alcohol intake during pregnancy. Fetal nicotine syndrome is now being studied and may include decreased birth size and later behavioral abnormalities. Adolescents with substance-abusing parents experience more stress than teens from non-substance-abusing families (Brown, 1989). Adolescents with substance-abusing parents report more negative life events and rate the events as more undesirable (Roosa, Beals, Sandler, & Pillow, 1990). Substance-abusing parents are less able to provide social or emotional support to children in their times of need (Holden, Brown, & Mott, 1988).

Several studies have viewed parental substance abuse as one of many factors contributing in varying degrees to family disharmony and dysfunction, which are then related to such negative outcomes as the initiation or escalation of substance abuse in the children (McCarthy & Anglin, 1990). The parent-child relationship is viewed as reciprocal in that the actions of the adolescent drug user may then lead to further deterioration of the parent-child bond. This deterioration of the parent-child bond may affect the next generation as well and may increase its risks for youthful drug use (Brook et al., 1990; Brook, Whiteman, & Finch, 1993; Kumpfer, 1993). The parents' failure to monitor children's behavior also may contribute to subsequent drug use by permitting association with deviant peers (Kandel & Andrews, 1987).

Interactions of Individual Personality, Parental, Peer, and Context Factors

In the previous section, we have identified numerous risk factors that are associated with later drug use. Certainly the goal of many prevention programs should be risk reduction, if possible, prior to the development of influences that increase the risk of drug use. Another approach is to enhance protective factors that serve to buffer such risks and lead ultimately to less drug use (Garmezy, 1983; Werner, 1989). A goal of future research should be the identification of protective factors that are capable of offsetting risks or enhancing other protective factors.

In research by Brook et al. (1990), the focus has been on two types of interaction of personality, parent, and peer factors. In the first (risk/protective), risk factors may be offset by protective factors in the adolescent's personality. In the second (protective/protective), one protective factor enhances another protective factor, so that the effect of the two combined is synergistic: that is, greater than the sum of the protective factors considered singly.

Several investigators (Brook et al., 1990; Garmezy, 1983; Rutter et al., 1990; Werner, 1989) have noted that protective factors can moderate the effects of risk conditions and can thereby both reduce vulnerability to noxious influences in the environment and enhance resiliency. Such protective conditions include a positive mutual attachment between parent and child, nondeviant siblings, academic achievement, and such traits of conventionality as low rebelliousness, low to moderate sensation seeking, and adherence to broad social norms. Moreover, the effect of one parent's use of drugs can be offset by nonuse of drugs by the other parent. Among African Americans, ethnic pride seems to operate as a protective factor to offset risk conditions. Similarly, ethnic pride also serves this purpose for Puerto Ricans. Protective factors in young adulthood include marriage and family responsibility.

Garmezy (1983), in a related study, noted that extreme stress can be offset by the child's temperament, by a supportive family, and by an external support system, which can all reinforce the child's efforts at coping.

In recent years, some attention has been paid to the role of gender as both a main and a moderating influence (Widner & Collins, 1993). Genetic factors and behavioral lack of control appear to be of less significance in the etiology of female alcohol problems as compared to those of males. With respect to family factors, alcohol abuse is similar in males and females. However, there do appear to be differences in parental monitoring. As expected, boys receive less monitoring than girls, and low monitoring is associated with more problem behavior (Barnes, Farrell, & Dintcheff, in press).

There is growing evidence that victimization, such as sexual victimization, is significant in the etiology of substance abuse, particularly among females. Among females, sexual molestation has been found to be related to alcohol use (Watts & Ellis, 1993). Miller, Downs, and Testa (1993) reported that alcoholic women were more likely to have experienced childhood sexual abuse and moderate to serious violence. Childhood sexual abuse is particularly common in certain "dually diagnosed" adolescents, those who suffer from both drug abuse and a psychiatric disorder (Brook, 1996). Advertising directed at women, which often portrays women as sexual objects, is believed to have influenced both tobacco use and alcohol consumption by women (Berman & Gritz, 1993).

Another major potential moderating variable is the developmental level of the child. Levels of development can be studied in many ways according to different psychological stages. (For example, one could examine stages of moral judgment or cognitive development.) Risk factors influencing the child may vary according to the period of development in which the risks are operative. For example, disruptions in the school setting may have very different implications when these occur during childhood instead of adolescence. Moreover, exposure to risks over a long period of development may differ substantially from exposure during a shorter developmental period.

Drug Use Interrelationships

Stability of Drug Use and Stage of Drug Use

There is considerable evidence that alcohol and drug use are quite stable behaviors. This has led some individuals to suggest that the best predictor of future drug behavior is past drug behavior. Kandel (1975) reported that adolescents move from tobacco and alcohol use to marijuana use and then to other illicit use of drugs. Involvement at one stage of drug use does not necessarily lead to drug involvement in the next stage, but youths who use one drug early are likely to use other drugs at an earlier age and are more likely to abuse drugs. The major period of risk for initiation into the use of legal drugs and marijuana is over by age 20 (Chen & Kandel, 1995). The risk for initiating the use of other illicit drugs (other than marijuana) lasts for a somewhat longer period than that for cigarettes, alcohol, and marijuana. Drug use, especially early drug use, is likely to be related to other deviant behavior (Kaplan, 1995). Cultural and social conditions such as drug availability may also affect the sequence of drug use.

Polysubstance Abuse and Comorbidity

Comorbidity is increasingly recognized as having adverse effects on substance abusers' drug use and mental and physical health, particularly at a time when almost all adolescent substance abusers are polysubstance abusers. Studies of clinical and epidemiologic samples have suggested that substance abuse and psychopathology are inextricably linked (Merikangas, Risch, & Weissman, 1994). Disorders that increase the risks of the development of alcoholism and drug abuse are bipolar affective illness, such as major depression; conduct disorders, especially those manifesting antisocial behavior; anxiety disorders, particularly phobic disorders; and childhood developmental disorders, including the spectrum of attention deficit disorder, oppositional disorder, and learning problems (Fergusson, Horwood, & Lynskey, 1994; Kaminer, 1991). Psychopathology can promote the use of drugs through the self-medication of psychiatric symptoms, and drug abuse can cause or lower the threshold for the development of psychiatric symptoms and disorders, most notably depression and antisocial behavior or antisocial personality disorder. Adolescents with dual or triple diagnoses are generally more symptomatic, have more severe academic and interpersonal difficulties, and are more difficult to treat than other adolescents.

Drug Use and Other Problem Behaviors

Drug use has been found to be related to a number of other deviant behaviors. Over the past two decades, substantial research has documented the interrelation of different problem behaviors (Elliott, Huizinga, & Ageton, 1985). The research has shown strong linkages between drug use and interpersonal aggression and theft, precocious sexual behavior, poor achievement, and dropping out of school. Many of the antecedents of different types of deviant behavior have been found to be similar. Broad social context factors (e.g., lack of adherence to social norms), family factors (e.g., high parental drug use or difficulty in the attachment relationship), personality and attitudinal factors (e.g., tolerance of deviance), and peer factors (e.g., peer drug use) have been found to be associated with different forms of deviance.

Drug Use and Crime

There is a strong statistical correlation between illegal drug use and criminal behavior (Inciardi, Horowitz, & Pottieger, 1993; Inciardi, McBride, McCoy, & Chitwood, 1994; McBride, Inciardi, Chitwood, McCoy, & the National AIDS Research Consortium, 1992). In almost all metropolitan areas, the data indicate that the majority of felony arrests in the United States involve current illegal drug users, most of whom are using cocaine. Studies of nonincarcerated drug-using populations indicate that the majority have extensive arrest and incarceration histories. Finally, general population surveys show a correlation between drug use and delinquency and criminal behavior. The relationship between drug use and delinquency may be related to the cost of drugs (Needle & Mills, 1994), the common etiology of drug use and delinquency, and the overlapping behavior of drug users and delinquents (Brook, Balka, Abernathy, & Hamburg, 1994).

Multiple Risks

The literature suggests that the more risks an individual is exposed to, the more likely he or she is to use or abuse drugs (Scheier & Newcomb, 1991). The effects of the accumulation of a number of risks in a person's life may be more important than those of any particular single risk.

Drug Use in Adult Life

Drug use initiation, escalation, or cessation may be delayed until later stages of development, and drug abuse may continue well into adulthood. Escalation from occasional use to heavy use or substitution of alcohol for other drugs can also be seen for persons age 20 to 30 and beyond. Work experience, marriage and children, and the vicissitudes of later adult life may have an impact on drug use, and the effects of drug use may, in turn, influence these life experiences.

Principles of Prevention: The Next Step

The research findings discussed here have a number of implications for prevention and treatment. Because sociocultural context, personal, and social factors all influence drug use, a multidisciplinary approach to drug use prevention is essential. Moreover, because the risk factors related to drug use derive from different domains, logic dictates that comprehensive prevention approaches are more likely to be effective than narrow approaches. Thus programs that target the individual's interaction with his or her environment are likely to be especially potent. In prevention programs, it is important to reduce the risk factors and enhance the protective factors.

Intervention Opportunities

The domain linkage findings suggest several possible targets for therapeutic or preventive intervention: the broad social context, the parent alone, the parent and the adolescent, the adolescent alone, and the peer group. If one wishes to intervene early in the causal chain of events, intervention should take place in the parent-child relationship in early childhood.

The foremost implication of the findings from research is that when a particular area of the child's life is strengthened (e.g., personality or family), a benefit accrues. First, these strengths (which we have deemed *protective* characteristics) may offset risks in other areas, such as those related to associating with drug-using peers. Second, protective characteristics enhance one another synergistically. In both cases, the likelihood of adolescent drug use is considerably reduced.

The next step is to apply the etiologic findings to the formulation of principles of prevention. General principles include the following:

1. Changes are more far-reaching if started at an early age.
2. Education for successful parenting must focus on discouraging drug use among parents and encouraging the development of a positive parent-child mutual attachment relationship.
3. Because poverty poses serious risks, an appropriate socioeconomic base is beneficial for the development of protective tendencies, such as a close parent-child bond or drug-resistant personality attributes, that will offset the risks for drug use.
4. The provision of adequate health care will move neighborhood and contextual factors in a positive direction to protect against drug use.

5. Programs focused on peer groups and on educational goals can have protective effects against drug use.

6. Because risk and protective factors are cumulative in their effects on drug use, a broad-based multidisciplinary approach to drug prevention and treatment is clearly necessary. Programs that reduce risks at the same time that they enhance protective factors from many domains will be most effective.

Currently, there is a great deal of interest in the study of adolescent drug use. Such attention is likely to broaden inquiry and yield a broader and firmer base of evidence, both of which augur well for future investigations, further comprehension of the etiology of drug use, and prevention programs. It is to be hoped that prevention programs that address the childhood and adolescent risk and protective factors identified in etiologic studies will result in reduced drug use and abuse as measured in future evaluations. Should this occur, empirical data then will be available to suggest that the benefits of prevention programs are far greater than anyone could have imagined.

References

Bachman, J. G., O'Malley, P. M., & Johnston, L. D. (1985). *Youth in transition: Vol. 6. Adolescence to adulthood—change and stability in the lives of young men.* Ann Arbor: University of Michigan, Institute for Social Research.

Bailey, S. L., & Hubbard, R. L. (1990). Developmental variation in the context of marijuana initiation among adolescents. *Journal of Health and Social Behavior, 31,* 58-70.

Barnes, G. M., Farrell, M. P., & Dintcheff, B. A. (in press). Family socialization effects on alcohol abuse and related problem behaviors among female and male adolescents. In R. Wilsnack & S. Wilsnack (Eds.), *Gender and alcohol.* New Brunswick, NJ: Rutgers Center of Alcohol Studies.

Barnes, G. M., & Welte, J. W. (1986). Patterns and predictors of alcohol use among 7-12th grade students in New York State. *Journal of Studies on Alcohol, 47,* 53-62.

Berman, B. A., & Gritz, E. R. (1993). Women and smoking: Toward the year 2000. In E. S. Lisansky Gomberg & T. D. Nirenberg (Eds.), *Women and substance abuse* (pp. 258-285). Norwood, NJ: Ablex.

Block, J., Block, J. H., & Keyes, S. (1988). Longitudinally foretelling drug usage in adolescence: Early childhood personality and environmental precursors. *Child Development, 59,* 336-355.

Boyle, M. H., Offort, D. R., Racine, Y. A., Szatmari, P., Fleming, J. R., & Links, P. S. (1992). Predicting substance use in late adolescence: Results from the Ontario Child Health Study follow-up. *American Journal of Psychiatry, 149,* 761-767.

Brook, D. W. (1996). Adolescents who abuse substances. In P. Kymissis & D. A. Halperin (Eds.), *Group therapy with children and adolescents* (pp. 243-264). Washington, D.C.: American Psychiatric Press.

Brook, J. S., Balka, E. B., Abernathy, T., & Hamburg, B. A. (1994). Sequence of sexual behavior and its relationship to other problem behaviors in African-American and Puerto Rican adolescents. *Journal of Genetic Psychology, 155*, 107-108.

Brook, J. S., Brook, D. W., Whiteman, M., Gordon, A. S., & Cohen, P. (1990). The psychosocial etiology of adolescent drug use and abuse. *Genetic, Social and General Psychology Monographs, 116*(Whole No. 2).

Brook, J. S., & Cohen, P. (1992). A developmental perspective on drug use and delinquency. In J. McCord (Ed.), *Advances in criminological theory: Vol. 3. Crime, facts, fictions, and theory* (pp. 231-251). New Brunswick, NJ: Transaction.

Brook, J. S., Nomura, C., & Cohen, P. (1989). Prenatal, perinatal, and early childhood risk factors and drug involvement in adolescence. *Genetic, Social and General Psychology Monographs, 115*, 221-241.

Brook, J. S., Whiteman, M., Brook, D. W., & Gordon, A. S. (1991). Sibling influences on adolescent drug use: Older brothers on younger brothers. *Journal of the American Academy of Child and Adolescent Psychiatry, 10*, 958-966.

Brook, J. S., Whiteman, M., & Finch, S. (1993). The role of mutual attachment in adolescent drug use: A longitudinal study. *Journal of the American Academy of Child and Adolescent Psychiatry, 32*, 982-989.

Brook, J. S., Whiteman, M., Gordon, A. S., & Brook, D. W. (1986). Father-daughter identification and its impact on her personality and drug use. *Developmental Psychology, 22*, 743-748.

Brook, J. S., Whiteman, M., Gordon, A. S., & Cohen, P. (1986). Dynamics of childhood and adolescent personality traits and adolescent drug use. *Developmental Psychology, 22*, 403-414.

Brown, S. A. (1989). Life events of adolescents in relation to personal and parental substance abuse. *American Journal of Psychiatry, 146*, 484-489.

Chasnoff, I. J. (1988). *Drugs, alcohol, pregnancy and parenting.* Boston: Kluwer.

Chen, K., & Kandel, D. (1995). The natural history of drug use from adolescence to the mid-30's in a general population sample. *American Journal of Public Health, 85*, 41-47.

Cloninger, C. R., Bohman, M., Sigvardsen, S., & von Knorring, A. L. (1985). Psychopathology in adopted-out children of alcoholics. *Recent Developments in Alcoholism, 3*, 37-51.

Cohen, P., & Brook, J. S. (1987). Family factors related to the persistence of psychopathology in childhood and adolescence. *Psychiatry, 50*, 332-345.

Dinwiddie, S. H., & Cloninger, C. R. (1991). Family and adoption studies in alcoholism and drug addiction. *Psychiatric Annals, 21*, 206-214.

Elliot, D. S., Huizinga, D., & Ageton, S. S. (1985). *Explaining delinquency and drug use.* Beverly Hills, CA: Sage.

Farrington, D. P., Gallagher, B., Morley, L., Ledger, R. J., & West, D. J. (1985). *Cambridge Study in Delinquent Development: Long term follow-up (first annual report to the Home Office, August 31, 1985).* Cambridge, UK: Cambridge University Press.

Fergusson, D. M., Horwood, L. J., & Lynskey, M. (1994). The childhood of multiple problem adolescents: A 15-year longitudinal study. *Journal of Child Psychology and Psychiatry, 35*, 1123-1140.

Fukui, S., Wada, K., & Iyo, M. (1994). Epidemiology of amphetamine abuse in Japan and its social implications. In A. K. Cho & D. S. Segal (Eds.), *Amphetamine and its analogs: Psychopharmacology, toxicology, and abuse* (pp. 459-478). San Diego: Academic Press.

Garmezy, N. (1983). Stressors of childhood. In N. Garmezy & M. Rutter (Eds.), *Stress, coping, and development in children* (pp. 43-84). New York: McGraw-Hill.

Gillis, J. S., Tareen, A. K., Chaudhry, H. R., & Haiden, S. (1994). Risk factors for drug misuse in Pakistan. *International Journal on the Addictions, 29*, 215-223.

Glantz, M. D., & Pickens, R. W. (1992). Vulnerability to drug abuse: Introduction and overview. In M. Glantz & R. Pickens (Eds.), *Vulnerability to drug abuse* (pp. 1-14). Washington, DC: American Psychological Association.

Goodwin, D. W. (1985). Alcoholism and genetics: The sins of the fathers. *Archives of General Psychiatry, 42,* 171-174.

Hawkins, J. D., Catalano, R. F., & Miller, J. Y. (1992). Risk and protective factors for alcohol and other drug problems in adolescence and early adulthood: Implications for substance abuse prevention. *Psychological Bulletin, 112,* 64-105.

Hawkins, J. D., Von Cleve, E., & Catalano, R. F., Jr. (1991). Reducing early childhood aggression: Results of a primary prevention program. *Journal of the American Academy of Child and Adolescent Psychiatry, 30,* 208-217.

Hirschi, T. (1969). *Causes of delinquency.* Berkeley: University of California Press.

Holden, M. G., Brown, S. A., & Mott, M. A. (1988). Social support network of adolescents: Relation to family alcohol abuse. *American Journal on Drug and Alcohol Abuse, 14,* 487-498.

Inciardi, J., Horowitz, R., & Pottieger, A. E. (1993). *Street kids, street drugs, street crime: An examination of drug use and serious delinquency in Miami.* Belmont, CA: Wadsworth.

Inciardi, J. A., McBride, D. C., McCoy, V. H., & Chitwood, D. (1994). Recent research on the crack-cocaine/crime connection. *Studies on Crime and Crime Prevention, 3,* 63-82.

Jessor, R., & Jessor, S. L. (1977). *Problem behavior and psychosocial development: A longitudinal study of youth.* San Diego: Academic Press.

Johnston, L. D., O'Malley, P. M., & Bachman, J. G. (1985). *Use of licit and illicit drugs by American high school students: 1975-1984.* Rockville, MD: National Institute of Drug Abuse.

Kaminer, Y. (1991). Adolescent substance abuse. In R. J. Frances & S. I. Miller (Eds.), *Clinical textbook of addictive disorders* (pp. 340-346). New York: Guilford.

Kandel, D. B. (1975). Stages in adolescent involvement in drug use. *Science, 190,* 912-914.

Kandel, D. B., & Andrews, K. (1987). Processes of adolescent socialization by parents and peers. *International Journal of Addictions, 22,* 319-342.

Kaplan, H. B. (1995). Drugs, crime, and other deviant adaptations. In H. B. Kaplan (Ed.), *Drugs, crime, and other deviant adaptations* (pp. 3-46). New York: Plenum.

Kumpfer, K. L. (1993). *Resiliency and AOD use prevention in high risk youth.* Unpublished manuscript, University of Utah.

Loeber, R. (1991). Antisocial behavior: More enduring than changeable? *Journal of the American Academy of Child and Adolescent Psychiatry, 30,* 393-397.

McBride, D. C., Inciardi, J. A., Chitwood, D. D., McCoy, C. B., & the National AIDS Research Consortium (1992). Crack use and correlates of use in a national population of street heroin users. *Journal of Psychoactive Drugs, 24,* 411-416.

McCarthy, W. J., & Anglin, M. D. (1990). Narcotics addicts: Effect of family and parental risk factors on timing of emancipation, drug use onset, pre-addiction incarcerations and educational achievement. *Journal of Drug Issues, 20,* 99-123.

McCord, J. (1981). Alcoholism and criminality. *Journal of Studies on Alcohol, 42,* 739-748.

Merikangas, K. R., & Gelernter, C. S. (1990). Co-morbidity for alcoholism and depression. *Psychiatric Clinics of North America, 13,* 613-632.

Merikangas, K. R., Risch, N. R., & Weissman, M. M. (1994). Co-morbidity and co-transmission of alcoholism, anxiety, and depression. *Psychological Medicine, 24,* 69-80.

Miller, B. A., Downs, W. R., & Testa, M. (1993). Interrelationships between victimization experiences and women's alcohol use. *Journal of Studies on Alcohol, 11,* 109-117.

Needle, R. H., & Mills, A. R. (1994). *Drug procurement practices of the out-of-treatment chronic drug abuser* (NIH Publication No. 94-3820). Rockville, MD: U.S. Dept. of Health and Human Services, Public Health Services, and National Institute of Health, National Institute on Drug Abuse.

Newcomb, M. D., & Bentler, P. M. (1986). *Consequences of adolescent drug use: Impact on the lives of young adults.* Newbury Park, CA: Sage.

Oetting, E. R., & Beauvais, F. (1987). Peer cluster theory, socialization characteristics and adolescent drug use: A path analysis. *Journal of Counseling Psychology, 34,* 205-213.

Oetting, E. R., & Lynch, R. S. (in press). Peers and the prevention of adolescent drug use. In W. J. Bukoski & Z. Amsel (Eds.), *Drug abuse prevention.* Westport, CT: Greenwood.

Olweus, D. (1980). Familial and temperamental determinants of aggressive behavior in adolescent boys: A causal analysis. *Developmental Psychology, 16,* 644-660.

Patterson, G. R., Chamberlain, P., & Reid, J. B. (1982). A comparative evaluation of a parent training program. *Behavior Therapy, 13,* 638-650.

Pickens, R. W., Svikis, D. S., McGue, M., Lykken, D. T., Heston, L. L., & Clayton, P. J. (1991). Heterogeneity in the inheritance of alcoholism. *Archives of General Psychiatry, 48,* 19-28.

Plomin, R. (1986). *Developmental genetics and psychology.* Hillsdale, NJ: Lawrence Erlbaum.

Robins, L. N. (1978). Sturdy childhood predictors of adult antisocial behavior: Replications from longitudinal studies. *Psychological Medicine, 8,* 611-622.

Robins, L. N. (1980). The natural history of drug abuse. *Acta Psychiatrica Scandanavica, 62*(Suppl. 284), 7-20.

Roosa, M. W., Beals, J., Sandler, L. N., & Pillow, D. R. (1990). The role of risk and protective factors in predicting symptomatology in adolescent self-identified children of alcoholic parents. *American Journal of Community Psychology, 18,* 725-741.

Rutter, M., MacDonald, J., Le Couteur, A., Harrington, R., Bolton, P., & Bailey, P. (1990). Genetic factors in child psychiatric disorders. II. Empirical findings. *Journal of Child Psychology and Psychiatry, 31,* 39-83.

Scarr, S., & Grajek, S. (1982). Similarities and differences among siblings. In M. E. Lamb & B. Sutton-Smith (Eds.), *Sibling relationships: Their nature and significance across the lifespan* (pp. 357-381). Hillsdale, NJ: Lawrence Erlbaum.

Scheier, L. M., & Newcomb, M. D. (1991). Psychosocial predictors of drug use initiation and escalation: An expansion of the multiple risk factors hypothesis using longitudinal data. *Contemporary Drug Problems, 18,* 31-73.

Simcha-Fagan, O., Gersten, J. C., & Langner, T. (1986). Early precursors and concurrent correlates of illicit drug use in adolescents. *Journal of Drug Issues, 16,* 7-28.

Wada, K., & Fukui, S. (1994). Demographic and social characteristics of solvent abuse patients in Japan. *American Journal on the Addictions, 3,* 165-176.

Watts, W. D., & Ellis, A. M. (1993). Sexual abuse and drinking and drug use: Implications for prevention. *Journal of Drug Education, 23,* 183-200.

Werner, E. E. (1989). High-risk children in young adulthood: A longitudinal study from birth to 32 years. *American Journal of Orthopsychiatry, 59,* 72-81.

Widner, G., & Collins, L. (1993). Gender, coping, and health. In H. W. Krohne (Ed.), *Attention and avoidance* (pp. 241-265). Seattle: Hogrefe-Huber.

Zuckerman, M. (1983). *Biological basis of sensation-seeking, impulsivity, and anxiety.* Hillsdale, NJ: Lawrence Erlbaum.

3

Modeling Adolescent Health Behavior

The Preadult Health Decision-Making Model

Lilly M. Langer

All societies recognize that adolescence, commonly defined as the movement from childhood to adulthood, marks one of the most significant stages in an individual's life. In the United States, part of the significance of this life stage is that it is associated with an elevated risk for a variety of maladies—in particular, adolescent substance abuse. Hence, if efforts to reduce risk for adolescents are to be effective, there is a need to understand this life stage. In light of this need, the objectives of this chapter are to discuss (a) adolescence as a phenomenon; (b) psychosocial and behavioral theories associated with adolescence, including theories on the concept of self; and (c) models of health behavior. More specifically, because the central focus of this chapter is adolescent substance abuse, this chapter reviews the extensive psychological and sociological literature on adolescent development and adolescent health behaviors—in particular, behaviors related to drugs, AIDS, and other sexually transmitted diseases (STDs) as public health problems. Also presented are a number of health decision-making models and an outline of the Preadult Health Decision-Making Model (PAHDM; Langer & Warheit,

1992). The PAHDM takes into account the differential processing of information from peers and parents and through critical or reflexive self-analysis.

Adolescence as a Phenomenon

The onset of adolescence is associated with puberty and extends from approximately 11 to 20 years of age (Nowels, Toister, & Braunstein, 1981). This life stage is characterized by developmental challenges that are social, psychological, and biological. DeJong (1972) contended that adolescents and young adults must complete three tasks: (a) breaking parental bonds, (b) establishing a position within a new reference group and defining their social self in the process, and (c) developing their own unique identity. Some of the issues related to these tasks are decision making, sexuality, personal values, occupational orientation, and peer relations.

A plethora of theories have been developed to explain the attitudes, beliefs, and behaviors associated with adolescence. However, there has been disagreement about whether adolescence should, in fact, be thought of as a distinct stage of growth (Ausubel, Montemayor, & Svajian, 1977). From a developmental perspective, some argue that adolescence is a stage and is, moreover, unique. As a basis for their arguments, they point to the numerous and generally sequential biopsychosocial changes that occur during this period. Stated most succinctly, according to the biological approach to adolescence, the behavioral changes that occur during this period are the result of hormonally induced physiological events. The endocrine changes that occur are thought to have been latent for many years and are genetically predetermined. These biological events, furthermore, are universally distributed, immune to cultural influence, and inevitable. Moreover, proponents of this approach insist that because the biological changes that occur during adolescence are common to the life cycle of all mammals, this period can be regarded as a phylogenetic phenomenon (Ausubel et al., 1977; Hall, 1882, 1904).

The biological changes associated with alterations in hormonal levels are manifested as physical changes in both form and function over a relatively short period of time in early adolescence. It is a commonly held belief that the biological changes that occur during adolescence make this period a time of turbulence and struggle (Hall, 1904; Offer & Offer, 1969, 1975; Offer, Ostrove, & Howard, 1981; Weiner, 1970). However, others have attempted to eradicate such a notion. Westley and Elkin (1957) noted that most teenagers do not fit the traditional stereotypes and appear to have little or no emotional difficulty during adolescence. A number of researchers have contended that the magnitude and intensity of disagreements between parents and their adolescent children have been exaggerated by the mass media (Banks, 1969; Harris, 1971).

During this transitional period when the individual is no longer a child but not yet an adult, he or she goes through numerous social and psychological changes as well. These changes mainly center on revising one's definition of self. From a psychosocial perspective, identity development during adolescence involves (a) differentiation of self from the previously held view of identity advanced by parents (Schachtel, 1959); (b) migration from the parental sphere of influence to the adolescent/peer universe—that is, a "decentration" (Piaget, 1954); and (c) a synthesis of parental and peer influences with the individual's idiosyncratic personal and social characteristics according to the individual's own decision-making "style."

Biopsychosocial changes for adults are usually gradual processes that span decades. In contrast, adolescence is a period of dramatic change that is compressed into a few brief "teen" years. Erikson (1959) viewed adolescence as a period of psychological moratorium: that is, a period when individuals are free to experiment with a variety of roles before deciding on their future. Substance use may be one example of such experimentation: Because the administration and use of drugs have been the exclusive province of adults, adolescents may view substance use as a relatively facile means of penetrating the experiential world of adults.

With biological, cognitive, and psychosocial changes fully under way, the relative stability that often typified the child's previous years becomes replaced by transition, change, and conflict. As the child begins to resemble an adult physically, he or she expects to be granted adult statuses. Adolescents at this stage in their psychosocial development frequently begin to reevaluate the tenets of parental and familial socialization in terms of competing options, perhaps for the first time. Often, peer group opinion carries the most weight during early adolescence (Erikson, 1950; Warheit et al., 1995). Acceptance by peers is of utmost importance, and the willingness to conform to group norms is especially characteristic of this time.

Although the adolescent will attempt to view matters from the perspective of parents and peers, he or she is "encapsulated" within his or her own unique phenomenal field. In other words, although an adolescent may have a general orientation, his or her decisions can never escape personal interests and concerns; the individual is to a certain extent directed by his or her own motivational system. Slowly, emotional ties with parents are loosened, and the adolescent begins to look to peers for explanations of existence and behavioral role models.

In previous generations, distinctions between right and wrong were delineated clearly through religious teachings. If persons sinned, they were fully aware they had done so and felt guilty. The current generation feel obliged to know right from wrong but are uncertain whether they understand this distinction (Borowitz, 1969). In contrast to preliterate societies, our society has no ritualized or legalized set of formal rules to socialize adolescents into adulthood. Furthermore, the strong emphasis on individuality in the United States coupled with the breakdown of the family has led to an adolescent period characterized by reliance on peers as a source of reference and self-definition. In this respect, the United States differs strikingly from preliterate societies, in which adolescence marked the disengagement from children/peers, followed by the association with adults and the assignment of adult tasks and statuses.

Hence, without a formalized set of socially sanctioned norms for adolescents, it is not surprising that for some teens this is quite a tumultuous period characterized by delinquent acts that are associated with a broad range of social problems, including minor and major crimes; the use of illicit drugs, alcohol, and cigarettes; AIDS/HIV; increased rates of other sexually transmitted diseases (STDs); and unplanned pregnancy. In fact, research findings indicate that over the past three decades, adolescents have become involved in the use of substances at increasingly younger ages (Bachman et al., 1991; Kandel & Logan, 1984; Palmer & Ringwalt, 1988; Rachal et al., 1975). Oetting and Beauvais (1990), summarizing findings of a number of national and local surveys, indicated that 65% of those in the seventh grade and 77.2% of those in the eighth grade had used alcohol at some time in their lives and that 10.4% of the seventh graders and 16.9% of the eighth graders had used marijuana. They also reported lifetime use of inhalants for 40.8% of the seventh and 50.9% of the eighth graders. Present prevalence trends highlight the seriousness of the issues related to current substance use among adolescents. In light of these issues, there is a great need to understand how the "lifeworld" of teenagers mediates their socialization and how adolescents make health decisions.

Theories of Adolescent Psychosocial Development

Historically, scientists from a variety of fields have endeavored to study and to explain the decision-making processes chosen by adolescents to handle the new tasks and responsibilities that accompany each stage of development. Although several theories have attempted to explain adolescent development and related behaviors (Baldwin, 1967), none has been able to account comprehensively for the development of non-normative attitudes, beliefs, and behaviors, including substance use, during adolescence. The following discussion contains a brief overview of several theoretical perspectives used to explain personality and behavior development during the life stage known as adolescence.

Personality Theories

Symbolic Interactionism

During the early part of the 20th century, modern social psychologists formulated a theory of the self known as *symbolic interactionism* (SI). Basic to SI is the contention that the self is a reflection of the view of others (Blumer, 1969; Cooley, 1902; Dewey, 1930; Mead, 1934; Stryker, 1980; Thomas & Thomas, 1928). Cooley (1902) maintained that personality emerges from "communication among those sharing extant social life, and that central to personality are the expectations of others" (Stryker & Statham, 1985). In accordance with theoretical traditions in sociology and social psychology, the adolescent's image of self emerges from interpersonal relationships. In 1902, Charles Horton Cooley developed the notion of the "looking glass" self. He argued that one's self-concept is significantly affected by the internalized imagined appraisals of others. Hence the self-concept based on a self-view is a social one that is developed through relationships with others. For example, if adolescents perceive that their peers view substance use as a sophisticated behavior and this perception is confirmed by the comments and actions of their peers, then adolescents who use substances will form a view of themselves as sophisticated.

SI, for example, could be used to explain the stage of adolescence during which the teenager becomes a group-oriented conformist who is overly concerned with acceptance by peers. Still, society and the individual are joined by a network of interpersonal communication. In terms of SI, interaction is symbolic, or based on the symbols/meanings that persons develop in the course of their conduct. Thus, from a SI perspective, the conformist behavior of the adolescent is simply a part of the continual process of identity development (Thomas & Weigert, 1971). The development of the self is the product of viewing oneself reflexively, as an object, and using the viewpoint of others to attach meaning to oneself.

Kuhn (1964) maintained that if one is familiar with the subjective definition of a person's identity, one can predict his or her behavior and interact with him or her. In other words, attitudes toward self are one of the best indicators of patterns of action. An underlying premise of SI is that the subjective component of the adolescent experience should be examined to gain insight into adolescent behavior. The symbols/meanings that adolescents assign to objects serve to organize their behavior into social acts (e.g., as noted above, the equation of drug use with sophistication and worldliness). Because significant symbols are the precursors to further behavior, they provide a means for adjusting activity (i.e., intervening) before behavior has occurred.

Developmental Perspective

Erikson (1959) argued that personality development is an ongoing process. Because adolescents undergo physiological, psychological, and social changes, identity formation is an especially complex process. Generally, an identity that provides a strong sense of self makes decision making easier for the late adolescent. During this time, parents, peers, and self are reappraised, independence is coveted, and, generally, ties to parents are loosened. Psychosocially, the stages of adolescence reflect critique, thesis, and synthesis. Both Erikson (1959) and Kohlberg (1966) perceived personality and decision making to be intertwined and influenced by the personal or ego identity and outside influences, which for the adolescent include (but are not limited to) peers and parents. Specifically, an adolescent must reach the stage of formal operational thought before he or she can evaluate, rationalize, and justify behavior.

Psychodynamic Perspective

Sigmund Freud's classic psychodynamic theories had a major influence on the field of personality development (Freud, 1905, 1938, 1923/1947).

Central to psychodynamic theories is an almost exclusive focus on unconscious dynamics and the early social and psychological experiences of the child. According to Freud, the infant enters the world governed by only the id, or biological self. Freud saw the emergence, very early on, of a second subsystem, which he termed the ego. Freud maintained that the ego emerged as a result of the dynamic interaction of the biological self or id with the third subsystem, the superego, or society and culture. As the child undergoes socialization, according to Freud, the superego initially reflects the parents' values and later on embodies the norms and values of society.

Behavioral Theories

Self-Esteem Motive Theory

The self-esteem motive is central to a number of theories of social behavior (Kaplan, 1975, 1980; Pepitone, 1964; Rosenberg, 1979, 1989; Webster & Sobieszek, 1974; Zetterberg, 1957). The major premise of self-esteem motive theory is that due to initial infant dependency on adults for the fulfillment of basic biological needs, an individual develops a need for human interaction, positive evaluations by others, and a favorable self-image. More specifically, adolescents are motivated to behave so as to avoid or reduce rejection, which they perceive will jeopardize goal attainment.

A large body of literature has been amassed by researchers who have offered a variety of theoretical postulates and models as a framework for understanding the etiology of non-normative behaviors, including substance use among adolescents. Some have focused on the negative personal and social consequences of low self-esteem, including self-rejection and derogation (Erikson, 1950; Jessor & Jessor, 1977; Kandel, 1983; Kandel & Logan, 1984; Kaplan, 1980, 1984; Kaplan, Johnson, & Bailey, 1986; Lettieri, 1984; Newcomb & Bentler, 1986; Padina & Schuela, 1983; Reckless, Dinitz, & Murray, 1956; Reiss, 1951; Rosenberg, 1989; Smith & Fogg, 1977, 1978; Wells & Rankin, 1983), and the role of factors relating to peer influence regarding substance use among adolescents (Brook, Whiteman, & Gordon, 1983; Combs, Paulson, & Richardson, 1991; Cousineau, Savard, & Allard, 1993; Diehlman, Butchart, Shope, & Miller, 1990-1991; Dinges & Oetting, 1993; Farrell & Danish, 1993; Forney, Forney, & Ripley, 1989; Huba & Bentler, 1980, 1984; Jessor & Jessor, 1977; Kandel & Logan, 1984; Kaplan,

1984; Maddahian, Bentler, & Newcomb, 1986; Newcomb & Bentler, 1986; Sarvela & McClendon, 1988; Warheit et al., 1995).

The literature cited above is an indication of the considerable attention that social scientists have given to explaining the relationships between self factors (i.e., self-esteem) and deviant behaviors and peer factors and illicit substance use among adolescents.

Summary and Synthesis of Theories

The foregoing discussion is but a glimpse into a vast body of literature on theories of adolescent personality development and how it is related to behavior; yet no consensus has been reached regarding how adolescents actually make behavioral decisions. Further, to date, there is a very limited body of empirical information regarding effective modeling of adolescent decision making. Attaining this level of understanding is difficult because not only are adolescents in a time of physical and cognitive transition, but their social environment is also in a process of accelerated change. For health planners to define the resources needed to provide effective interventions for adolescents, these experts must first be able to model adolescent health behavior effectively by defining the forces that influence attitudes, beliefs, and behaviors.

Models of Health Behavior

The theories discussed so far are, like all other theories, interrelated sets of concepts, variables, statements, and formats (Turner, 1986). To render a theory testable, one must quantify it and specify the relationships of its various elements. Through this process, theories can be used to develop models. The importance of the conceptual delineation involved in modeling is especially clear in the case of a social phenomenon as complex as health decision making. In a society in which the definition of self is derived from peers, it is not surprising that health behaviors are also obtained from the attitudes and behaviors of peers. Given the seriousness of social problems related to issues such as substance abuse, AIDS, and teen pregnancy, it is clear that there is a crucial need for models that determine health decision elements and their interactions among adolescents as precisely as possible. With these models, effective intervention becomes more possible.

Rationale for Health Behavior Modeling

Traditionally, one of the goals of educators in the United States has been enlightenment through socialization. However, historically, the specific task of health behavior socialization was a parental responsibility. More recently, educators have undertaken increased responsibility for this formidable task as part of their health curriculum. The topics addressed by health educators now include a host of drug- and alcohol-related issues, such as pregnancy, STDs, sexual decision making, sexual communication, and, most recently, AIDS. Some researchers (Scales, 1983) maintain that education that provides only facts does not address the fundamental need of students to understand more fully the real consequences of their behavior. Accurate knowledge and information seem to be necessary but not sufficient to effect a change in attitudes and behaviors. Polis (1985) suggested that educators should assist students in developing "skills of critical inquiry" so that teenagers can begin to take the perspective of other persons in a given situation and thus enhance their sense of self-efficacy. To provide these skills, educators must recognize various orientations with regard to decision making of their students. Understanding an adolescent's worldview is crucial for developing effective health education programs.

The links between knowledge, attitudes, beliefs, skills, and behaviors have long baffled researchers and health professionals. As noted, several theories have addressed self-destructive behaviors and issues of risk. The persistent prevalence and incidence of preventable diseases associated with discretionary behaviors such as substance use indicate that no "theoretical panacea" has been found to account for these behaviors. What may be on the horizon is an integrated, unified theory that is made up of various components of several current theories.

The following is a discussion of some of the theoretical models in the health education and prevention literature. These models are presented to provide the reader with a historical overview of some of the various efforts to clarify processes of health decision making.

Social Learning Model

The basic components of social learning theory (SLT), as first delineated by Rotter (1954), are behavioral potential, expectancy, reinforcement value, and the psychological situation. According to SLT, the expectation and perceived value of a given consequence determine the probability that a given behavior will be performed. Each decision is thus considered situationally specific because the individual assigns subjective values to consequences. Therefore it can be reasoned that behavioral changes result from increasing the strength of the perceived relationships between a behavior and its consequences, in addition to changing how these consequences are evaluated. Moreover, one's ability to perform a behavior becomes a major element in formulating an expectation. Strecher, DeVellis, Becker, and Rosenstock (1986) used the terms *outcome expectations* and *efficacy expectations* to describe decision making, and Bandura (1977a) argued that the influence of self-efficacy affects all dimensions of behavior. In fact, Bandura noted that locus of control, or conviction that outcomes are or are not determined by one's own action, affects self-efficacy and behavior in a number of ways.

Many of the proponents of learning theory have posited a stimulus-response type of explanation of child development. According to this position, mere exposure to a particular situation is sufficient to stimulate and thus to explain behavior. The individual is perceived as an object acted on by external forces. By emphasizing social interaction and deemphasizing the element of external reinforcement, social learning theories differ from other learning theories. A large body of empirical literature has developed in support of its claims (Bandura & Walters, 1959; Dollard, Doob, Miller, Mowrer, & Sears, 1939; Hull, 1931; Hull et al., 1940; Miller & Dollard, 1941; Sears, 1951; Skinner, 1950). Social learning theory is especially relevant when considering adolescents who have been socialized by Western culture to believe in an external locus of control. For example, adolescents, especially those who are disadvantaged, may grow up believing that they have little or no control over their environment or their future. After being exposed regularly to the sale and use of illicit drugs, they may become convinced that external forces will determine their fate and that they too will be compelled to become users.

Skinner's reinforcement theory (1976) added the element of external reinforcement to social learning. Skinner argued that rewarded behaviors tend to be learned and repeated, whereas actions that are punished are extinguished. Bandura (1977b) introduced another concept known as *observational learning.* He maintained that learning consists of cognitive and social interaction that involves attention to the modeled behavior. Repetition of the modeled behavior involves retention or memory processing, motivation, and the rehearsing and reinforcing of the modeled behavior. For example, role playing can be seen as a method for developing skills at negotiation and perceived self-efficacy (Allensworth & Symons, 1989).

Although SLT has been useful to a degree in predicting health behaviors such as alcohol and drug use (Akers, Krohn, Lanza-Kaduce, & Radosevich, 1979), programs based on this theory have been only moderately successful in reducing the onset of behaviors such as regular tobacco use (Hansen, Malotte, & Fielding, 1988). According to some researchers, this model's predictive strength is relatively weak when compared to models such as the health belief model (Wallston & Wallston, 1984).

Health Belief Model

The basic premise of the health belief model (HBM) is that behavioral change results from knowledge related to health when three conditions are met. First, the person must believe that he or she is threatened by a particular health risk, whether because of his or her personal susceptibility or because of the severity of the risk itself. Second, a risk-reducing action must be viewed as providing a greater potential benefit than its potential cost. And third, environmental cues, such as the death of a friend or family member, must be present that stimulate a decision to reduce health risks. In contrast to social learning models, the HBM originally resulted from applied research in health education (Janz & Becker, 1984; Leventhal & Hirschman, 1982). This widely used social psychological model accounted for some dimensions of preventive health behavior. Since its inception, it has been applied to educational efforts aimed at altering sexual behavior (Becker & Joseph, 1988; Eisen & Zellman, 1986; Eisen, Zellman, & McAlister, 1985; Hingson, Strunin, Berlin, & Heeren, 1990; Simon & Hingson, 1984; Strunin & Hingson, 1992).

Findings show that the HBM is only moderately accurate in predicting preventive health outcomes (Becker et al., 1977; Janz & Becker, 1984). Zimmerman (1989) found that the strongest predictor of whether an individual would engage in a particular health behavior was the ratio of perceived benefit to perceived cost. The weakest predictor of health promotion or risk reduction was the severity of negative health consequences. The use of scare tactics alone was generally found to be a poor method for instigating behavior change. High levels of fear without specific plans for action were as ineffective as low levels of fear in catalyzing action (Zimmerman, 1989). The findings of a survey of 189 Louisiana teenagers and 80 family physicians

(Manning & Balson, 1989) illustrated that a physician's ability to predict teenagers' beliefs on the basis of the major dimensions of the HBM was minimal.

Studies that have attempted to establish that knowledge is essential to assessing perceived susceptibility, perceived risk, and cost/benefit have produced inconsistent findings (Catania, Kegeles, & Coates, 1990). Although evidence supports the role of susceptibility in evaluating risk, those findings are not entirely consistent. Cost/benefit, as applied to a variety of health behaviors, has been a central component of the HBM. However, in contrast to its various other applications, the concept of cost/benefit may not be relevant to adolescent sexual behaviors in or not in the context of drug use (Langer & Tubman, in press). For example, a change to less risky sexual practices may be dependent on a nonrational perception of risk or the label that has been attached to a particular health problem such as substance use or AIDS. Gardner (1993) has suggested that uncertainty about the future is an incentive for adolescents to participate in a wide range of risk-taking behaviors because the immediate costs of not participating in risky behavior may outweigh the immediate benefits. The long-term benefits of nonparticipation (e.g., health status, status in one's peer group, potential income) may be discounted due to a lack of reliable information needed to predict future outcomes in terms of health, income, or longevity. This particular pattern of evaluating the costs and benefits of risk-taking behavior may be accentuated among adolescents who perceive their futures as being particularly uncertain (e.g., minority substance abusers).

Ajzen-Fishbein Model

The primary focus of the Ajzen-Fishbein model (AFM) is how the advice of others may serve as a catalyst for positive or negative changes in health behaviors. This model has been used by social psychologists who have studied the relationship between health attitudes and behaviors (Ajzen, 1982; Ajzen & Fishbein, 1980; Fishbein & Ajzen, 1975). For example, according to the AFM, an adolescent's decision to smoke may be predicated on norms perceived to be held by a significant other or peer group. Central to this model is the assumption that a behavior is dependent on one's intention to engage in a specific action. In fact, this premise was elaborated on by Prochaska, DiClemente, and Norcross (1992) in their research involving stages of change. More specifically, these researchers posited that modification of addictive behaviors involves progression through five stages: (a) precontemplation (no intention to change), (b) contemplation (awareness that a problem exists), (c) preparation (intention to take action), (d) action (modification of behavior), and (e) maintenance (work toward prevention of relapse). Individuals typically recycle through these stages several times before termination of the addiction. Further, the findings indicated that the underlying structure of change is neither technique oriented nor problem specific.

In the AFM, behavioral intention consists of three elements: (a) an evaluation of the consequences of the particular action, (b) an estimation of the normative judgment of significant others regarding this action, and (c) a willingness to conform to the wishes of those significant persons. The utility of this model has been demonstrated in a variety of health behavior studies, including research on weight reduction (Saltzer, 1981; Sejwacz, Ajzen, & Fishbein, 1980) and cigarette smoking (Chassin et al., 1981).

When the AFM is applied to adolescents and AIDS, the perceived consequences could include the belief that sex without drugs or the use of a condom might be less satisfying. Thus a nonconforming male adolescent might experience real or perceived loss of status among members of his peer or reference group. This adolescent's decision to be vigilant with regard to avoiding health risks would then depend on his or her willingness to conform to or deviate from peer norms.

The health behavior decision-making process is very complex. Research has shown that the impact of cognition is not necessarily mediated by attitudes (Liska, 1984). Liska suggested that this may occur because cognitions are frequently too complex and the cognitive processing capacities of individuals too variable for thoughts to be completely transformed into attitudes. In addition, he noted that according to the AFM, social structure is conceptualized as a background variable, with its effect on behavior mediated by attitudes, subjective norms, and intentions. This might be the case when behavior depends on motivation alone. However, much of behavior also depends on resources, especially regarding drug use among adolescents. For example, if an adolescent is motivated to use illicit drugs and does not have the money or social connections to acquire them, motivation can be stymied. Resources and opportunities that directly influence behavior may be determined by social structure. Behavior then becomes the medium through which attitudes, norms, and intentions are expressed.

Bentler and Speckart (1981) showed that when prior behavior is taken into account, the predictive components of the model are reduced. For example, individuals who use substances as a means of dealing with challenging life events reinforce this behavior each time they repeat it. Hence individuals who have patterned substance abuse behavior are more likely to repeat the behavior regardless of the attitudes of significant others. Bentler and Speckart (1981) maintained that although ongoing and new behaviors must be distinguished, prior behavior must not be simply controlled; rather, models must be developed that incorporate a scheme that accounts for diverse behavioral patterns.

According to the AFM, social networks or directedness may be a powerful force in labeling health problems (Gross & McMullen, 1983). Moreover, behavioral changes may be interpreted as changes to more, less, or equally pleasurable activities. For the adolescent who lacks a future perspective, however, such personal assessments may be regarded as inconceivable. Therefore, if health risk reduction education is to result in behavior change, instruction must include ways to portray low-risk behaviors as pleasurable. It must foster the idea that adolescents are capable of making the desired changes. Further, adolescents must become confident that they possess the skills required to initiate and persist in behavior change.

Decision-Making Model

Decision theory involves a large corpus of literature that details the intricacies of how people make particular decisions. Although many of the procedures appear to be quite complex, there seem to be some common underlying principles (Behn & Vaupel, 1983; Raiffa, 1968; von Winterfeldt & Edwards, 1986; Watson & Buede, 1987). In general, decision making involves the reconciliation of conflicting objectives, while incorporating the element of uncertainty that is related to generating particular outcomes.

The decision-making model (DMM) proposed by Janis and Mann (1977) is specific neither to adolescent development nor to health-related decisions. Rather, it provides a general framework for considering the relationship between knowledge, attitudes, beliefs, and behaviors. Central to the DMM are five coping patterns associated with decisional conflict:

1. The decision maker ignores messages of risk/loss and persists in previous behavior.
2. The decision maker uncritically adopts the most salient recommended course of action.

3. The decision maker engages in defensive avoidance by, for example, procrastinating, shifting responsibility, or rationalizing.
4. The decision maker searches frantically for a way out of the dilemma by adopting a hypervigilance that, in its extreme form, resembles panic.
5. The decision maker is vigilant in searching for relevant information and weighs alternatives before making a choice.

Although the first two coping mechanisms presuppose a short period of conflict, when an issue is of a vital nature they often lead to defective decision making. Similarly, defensive avoidance and hypervigilance can be adaptive in certain circumstances but generally lead to serious losses. Janis and Mann (1977) indicated that with the exception of split-second responses, only the fifth pattern leads to worthwhile decisions. In fact, vigilance is seen only under three conditions: when the risks of alternate choices are known, when better alternatives are thought to exist, and when there is adequate time for deliberation before a decision must be made.

According to this model, the individual must be challenged by some disturbing information or event that alerts him or her to an imminent loss. This challenge may assume the form of an impressive communication or a disturbing event. However, caution is advised in terms of using scare tactics. If fear exceeds an optimal level, adherence to warnings begins to diminish. Janis and Mann (1977) maintained that optimal levels of fear arousal may vary according to the type of threat and the personalities involved.

According to DMM, changing one's behavior to avoid harmful health behavior outcomes involves decision making. Often decisions concerning one's health are mediated by conflict. For example, when decisions are made by adolescents concerning the use of drugs or postponing of sexual activity, these choices require the acceptance of short-term inconveniences to achieve long-term objectives. If circumstances allow adequate time, adolescents who make these types of choices may experience a great deal of conflict before they make up their minds and act. The greater the perceived costs, the greater the stress that is engendered by decisional conflict.

Summary of Models

The health behavior models presented in this chapter represent attempts both to define and to understand the dynamics of the forces that shape human behavior. Although many of the psychosocial health behavior models are useful in identifying some of the decisions that underlie a commitment to personal change, they all presume high levels of cognition and rationality. However, actually altering behaviors such as substance use, sexual behavior, and overeating is complex, and individuals usually have an investment in their behavior on some level. Further, some types of behaviors are not unilateral. For example, most sexual behaviors and drug sharing require mutual and simultaneous commitments to action on the part of two participants. Certainly, being under the influence of drugs makes this an even more complex process. In contrast, behaviors such as overeating, smoking cessation, and alcohol abstinence involve only one person's discontinuing a single behavior. Moreover, much of human behavior is not accompanied by a conscious level of cognition. Therefore existing sociomedical models, though effective in understanding simple or single-person health decisions, are inadequate in explaining complex behaviors, especially those that are simultaneous and socially interactive.

Who influences the decisions adolescents make, to what extent, and why are questions that researchers have been attempting to answer for a long time. Examination of the relationships of reference groups to the attitudes, beliefs, and behaviors of adolescents encompasses a large and ever-expanding body of literature. Most research endeavors in this area have focused primarily on peer versus parent influence with regard to issues such as morals, autonomy, deviance, sexuality, substance abuse, self-esteem, and achievement (Bowerman & Kinch, 1959; Dielman, Campanielli, Shope, & Butchart, 1987; Fasick, 1984; Fisher, 1986; Floyd & South, 1972; Jensen, 1973; Jorgensen & Sonstegard, 1984; Juhasz & Sonnenshein-Schneider, 1987; Larson, 1972; Shah & Zelnick, 1981; Steinberg & Silverberg, 1986; Young & Ferguson, 1979). However, additional studies have included various other decision-making referents, such as the church, teachers, partners, and self (Daugherty & Burger, 1984; Maslow, 1954, 1964, 1968; Thompson & Spanier, 1978; Wilson, 1988). Not only have researchers clearly identified different decision-making styles, but they have suggested, and in some cases empirically tested, biopsychosocial factors that correlate to specific decision-making orientations (Erikson, 1950; Freud, 1947, 1962; Lidz, 1983; Lindzey & Borgatta, 1954; Mead, 1934; Piaget, 1954; Webster & Sobieszek, 1974).

Historically, these decision-making models have been predicated on the assumption that the subjects are free adults. But in today's society, adolescents have not been allowed to engage in certain behaviors until they have become adults, as represented by completing school or finding a job. As McCall and Simmons (1966) noted, adults impinge on the world of the child to a greater degree than the child can invade the world of adults. Given this asymmetry, the preadult stage of psychosocial development can be viewed as embodying an artificial prereality controlled by adults.

Environment impinges on behavior for adults as well as adolescents. However, the ground rules are different in varying social and cultural environments for the individual at these two life stages. For example, alcohol use among adults and teenagers 18 years of age or older is legally and socially acceptable. However, this same substance is forbidden to be sold to individuals under the age of 18 under any circumstance (although it is not illegal for an adolescent of any age to consume alcohol). The use of illicit drugs, on the other hand, is not legally sanctioned for either adults or adolescents.

Because earlier health behavior models were designed to predict and control behaviors in the qualitatively less restrictive environments of adults, they may not be relevant in the more restrictive domain of adolescents. Health decision-making models that fail to take into account the differences between the environment of adolescents and adults may fail to explain behavior.

The realization that decisions are often socially interactive has led me to posit the preadult health decision-making model (PAHDM) as a synthesis of the psychological modeling of maturation and influence, on the one hand, and the social/medical understanding of influence, on the other. This perspective is in contrast to the more narrow perspectives that characterize the models just discussed. For example, the health belief model emphasizes rational response to external cues and the evaluation of risk/benefit, while deemphasizing the interactive and maturational aspect of decision making. Strongly influenced by SI, the central premise of the PAHDM is that adolescents are in a process of self-development and that to understand their decision making, the concept of an emerging self as it interacts with their lifeworld must be taken into account. The PAHDM is socially sensitive in that it takes into account the element of interaction and the element of interpretation and is fluid and open to change.

The following discussion elaborates the PAHDM and illustrates its role in health behavior intervention.

The PAHDM as an Adolescent Health Behavior Model

Directedness as Related to Adolescent Decision Making: The Conceptual Model

Although many factors can be used to explain health attitudes, beliefs, and behaviors, the focus here is on directedness as a central component in a model of adolescent health decision making. More specifically, the focus is on how biopsychosocial/environmental factors and reference groups associated with decision making direct and reinforce the attitudes, beliefs, and behaviors related to risk. The PAHDM is related to and parallels Riesman's typological classifications of tradition-directed, inner-directed, and other-directed persons, as described in his classic work *The Lonely Crowd* (1950).

Culture affects all aspects of self-expression. Understanding this influence is difficult because individuals have their own modes of reacting to socialization and therefore develop their own decision-making styles. Although the classifications of directedness in the PAHDM are similar to those of Riesman (1950), they are fundamentally different from Riesman's in that his are based on the population S-curve; that is, they are categorical and staged. Though it may appear that the macro stages of population growth and decline identified by Riesman roughly parallel phases of adolescent development as delineated in the PAHDM, this is not the case. The PAHDM is a dynamic process model that represents variations in directedness that are assumed to exist along a continuum; Riesman's static model is not. The assumptions of the PAHDM are that human behavior is learned, rational, modifiable, and synergistic and that it involves cognitive, emotional, and symbolic processes, which continually interact. Moreover, in keeping with Mead's work (1934), the self is seen as consisting of a basic core of states and traits that are relatively fixed (the I) in addition to a dynamic, changing set of attitudes, beliefs, and values that are modifiable within varying social contexts (the me). Although a positive linear relationship may not always exist between knowledge and behavior, this model postulates that when conditions are modified and information is provided, behavior can be altered in a variety of ways. This is thought to be more so among those whose sense of self has not been fixed in place by age, experience, or maturation. The assumptions of the PAHDM make intervention possible at a variety of points, whereas staged models militate against change.

Essentially, the PAHDM is intended to provide a theoretically and empirically driven model that can be used in altering risky attitudes and behaviors of adolescents. If the PAHDM is found to have validity and reliability, it could be used in programs designed to reduce the risk behaviors related to HIV.

It should be noted that when the PAHDM was proposed to the literature in 1992 (Langer & Warheit, 1992), it was not presented as a definitive model of adolescent health behavior; rather, it was intended to stimulate empirical studies that would provide tested data to substantiate the untested relationships posited in the model or modify them accordingly. Since that time, a number of studies have been performed testing various aspects of the PAHDM, and as a result, the model represented in Figure 3.1 is a revised version of the original PAHDM.

The PAHDM is primarily a bilateral conceptual framework. Specifically, it focuses on two major aspects of decision making: (a) *inputs,* considered to be knowledge and beliefs and (b) *outputs,* considered to be attitudes and behaviors. Both inputs and outputs are shown to be mediated at different points by biopsychosocial/environmental factors that exist along a developmental time sequence. That is, past, present, and self-perceived future factors are considered by the PAHDM to intervene or mediate adolescent decision making at either the input stage (prior to any cue to action) and/or the decision-making stage. Further, it is suggested that biopsychosocial factors may influence whether the cue to action will occur at all.

The PAHDM is a decision-making model in which the adolescent is depicted by two concentric circles representing the two categories of decision-making orientation or directedness: peer-directed and parent/self-directed. Peer-directedness is exemplified by individuals whose decision-making processes are most strongly influenced by peers, rather than parents or self. Parent/self-directed individuals are defined as those who are most strongly influenced by parents and self, rather than peers, when making decisions. In accordance with Riesman (1950), it should be noted that the overlap of peer- and parent/self-directed styles is intended to indicate that pure types are not being suggested. In other words, an empirical rather than an ideal type construct is being suggested. Some studies have reported significant differences in the HIV-related attitudes and behavior of peer-, parent-, and self-directed adolescent decision makers (Langer, Zimmerman, Warheit, & Duncan, 1993) and in their risk for cardiovascular disease

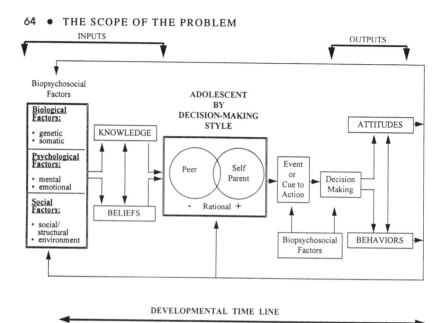

Figure 3.1. The Preadult Health Decision-Making Model (PAHDM)

(Bromfield, 1994). However, on the basis of previous empirical testing that has shown little or no significant difference between self- and parent-directed decision makers with regard to a variety of risk-related attitudes and behaviors (Langer et al., 1993), current studies have retained the category of peer-directed decision making but have collapsed the categories of self-and parent-directed decision making into a single decision-making style that is considered the more "rational" (Langer & Tubman, in press). These unpublished findings confirm the need to focus on decision making as an important component of any effective behavior change intervention.

Although many of the relationships specified in Figure 3.1 have been verified empirically (Bromfield, 1994; Langer et al., 1993; Langer & Tubman, in press), a number are in the process of being tested, and a number have not yet been tested.

Inputs

As shown in Figure 3.1, biopsychosocial factors related to knowledge and beliefs are considered to be input factors that have a reciprocal relationship and influence the decision-making style of the individual prior to a cue to action. For example, biological factors can influence decision-making style not only directly but also through their influence on beliefs, as in the case of one's physical stature influencing one's self-concept (e.g., one's sense of one's physical desirability to others).

It has been argued by Fishbein and Ajzen (1975) that beliefs and attitudes are highly correlated (correlations between .60 and .80) and thus may represent the same phenomenon. However, it has been suggested by Liska (1984) that this high correlation is the result of systematic measurement error, and other studies suggest that substantial variation exists between attitudes and beliefs (Bagozzi, 1978; Bagozzi & Burnkrant, 1979; Kothandapani, 1971). Furthermore, still others have found that beliefs are predictors of attitudes (Bagozzi & Burnkrant, 1979; Schlegel & DiTecco, 1982; Triandis, 1977).

As noted previously, the literature supports knowledge as an input in this model. Moreover, knowledge and beliefs are shown to be contingent on psychosocial factors such as personality (Albrecht & Warner, 1975; Brook, Lukoff, & Whiteman, 1978), need for approval (Albrecht & Warner, 1975; Crowne & Marlowe, 1964), self-efficacy (Bandura, 1977a, 1982; Coelho, 1984; Schunk & Carbonari, 1984), self-esteem (Orr, Wilbrandt, Brack, Rauch, & Ingersoll, 1989; Rosenberg, Schooler, & Schoenbach, 1989), self-concept (Burke & Reitzes, 1981; Swann & Read, 1981), and social environment and socioeconomic class (Coates & Perry, 1980; Kohn, 1959, 1963, 1969; Lewis & Lewis, 1984; Stinchcombe, 1964; Zuehlke, 1981). Biological factors such as a birth defect, illness, and/or hormonal imbalance can also be associated with psychological and social factors and with the processing of knowledge and beliefs. This is an extremely abbreviated list in terms of both variables and related studies. Clearly, an exhaustive delineation would be beyond the scope of this chapter. However, the extensive number of variables that are possible contributors to an adolescent's decisions emphasizes the complexity of the task of modeling health behavior decision making.

Irwin and Millstein (1986) proposed a model of adolescent risk-taking behavior that included some of the components of the PAHDM. For example, because they maintained that specific areas of psychosocial development appear to be affected by timing of biological maturation, they included biological development as a component of their model. The factors they included in their proposed model are compatible with some of those proposed by the PAHDM. However, one of the major differences between their risk-taking model and the PAHDM is that their model is depicted as recursive and, in addition, omits the reciprocal interaction of attitudes with behaviors.

How the confluence of biopsychosocial factors, especially one's current social structure, affects the decision-making orientation and process of adolescents (or adults) is not well delineated in the current scientific literature. This gap in our understanding represents a serious challenge to understanding adolescent health behavior decision making. Most health behavior modeling has attempted to develop an effective, but parsimonious, model for predicting and preventing risky health behaviors. To date, such a model has not been developed for the following reasons:

1. Researchers have found that behaviors result from a confluence of numerous interactions and contingency factors.
2. Some of the factors are related recursively and others nonrecursively.
3. When a large number of the contingency factors and interactions were included in the model, investigators were faced with the problem of multicollinearity (Songer-Nocks, 1976) and a model that was unwieldy and impractical.

Unlike the Ajzen-Fishbein model, the PAHDM is a dynamic and nonrecursive model. Further, unlike the health belief model, biopsychosocial and decision-making directedness/orientation are considered important factors to be taken into account along a time line that exists before, during, and after a cue to action. Still another major assumption of the PAHDM is that health behavior modeling for adolescents must exist along a developmental time line to take into account developmental and social structural differences that, as noted previously, have been well documented in the literature.

Outputs

As shown in Figure 3.1, attitudes and behaviors are considered as outputs in the PAHDM. However, researchers have raised questions regarding the relationship between attitudes and behaviors. Some have shown that attitudes are predictors of behaviors (Albrecht & Carpenter, 1976; Bentler & Speckart, 1979; Schwartz & Tessler, 1972). Others have shown that behavior affects attitudes (Bem, 1972; Felson & Bohrnstedt, 1980; Jones & McGillis, 1976; Zanna & Olson, 1982) and that reciprocal effects exist between attitudes and behaviors but that the attitude effect is somewhat stronger than the behavioral effect in the reciprocal relationship (Andrews & Kandel, 1979; Bentler & Speckart, 1981; Kahle & Berman, 1979). Further, it has been reported that the magnitude of the reciprocal effects may be mediated by social/structural contingency conditions such as the amount of time that has lapsed (Warner & DeFleur, 1969). Keep in mind that because this is a nonrecursive model, attitudes and behaviors that result from a particular decision-making style (shown as outputs) can also be conceptualized as inputs that influence subsequent biopsychosocial factors, which are shown as the inputs to future decision-making processes. An example of this type of variable that currently is being investigated is sexual coercion as it relates to substance abuse and subsequent HIV-related risky sexual behaviors.

Discussion

Not only is the PAHDM based on the fundamental sociological principles reflected in current health behavior models; it also includes the psychological variables of maturation and developmental phasing that affect the transition from childhood to adulthood. A unique feature of adolescent, as opposed to adult, decision making is that decision-making styles of adolescents are more reflective of their development (i.e., their change from the child to adult state), whereas in adults, decision making may be more reflective of ideology or personality. This point, which is central to the PAHDM, underscores the importance of developing a health behavior model that is relevant to the adolescent.

The results of empirical studies aimed at testing the PAHDM indicate that decision-making directedness of adolescents is a significant predictor of AIDS-related knowledge, attitudes, beliefs, skills, and behaviors; drug- and alcohol-related risky sexual behaviors; and behaviors that increase risk for cardiovascular disease (Bromfield, 1994; Langer et al., 1993; Langer & Tubman, in press; Tubman & Langer, 1995). These findings have both basic and applied scientific implications not only for health planning but also for our understanding of developmental issues and the psychosociological research methods applied to youth.

Risk reduction interventions, cited previously, have shown that educating adolescents about issues such as substance abuse and sexual behavior has not always been translated into behavioral change. Hence there exists a need to reexamine the current health behavior models used to plan interventions in terms of how relevant these interventions are when applied to adolescents as a group. Decision making among adolescents, as well as adults, is multifaceted, and if health professionals are to develop effective interventions for this age group, they must attend carefully to contextual meanings. Although terms for particular behaviors have a stable meaning among some health researchers, the contextual meaning of terms for teenagers may vary greatly. Furthermore, the interactional patterns of adolescents include a great deal of peer processing, parental discussions, interaction with other adults, and, for some, a unique combination of these factors. In accordance with the PAHDM, an intervention is more likely to be successful if it is designed in such a way as to gain maximum processing and reinforcements from a student's support group, no matter how this social network is constituted.

To gain greater insight into adolescent decision making, it is necessary to define more clearly health behavior modeling as this work has been carried out by other health behavior researchers. As discussed earlier, the effectiveness of current state-of-the-art health models in predicting and changing health behaviors and attitudes has been found to be extremely limited when applied to adolescent decision making. Issues such as the evaluation of risks and benefits, the dissuasive power of potential negative consequences, the persuasive power of health information, and the relative importance assigned to the opinions of family members or peers may place health behavior modeling for preadults into a frame distinctly different from that appropriate for adults. Interventions based on traditional health models seem to show adequate effectiveness in changing knowledge and beliefs. What they fail to do is affect attitudes and behaviors.

The PAHDM offers a potential mechanism by which to modify attitudes and behaviors through formulating content in terms that are consonant with an adolescent's frame of reference and subcultural worldview rather than through the indirect mechanism of the modification of knowledge. Attitudes and behavior may be independent of specific knowledge on a given question. For example, a person's decision to be drug-free may have little relationship to his or her degree of drug knowledge. More broadly, a person's degree of religious faith and the behavior constraints he or she observes may have little or no relationship to his or her theological sophistication. Further, it is important to assess adolescents' perceptions of their own mortality. If an adolescent is exposed to an environment characterized by frequent violence and the untimely death of peers, an intervention that includes warnings of the risk of early death if risky behaviors are not curtailed may have little impact because the adolescent thinks he or she is going to die soon anyway. In fact, if adolescents do not witness premature dying in their own environment, they are likely to be exposed to it via the popular media.

The PAHDM fundamentally acknowledges that adolescent health decision making is based not only on a standard protocol of assessing health risks in a response to a cue to action, but also on systematic differential processing of information from peers and parents and through critical or reflexive self-analysis. Many open questions exist at the moment as to the specifics of the preadult judgment process, the sequential relationship of critical factors, and points for potential influence by multidimensional intervention that may be addressed with further refinement of the PAHDM. The current phase of PAHDM development is focusing on process models with identified critical points amenable to hypothesis testing. It is important to emphasize the need for additional research in the area of adolescent health decision making so that reliable measures can be established to test these hypotheses.

In light of the many potential maladies that adolescents face today, future preadult health risk research, whether considering drug addiction, sexually transmitted diseases such as AIDS, or other issues such as pregnancy or suicide, should incorporate the concept of maturation and/or differences in information processing among adolescents. As noted previously, a large corpus of literature in the area of adolescent risk behavior confirms that to date no unified theory has been developed that explains how adolescents make decisions that put them at risk. As a result, the trend in risk reduction research has been more toward identifying risk factors. The PAHDM follows this trend in that decision-making style can be identified as a modifiable risk factor with associated precursor risk factors. In fact, the outputs (i.e., attitudes and behaviors resulting from a particular decision) can be seen as precursor risk factors in this nonrecursive model.

If we understand the processes by which adolescents make health decisions, intervention dollars may be more effectively spent in the design and implementation of programs that are not confined to a single dimension of information dissemination but rather include several dimensions that take into account the context of the youth culture. The development of rational decision-making skills in the context of this youth culture should be an integral component of interventions aimed at behavior change in this group.

As shown in the depiction of the PAHDM (Figure 3.1), there are a variety of points of intervention. However, for an intervention that focuses on the development of decision-making skills to be effective, it is important for adolescents to understand their own unique process of decision making. Understanding one's decision-making process involves much more than just skill training; it involves an understanding of how individuals appraise the many life events to which they are exposed. Inputs in the PAHDM can be conceptualized as constituting the adolescent's appraisal arena. The appraisal arena is made up of a confluence of factors that are, in large part, the result of the process of socialization. Our Western society has socialized individuals to believe that they must look outside themselves for "expert advice." This belief is commonly referred to as an "outer locus of control." The consequences of believing that others have the "answers" to challenging life events are feelings of vulnerability and the need to search for external sources for assuagement (e.g., drugs, alcohol, sex, material goods). Feelings of powerlessness or lack of control over daily life may promote risk taking because risk taking, per se, often involves the exercise of personal control over deliberately created chaos (Lyng, 1993). Lyng asserted that adolescents, in walking the line between safety and disaster, may create opportunities to practice skills, such as concentration, maintenance of control, and resisting paralysis from fear, that may be critical to the development of their autonomy. While focusing on the potential peril associated with risk taking, researchers often lose sight of the phenomenological aspects of risk taking and the potentially adaptive functions that risk taking may serve. Obtaining an understanding of the norms and values of subcultures of substance-abusing adolescents would provide useful information for intervention planners.

Before interventions can be effective in adolescent risk reduction through the altering of their decision-making processes, adolescents must learn how to turn inward and thereby come to know themselves as unique individuals biopsychosocially. Further, we must empower adolescents with confidence in the belief that they are experts on knowing how to avoid personal risk. These are the type of skills that will allow adolescents to become their own interventionists equipped with the ability to reappraise and alter their beliefs and their decision-making processes as situations arise. With this vision as an inspiring goal, efforts aimed at developing risk-reducing decision-making skills into preadult decision making offer a promising component for intervention design.

References

Ajzen, I. (1982). On behaving in accordance with one's attitude. In M. P. Zanna, E. T. Higgins, & C. P. Herman (Eds.), *Consistency in social behavior: The Ontario Symposium* (Vol. 2). Hillsdale, NJ: Lawrence Erlbaum.

Ajzen, I., & Fishbein, M. (1980). *Understanding attitudes and predicting social behavior.* Englewood Cliffs, NJ: Prentice Hall.

Akers, R. L., Krohn, M. D., Lanza-Kaduce, L., & Radosevich, M. (1979). Social learning and deviant behavior: A specific test of a general theory. *American Sociological Review, 44,* 636-655.

Albrecht, S., & Carpenter, K. (1976). Attitudes as predictors of behavior versus behavior intentions: A convergence of research traditions. *Sociometry, 39,* 1-10.

Albrecht, S., & Warner, L. (1975). The interactive effects of situational and personality factors on attitude-behavior consistency. *Youth and Society,*

Allensworth, D. D., & Symons, C. W. (1989). A theoretical approach to school-based HIV prevention. *Journal of School Health, 59*(2), 59-65.

Andrews, P., & Kandel, D. B. (1979). Attitude and behavior: A specification of the contingency consistency hypothesis. *American Sociological Review, 44,* 280-297.

Ausubel, D. P., Montemayor, R., & Svajian, P. N. (1977). *Theory and problems of adolescent development.* New York: Grune & Stratton.

Bachman, J. G., Wallace, J. M., O'Malley, P. M., Johnston, L. D., Kurth, C. L., & Neighbors, H. W. (1991). Racial/ethnic differences in smoking, drinking, and illicit drug use among American high school seniors. 1976-89. *American Journal of Public Health, 81,* 372-377.

Bagozzi, R. P. (1978). The construct validity of the affective, behavioral and cognitive components of attitude by the analysis of covariance structures. *Multivariate Behavioral Research, 13,* 9-31.

Bagozzi, R. P., & Burnkrant, R. E. (1979). Attitude organization and the attitude-behavior relationship. *Journal of Personality and Social Psychology, 37,* 913-919.

Baldwin, A. L. (1967). *Theories of child development.* New York: John Wiley.

Bandura, A. (1977a). Self-efficacy: Toward a unifying theory of behavioral change. *Psychological Review, 84,* 191-215.

Bandura, A. (1977b). *Social learning theory.* Englewood Cliffs, NJ: Prentice Hall.

Bandura, A. (1982). The self and mechanisms of agency, In M. Schuls (Ed.), *Psychological perspectives on the self* (Vol. 1). Hillsdale, NJ: Lawrence Erlbaum.

Bandura, A., & Walters, R. H. (1959). *Adolescent aggression.* New York: Ronald.

Banks, L. (1969). *Youth in turmoil.* New York: Time-Life.

Becker, M. H., Haefner, D. P., Kasl, S. V., Kirscht, J. P., Maiman, L. A., & Rosenstock, I. M. (1977). Selected psychosocial models and correlates of individual health-related behaviors. *Medical Care, 15*(Suppl.), 27-46.

Becker, M. H., & Joseph, J. G. (1988). AIDS and behavioral change to reduce risk: A review. *American Journal of Public Health, 78,* 394-410.

Behn, R. D., & Vaupel, J. (1983). *Quick analysis for busy decision-makers.* New York: Basic Books.

Bem, D. J. (1972). Self-perception theory. *Advances in Experimental Social Psychology, 6,* 2-62.

Bentler, P. M., & Speckart, G. (1979). Models of attitude-behavior relations. *Psychological Review, 86,* 452-464.

Bentler, P. M., & Speckart, G. (1981). Attitudes "cause" behavior: A structural equation analysis. *Journal of Personality and Social Psychology, 40,* 226-238.

Blumer, H. (1969). *Symbolic interactionism: Perspective and method.* Englewood Cliffs, NJ: Prentice Hall.

Borowitz, R. (1969). *Choosing a sex ethic.* New York: Schocken.

Bowerman, C., & Kinch, J. (1959). Changes in family and peer orientation of children between the fourth and tenth grades. *Social Forces, 37,* 206-211.

Bromfield, P. E. (1994). *Knowledge, attitudes, behavior, and decision-making orientation relating to cardiovascular health in high school students.* Unpublished master's thesis, Western Michigan University at Kalamazoo.

Brook, J. S., Lukoff, I. F., & Whiteman, M. (1978). Family socialization and adolescent personality and their association with adolescent use of marijuana. *Journal of Genetic Psychology, 183,* 261-271.

Brook, J. S., Whiteman, M., & Gordon, A. S. (1983). Stages of drug use in adolescence: Personality, peer, and family correlates. *Developmental Psychology, 19,* 269-277.

Burke, P., & Reitzes, D. (1981). The link between identity and role performance. *Social Psychology Quarterly, 44*(2), 83-92.

Catania, J. A., Kegeles, S. M., & Coates, T. J. (1990). Toward an understanding of risk behavior: An AIDS risk reduction model (ARRM). *Health Education Quarterly, 17,* 53-72.

Chassin, L., Presson, C. C., Bensenberg, M., Corty, E., Olshansky, R. W., & Sherman, S. J. (1981). Predicting adolescents' intentions to smoke cigarettes. *Journal of Health and Social Behavior, 22,* 445-455.

Coates, T., & Perry, C. (1980). Multifactor risk reduction with children and adolescents. In D. Upper & S. Ross (Eds.), *Behavior group therapy: An annual review.* Champaign, IL: Research Press.

Coelho, R. J. (1984). Self-efficacy and cessation of smoking. *Psychological Reports, 54,* 309-310.

Combs, R. H., Paulson, M. J., & Richardson, M. A. (1991). Peer versus parental influence on substance use among Hispanic and Anglo children and adolescents. *Journal of Youth and Adolescence, 20,* 73-88.

Cooley, C. H. (1902). *Human nature and the social order.* New York: Scribner's.

Cousineau, D., Savard, M., & Allard, D. (1993). Illicit drug use among adolescent students: A peer phenomenon? *Canadian Family Physician, 39,* 523-528.

Crowne, D., & Marlowe, D. (1964). *The approval motive.* New York: John Wiley.

Daugherty, L., & Burger, J. (1984). The influence of parents, church, and peers on the sexual attitudes and behaviors of college students. *Archives of Sexual Behavior, 13,* 351-359.

DeJong, A. J. (1972). *Making it to adulthood.* Philadelphia: Westminster.

Dewey, J. (1930). *Human nature and conduct.* New York: Modern Library.

Dielman, T. E., Butchart, A. T., Shope, J. T., & Miller, M. (1990-1991). The environmental correlates of adolescent substance use and misuse: Implications for prevention programs. *International Journal of the Addictions, 25,* 855-880.

Dielman, T., Campanielli, P., Shope, J., & Butchart, A. (1987). Susceptibility to peer pressure, self-esteem, and health locus of control as correlates of adolescent substance abuse. *Health Education Quarterly, 14,* 207-221.

Dinges, M. M., & Oetting, E. R. (1993). Similarity in drug use patterns between adolescents and their friends. *Adolescence, 28,* 253-266.

Dollard, J., Doob, L. S., Miller, N. E., Mowrer, O. H., & Sears, R. R. (1939). *Frustration and aggression.* New Haven, CT: Yale University Press.

Eisen, M., & Zellman, G. L. (1986). Predicting adolescents' sexuality knowledge. *Health Education Quarterly, 13,* 9-22.

Eisen, M., Zellman, G. L., & McAlister, A. L. (1985). Adolescents' fertility control. *Health Education Quarterly, 12,* 185-210.

Erikson, E. H. (1950). *Childhood and society.* New York: Norton.

Erikson, E. H. (1959). The problem of ego identity. In M. Gold & E. Douvan (Eds.), *Adolescent development: Readings in research and theory* (p. 19). New York: International Universities Press.

Farrell, A. D., & Danish, S. J. (1993). Peer drug associations and emotional restraint: Causes or consequences of adolescent drug use? *Journal of Consulting and Clinical Psychology, 61,* 327-334.

Fasick, F. (1984). Parents, peers, youth culture and autonomy in adolescence. *Adolescence, 21,* 143-157.

Felson, R., & Bohrnstedt, G. (1980). Attributions of ability and motivation in a natural setting. *Journal of Personality and Social Psychology, 39,* 799-805.

Fishbein, M., & Ajzen, I. (1975). Misconceptions about the Fishbein model: Reflections on a study by Songer-Nocks. *Journal of Experimental Social Psychology, 12,* 579-584.

Fisher, T. (1986). An exploratory study of parent-child communication about sex and the sexual attitudes of early, middle, and late adolescents. *Journal of Genetic Psychology, 147,* 543-557.

Floyd, H., & South, D. (1972). Dilemma of youth: The choice of parents or peers as a frame of reference for behavior. *Journal of Marriage and the Family, 34,* 627-634.

Forney, M. A., Forney, P. D., & Ripley, W. K. (1989). *Predictor variables of adolescent drinking.* Paper presented at the annual meeting of the Eastern Educational Research Association, Miami Beach, FL.

Freud, S. (1938). *The basic writings of Sigmund Freud* (A. A. Brill, Ed.). New York: Random House.

Freud, S. (1947). *The ego and the id* (Vol. 19). London: Hogarth. (Originally published 1923)

Freud, S. (1962). Three essays of the theory of sexuality. In *Three contributions to the theory of sex.* New York: Dutton.

Freud, S. (1986). *The standard edition of the complete psychological works of Sigmund Freud: Vol. 7. Three essays of the theory of sexuality* (A. Freud, Trans. assisted by A. Strachey and A. Tyson). London: Hogarth.

Gardner, W. (1993). A life-span rational-choice theory of risk taking. In N. J. Bell & R. W. Bell (Eds.), *Adolescent risk taking (pp. 66-83). Newbury Park, CA: Sage.*

Gross, A., & McMullen, P. (1983). Models of the help seeking process. In B. DePaulo, A. Nadler, & J. Fisher (Eds.), *New directions in helping: Help seeking* (Vol. 2). New York: Academic Press.

Hall, G. S. (1882). *The moral and religious training of children. Princeton Review,* 26-48.

Hall, G. S. (1904). *Adolescence: Its psychology and its relations to physiology, anthropology, sociology, crime, religion, and education.* New York: D. Appleton.

Hansen, W. B., Malotte, C. K., & Fielding, J. E. (1988). Evaluation of a tobacco and alcohol abuse prevention curriculum for adolescents. *Health Education Quarterly, 15,* 93-114.

Harris, L. (1971, January). Change, yes—upheaval, no. *Life,* pp. 22-27.

Hingson, R. W., Strunin, L., Berlin, B. M., & Heeren, T. (1990). Beliefs about AIDS, use of alcohol and drugs, and unprotected sex among Massachusetts adolescents. *American Journal of Public Health, 80,* 295-299.

Huba, G. J., & Bentler, P. M. (1980). The role of peer and adult models for drug taking at different stages in adolescence. *Journal of Youth and Adolescence, 9,* 449-465.

Huba, G. J., & Bentler, P. M. (1984). Causal models of personality, peer cultural characteristics, drug use, and criminal behavior over a five year span. In D. W. Goodwin, K. T. Van

Duesen, & S. A. Mednick (Eds.), *Longitudinal research in alcoholism* (pp. 73-94). Boston: Kluwer-Nijhof.

Hull, C. L. (1931). Goal attraction and directing ideas conceived as habit phenomena. *Psychological Review, 38,* 489-503.

Hull, C. L., Hovlund, C. I., Ross, R. T., Hall, M., Perkins, D. T., & Fitch, F. B. (1940). *Mathematico-deductive theory of role learning.* New Haven, CT: Yale University Press.

Irwin, C. E., & Millstein, S. G. (1986). Biopsychosocial correlates of risk-taking behaviors during adolescence. *Journal of Adolescent Health Care, 7*(Suppl.), 82S-96S.

Janis, I. L., & Mann, L. (1977). *Decision-making: A psychological analysis of conflict, choice, and commitment.* New York: Free Press.

Janz, E. E., & Becker, M. (1984). The health belief model: A decade later. *Health Education Quarterly, 11,* 1-47.

Jensen, G. (1973). Parents, peers, and delinquent action: A test of the differential association perspective. *American Journal of Sociology, 78,* 562-575.

Jessor, R., & Jessor, S. L. (1977). *Problem behavior and psychosocial development: A longitudinal study of youth.* New York: Academic Press.

Jones, E. E., & McGillis, D. (1976). Correspondent inferences and the attribution curve: A comparative appraisal. In J. H. Harvey, W. J. Iches, & R. F. Kidd (Eds.), *New directions in attribution research* (Vol. 1, pp. 389-420). Hillsdale, NJ: Lawrence Erlbaum.

Jorgensen, S. R., & Sonstegard, J. S. (1984, February). Predicting adolescent sexual and contraceptive behavior: An application and test of the Fishbein model. *Journal of Marriage and the Family, 46,* 43-55.

Juhasz, A., & Sonnenshein-Schneider, M. (1987). Responsibility and control: The basis of sexual decision making. *Personnel and Guidance Journal, 53,* 181-185.

Kahle, L. R., & Berman, J. J. (1979). Attitudes cause behavior: A cross-lagged panel analysis. *Journal of Experimental Social Psychology, 37,* 314-321.

Kandel, D. B. (1983). Socialization and adolescent drinking. *Child Health, 2,* 66-75.

Kandel, D. B., & Logan, J. A. (1984). Patterns of drug use from adolescence to young adulthood: I. Periods of risk for initiation, continued use, and discontinuation. *American Journal of Public Health, 74,* 660-666.

Kaplan, H. B. (1975). *Self-attitudes and deviant behavior.* Pacific Palisades, CA: Goodyear.

Kaplan, H. B. (1980). *Deviant behavior in defense of self.* New York: Academic Press.

Kaplan, H. B. (1984). Pathways to adolescents drug use: Self-derogation, peer influence, weakening of social control and early substance use. *Journal of Health and Social Behavior, 25,* 270-289.

Kaplan, H. B., Johnson, R. J., & Bailey, C. A. (1986). Self-rejection and the explanation of deviance: Refinement and elaboration of a latent structure. *Social Psychology Quarterly, 49,* 110-128.

Kohlberg, L. A. (1966). A cognitive-developmental analysis of children's sex role concepts and attitudes. In E. E. Maccoby (Ed.), *The development of sex differences* (pp. 223-321). Stanford, CA: Stanford University Press.

Kohn, M. L. (1959). Social class and the exercise of parental authority. *American Sociological Review, 24,* 352-366.

Kohn, M. L. (1963). Social class and parent-child relationships: An interpretation. *American Journal of Sociology, 68,* 471-480.

Kohn, M. L. (1969). *Class and conformity: A study in values.* Homewood, IL: Dorsey.

Kothandapani, V. (1971). Validation of feeling, belief, and intention to act as three components of attitude and their contribution to the prediction of behavior. *Journal of Personality and Social Psychology, 19,* 521-533.

Kuhn, M. H. (1964). Major trends in symbolic interaction theory in the past twenty-five years. *Sociological Quarterly, 5,* 61-84.

Langer, L. M., & Tubman, J. G. (in press). Psychosocial and situational factors associated with alcohol and non-alcohol HIV-related risky sexual behaviors among adolescents in treatment for substance abuse. *American Journal of Orthopsychiatry.*

Langer, L. M., & Warheit, G. J. (1992). The pre-adult health decision-making model: Linking decision-making directedness/orientation to adolescent health related attitudes and behaviors. *Adolescence, 27,* 919-948.

Langer, L. M., Zimmerman, R. S., Warheit, G. J., & Duncan, R. C. (1993). An examination of the relationship between adolescent decision-making orientation and AID-related knowledge, attitudes, beliefs, behaviors, and skills. *Health Psychology, 12,* 227-234.

Larson, L. (1972). The relative influence of parent-adolescent affect in predicting the salience hierarchy among youth. *Pacific Sociological Review, 15,* 83-102.

Lettieri, D. J. (1984, September). *Review of theories of adolescent substance abuse.* Paper presented at the meeting of the Research Society on Alcoholism, Santa Fe.

Leventhal, H., & Hirschman, R. S. (1982). Social psychology and prevention. In G. S. Sanders & J. Suis (Eds.), *Social psychology of health and illness* (pp. 183-226). Hillsdale, NJ: Lawrence Erlbaum.

Lewis, C. E., & Lewis, M. A. (1984). Peer pressure and risk-taking behaviors in children. *American Journal of Public Health, 74,* 580-584.

Lidz, T. (1983). *The person: His and her development throughout the life cycle.* New York: Basic Books.

Lindzey, G., & Borgatta, E. F. (1954). Sociometric measurement. In G. Lindzey (Ed.), *Handbook of social psychology* (pp. 405-448). Reading, MA: Addison-Wesley.

Liska, A. E. (1984). A critical examination of the causal structure of the Fishbein/Ajzen attitude-behavior model. *Social Psychology Quarterly, 47,* 61-74.

Lyng, S. (1993). Dysfunctional risk taking: Criminal behavior as edgework. In N. J. Gell & R. W. Bell (Eds.), *Adolescent risk taking* (pp. 107-130). Newbury Park, CA: Sage.

Maddahian, E., Bentler, P. M., & Newcomb, M. D. (1986). Adolescent substance use: Impact of ethnicity, income, and availability. *Advances in Alcohol Substance Abuse, 5,* 63-78.

Manning, D. T., & Balson, P. M. (1989). Teenagers' beliefs about AIDS education and physicians' perceptions about them. *Journal of Family Practice, 29,* 173-177.

Maslow, A. H. (1954). *Motivation and personality.* New York: Harper.

Maslow, A. H. (1964). *Religions, values and peak experiences.* Columbus: Ohio State University Press.

Maslow, A. H. (1968). *Toward a psychology of being.* New York: van Nostrand Reinhold.

McCall, G. J., & Simmons, J. L. (1966). *Identities and interactions.* New York: Free Press.

Mead, G. H. (1934). *Mind, self, and society* (C. W. Morris, Ed.). Chicago: University of Chicago Press.

Miller, N. E., & Dollard, J. (1941). *Social learning and imitation.* New Haven, CT: Yale University Press.

Newcomb, M. D., & Bentler, P. M. (1986). Substance abuse and ethnicity: Differential impact of peer and adult models. *Journal of Psychology, 120,* 83-95.

Nowels, A., Toister, R. P., & Braunstein, J. J. (1981). An introduction to adolescent development. In J. H. Braunstein & R. P. Toister (Eds.), *Medical applications of the behavioral sciences* (pp. 363-382). Chicago: Year Book.

Oetting, E. R., & Beauvais, F. (1990). Adolescent drug use: Findings of national and local surveys. *Journal of Consulting and Clinical Psychology, 58,* 385-394.

Offer, D., & Offer, J. (1969). *The psychological world of the teenager: A study of normal adolescent boys.* New York: Basic Books.

Offer, D., & Offer, J. (1975). *From teenage to young manhood: A psychological study.* New York: Basic Books.

Offer, D., Ostrove, E., & Howard, K. I. (1981). *The adolescent: A psychological self-portrait.* New York: Basic Books.

Orr, D., Wilbrandt, M., Brack, C., Rauch, S., & Ingersoll, G. (1989). Reported sexual behaviors and self-esteem among young adolescents. *American Journal of Diseases of Children, 143,* 86-90.

Padina, R. J., & Schuela, J. A. (1983). Psychosocial correlates of alcohol and drug use of adolescent students and adolescents in treatment. *Journal of Studies in Alcohol, 44,* 950-973.

Palmer, J. H., & Ringwalt, C. L. (1988). Prevalence of alcohol and drug use among North Carolina public school students. *Journal of School Health, 58,* 288-291.

Pepitone, A. (1964). *Attraction and hostility.* New York: Prentice Hall.

Piaget, J. (1954). *The construction of reality in children.* New York: Basic Books.

Polis, C. A. (1985). Value judgements and world views in sexuality education. *Family Relations, 34,* 285-290.

Prochaska, J. O., DiClemente, C. C., & Norcross, J. C. (1992). In search of how people change: Applications to addictive behaviors. *American Psychologist, 47,* 1102-1114.

Rachal, J. V., Williams, J. R., Beham, M. L., Cavanaugh, N., Moore, R. P., & Eckerman, W. C. (1975) *A national study of adolescent drinking behaviors, attitudes and correlates* (NTIS No. PB-246-002). Rockville, MD: Department of Health Service, Alcohol, Drug Abuse and Mental Health Administration, NIAAA.

Raiffa, H. (1968). *Decision analysis.* Reading, MA: Addison-Wesley.

Reckless, W. C., Dinitz, S., & Murray, E. (1956). Self-concept as an insulator against delinquency. *American Sociological Review, 21,* 744-746.

Reiss, A. J. (1951). Delinquency as the failure of personal and social controls. *American Sociological Review, 16,* 196-206.

Riesman, D. (1950). *The lonely crowd.* New Haven, CT: Yale University Press.

Rosenberg, M. (1979). *Conceiving the self.* New York: Basic Books.

Rosenberg, M. (1989). Self-esteem and adolescent problems. *American Sociological Review, 54,* 1004-1018.

Rosenberg, M., Schooler, C., & Schoenbach, C. (1989). Self-esteem and adolescent problems: Modeling reciprocal effects. *American Sociological Review, 54,* 1004-1018.

Rotter, J. P. (1954). *Social learning and clinical psychology.* Englewood Cliffs, NJ: Prentice Hall.

Saltzer, E. B. (1981). Cognitive moderators of the relationship between behavioral intention and behavior. *Journal of Personality and Social Psychology, 41,* 260-271.

Sarvela, P. D., & McClendon, E. J. (1988). Indicators of rural youth drug use. *Journal of Youth and Adolescence, 17,* 335-347.

Scales, P. (1983). Sense and nonsense about sexuality education: A rejoinder to the Shornack's critical view. *Family Relations, 32,* 287-296.

Schachtel, E. (1959). *Metamorphosis.* New York: Basic Books.

Schlegel, R. P., & DiTecco, D. (1982). Attitudinal structures and the attitude-behavior relation. In M. P. Zanna, E. T. Higgins, & C. P. Herman (Eds.), *Consistency in social behavior* (pp. 17-50). Hillsdale, NJ: Lawrence Erlbaum.

Schunk, D., & Carbonari, J. (1984). Self-efficacy models. In J. Matarazzo, S. Weiss, J. Herd, N. Miller, & S. Weiss (Eds.), *Behavioral health: A handbook of health enhancement and disease prevention* (pp. 230-247). New York: John Wiley.

Schwartz, S. H., & Tessler, R. C. (1972). A test of a model for reducing measured attitude-behavior discrepancies. *Journal of Personality and Social Psychology, 24,* 225-236.

Sears, R. R. (1951). A theoretical framework for personality and social behavior. *American Psychologist, 6,* 476-483.

Sejwacz, D., Ajzen, I., & Fishbein, M. (1980). Predicting and understanding weight loss: Intention, behaviors, and outcomes. In I. Ajzen & M. Fishbein (Eds.), *Understanding attitudes and predicting social behavior* (pp. 101-112). Englewood Cliffs, NJ: Prentice Hall.

Shah, F., & Zelnik, M. (1981). Parent and peer influence on sexual behavior, contraceptive use, and pregnancy experience of young women. *Journal of Marriage and the Family, 43,* 339-348.

Simon, L., & Hingson, R. (1984). Acquired immunodeficiency syndrome and adolescents: Knowledge, beliefs, attitudes, and behaviors. *Pediatrics, 11,* 403-408.

Skinner, B. F. (1950). Are theories of learning necessary? *Psychological Review, 57,* 193-216.

Skinner, B. F. (1976). *About behaviorism.* New York: Random House.

Smith, G. M., & Fogg, C. P. (1977). Psychological antecedents of teenager drug use. In R. G. Simmons (Ed.), *Research in community mental health* (Vol. 1, pp. 87-102). Greenwich, CT: JAI.

Smith, G. M., & Fogg, C. P. (1978). Psychological predictors of early use, late use, and non-use of marijuana among teenage students. In D. K. Kandel (Ed.), *Longitudinal research on drug use: Empirical findings and methodological issues.* Washington, DC: Hemisphere.

Songer-Nocks, E. (1976). Situational factors affecting the weighting of predictor components in the Fishbein model. *Journal of Experimental Social Psychology, 12,* 56-69.

Steinberg, L., & Silverberg, S. (1986). The vicissitudes of autonomy in early adolescence. *Child Development, 57,* 841-851.

Stinchcombe, A. L. (1964). *Rebellion in high school.* Chicago: Quadrangle.

Strecher, V. J., DeVellis, B. M., Becker, M. H., & Rosenstock, I. M. (1986). The role of self-efficacy in achieving health behavior change. *Health Education Quarterly, 13,* 73-91.

Strunin, L., & Hingson, R. W. (1992). Alcohol, drugs, and adolescent sexual behavior. *International Journal of Addictions, 27,* 129-148.

Stryker, S. (1980). *Symbolic interactionism: A social structural version.* Menlo Park, CA: Benjamin/Cummings.

Stryker, S., & Statham, A. (1985). Symbolic interaction and role theory. In G. Lindzey & E. Aronson (Eds.), *Handbook of social psychology* (pp. 311-378). New York: Random House.

Swann, W., & Read, S. (1981). Acquiring self-knowledge: The search for feedback that fits. *Journal of Personality and Social Psychology, 6,* 1119-1128.

Thomas, W. I., & Thomas, D. (1928). *The child in America.* New York: Knopf.

Thomas, D. L., & Weigert, A. J. (1971). Socialization and adolescent conformity to significant others: A cross-national analysis. *American Sociological Review, 36,* 835-846.

Thompson, L., & Spanier, G. (1978). Influence of parents, peers, and partners on the contraceptive use of college men and women. *Journal of Marriage and the Family, 40,* 481-491.

Triandis, H. (1977). *Interpersonal behavior.* Monterey, CA: Brooks/Cole.

Tubman, J. G., & Langer, L. M. (1995). About last night: The social ecology of sexual behavior with and without concurrent alcohol use among adolescents in treatment for substance abuse. *Journal of Substance Abuse 7*(4), 449-461.

Turner, J. H. (1986). *The structure of sociological theory* (4th. ed.). Chicago: Dorsey.

von Winterfeldt, D., & Edwards, W. (1986). *Decision analysis and behavioral research.* New York: Cambridge University Press.

Wallston, B. S., & Wallston, K. A. (1984). Social psychological models of health behavior: An examination and integration. In A. Baum, S. E. Taylor, & J. E. Singer (Eds.), *Handbook of psychology and health* (Vol. 4, pp. 23-53). Hillsdale, NJ: Lawrence Erlbaum.

Warheit, G. J., Biafora, F. A., Zimmerman, R. S., Gil, A. G., Vega, W. A., & Apospori, E. (1995). Self-rejection/derogation, peer factors, and alcohol, drug, and cigarette use among a sample of Hispanic, African-American, and white non-Hispanic adolescents. *International Journal of the Addictions, 30,* 97-116.

Warner, L., & DeFleur, M. (1969). Attitude as an interactional concept: Social constraint and social distance as intervening variables between attitudes and action. *American Sociological Review, 34,* 153-169.

Watson, S., & Buede, D. (1987). *Decision synthesis.* New York: Cambridge University Press.

Webster, M., & Sobieszek, B. (1974). *Sources of self evaluation: A formal theory of significant others and social influence.* New York: John Wiley.

Weiner, I. (1970). *Psychological disturbance in adolescence.* New York: Wiley-Interscience.

Wells, L. E., & Rankin, J. H. (1983). Self-concept as a mediating factor in delinquency. *Social Psychological Quarterly, 46,* 11-22.

Westley, W. A., & Elkin, F. (1971). The protective environment and adolescent socialization. In M. Gold & E. Douvan (Eds.), *Adolescent development: Readings in research and theory.* Boston: Allyn & Bacon. (Reprinted from *Social Forces,* 35, 243-249.)

Wilson, S. (1988). The real self controversy: Toward an integration of humanistic and interactionist theory. *Journal of Humanistic Psychology, 28,* 39-65.

Young, J., & Ferguson, L. (1979). Developmental changes through adolescence in the spontaneous nomination of reference groups as a function of decision content. *Journal of Youth and Adolescent, 8,* 239-252.

Zanna, M. P., & Olson, J. M. (1982). Individual differences in attitudinal relations. In M. P. Zanna, E. T. Higgins, & C. P. Herman (Eds.), *Consistency in social behavior* (pp. 75-104). Hillsdale, NJ: Lawrence Erlbaum.

Zetterberg, H. L. (1957). Compliant actions. *Acta Sociologica, 3,* 179-201.

Zimmerman, R. S. (1989). AIDS: Social causes, patterns, "cures," and problems. In K. McKinney & S. Sprecher (Eds.), *Human sexuality: The societal and interpersonal context* (pp. 286-317). Norwood, NJ: Ablex.

Zuehlke, M. (1981). *Adolescent peers as facilitators of contraceptive use.* Paper presented at the annual meeting of the American Psychological Association, Los Angeles.

PART 2
Prevention Initiatives

4

Prevention Technologies for Drug-Involved Youth

Mario A. Orlandi

An extensive body of research has accumulated over the past three decades aimed at clarifying the epidemiology and etiology of alcohol, tobacco, and other drug (ATOD) use and related problems (Botvin & Botvin, 1992; Tobler, 1992; see Chapters 1, 2, & 3). As the result of significant advances in our understanding of specific epidemiological and etiological principles, a variety of intervention technologies have evolved to prevent or control ATOD use and the massive burden that it places on our society. This chapter briefly reviews intervention approaches designed to minimize the impact of ATOD use.

Overall findings that relate to the causes and correlates of ATOD use have considerable significance for the focus and timing of preventive interventions (Brook, Brook, Gordon, Whiteman, & Cohen, 1990). Because ATOD use follows a developmental progression, the importance of early intervention is underscored (Zigler, Tanssig, & Black, 1992). Similarly, the evidence that different types of problem behaviors are learned socially and that they are part of a general syndrome of highly associated behaviors suggests that they may have common causes and should be approached comprehensively. If prevention programs are sufficiently comprehensive to target these underlying determinants effectively, it may be possible to develop interventions that address multiple behaviors simultaneously, obviating the need to develop separate interventions for specific problems (Botvin, 1982; Orlandi, Landers, Weston, & Haley, 1990; Swisher, 1979). A number of the approaches that have evolved from our etiological understanding are reviewed in the section that follows.

Traditional Intervention Approaches

A variety of intervention strategies developed during the 1960s and 1970s were based on the assumption that either providing adolescents with specific information or distracting them with alternative activities would deter the onset of ATOD use. The informational approaches took various forms, ranging from general facts about negative consequences to specific appeals to morality. The alternatives approach was based on the belief that adolescents would not engage in unhealthy behavior if healthy outlets were made readily available.

What these traditional approaches lacked was an appreciation for the fact that ATOD use is learned within and influenced by youths' social context and that vulnerable youth generally lack the skills needed to resist these influences (Dryfoos, 1993). Several examples are described.

Information Education

Information education is probably the most common approach to ATOD use prevention. This approach uses factual information concerning the nature, pharmacology, and adverse consequences of tobacco, alcohol, and drug use. It is based on the belief that once individuals are aware of the hazards of using tobacco, alcohol, and drugs, they will develop antidrug attitudes and make a rational and logical decision not to use drugs (Berberian, Gross, Lovejoy, & Paparella, 1976).

Such programs have primarily taken the form of either public information campaigns or school-based programs. Government agencies, community groups, and such voluntary organizations as the American Cancer Society and the National Council on Alcoholism have produced a multitude of pamphlets, leaflets, posters, and public service announcements. School programs have typically consisted of drug education classes, classroom presentations, assembly programs featuring guests speakers, and films.

Fear Arousal

In contrast with approaches designed merely to disseminate factual information, some approaches have attempted to generate fear by dramatizing the risks associated with ATOD use. These approaches have attempted to communicate that drugs are dangerous and that those individuals foolish enough to use them will suffer grave consequences (Schaps, Bartolo, Moskowitz, Palley, & Churgin, 1981). In a classic example of this approach, films have been shown to students prior to prom night that graphically illustrate the possible fate of those who drink and drive.

Moral Appeal

Another approach is to place ATOD use in a moral or ethical framework. This approach involves lecturing to students about the evils of smoking, drinking, or using drugs. Many early prevention efforts either relied on this approach exclusively or combined it with information education and fear arousal (Swisher & Hoffman, 1975). This approach has remained popular largely because it is simple and does not require complicated intervention protocols.

Affective Education

ATOD education shifted emphasis away from an informational approach during the mid-1970s toward a focus on personal and social growth. The underlying assumption of this affective education approach is that ATOD use can be prevented by increasing the fulfillment of basic personal needs through existing social institutions (Swisher, 1979). Affective education programs have included classroom activities intended to increase self-esteem, communication skills, values clarification, and decision making.

Alternatives

Another approach that gained popularity in the 1970s offered adolescents opportunities designed to serve as "alternatives" to drug use (Schaps et al., 1981). Such approaches have included a variety of recreational, educational, and community service activities. For example, a number of drug-free youth centers have been established that feature arts, crafts, music, and sports activities. Some programs promote wilderness or outdoor experiences designed to enhance self-efficacy while giving participants a chance to experience a "natural high." Other approaches attempt to match specific alternatives with an individual's unfulfilled needs. For example, the desire for more sensory stimulation might be satisfied through music, art, and nature studies.

Effectiveness of Traditional Approaches

Empirical evidence has consistently shown that these traditional approaches to ATOD problem prevention are not effective (Berberian et al., 1976; Dorn & Thompson, 1976; Schaps et al., 1981; Swisher & Hoffman, 1975). Such studies have shown that information education programs are capable of increasing knowledge and changing attitudes toward ATOD use. However, they do not reduce or prevent related behaviors. In fact, there is even some evidence that such approaches may lead to increased usage through the stimulation of curiosity (Mason, 1973; Swisher, Crawford, Goldstein, & Yura, 1971).

Because fear arousal and moral appeals are typically used in conjunction with informational approaches, no evidence is available concerning their independent effects on substance use. However, because virtually all of the studies that have reported on the evaluation of information education approaches have found no evidence of prevention effects on behavior, it is unlikely that either of these approaches would yield any effects if used independently. Clearly, therefore, purely informational approaches have not changed ATOD use behavior, and given what we now know regarding etiology, this is most likely due to a narrow focus that ignores factors that are most salient for prevention.

Similarly, studies that have reported on the evaluation of affective education and alternatives approaches have in some instances been able to demonstrate an impact on one or more of the correlates of ATOD use but have found no evidence of prevention effects on behavior (Dryfoos, 1993; Gorman, 1995; Kim, 1988; Schaps et al., 1981).

Psychosocial Intervention Approaches

Unlike traditional approaches, which focus on information education, fear arousal, moral persuasion, or alternatives, the most promising substance abuse prevention interventions currently available are those that focus primary attention on both psychological and social (psychosocial) factors (Brook et al., 1990). Psychosocial approaches to substance abuse prevention include resistance skills training, psychological inoculation, personal skills training, and social skills training (Botvin & Botvin, 1992).

These approaches differ from traditional approaches in several important ways. First, they are based on a more complete understanding of the causes of ATOD use among adolescents; second, they are grounded in accepted theories of human behavior; third, they utilize tested intervention techniques; and, fourth, empirical studies testing these approaches have emphasized methodological rigor and have employed increasingly sophisticated research designs (Coie et al., 1993).

Early studies testing these psychosocial approaches were focused on cigarette smoking. This focus was justified because cigarette smoking is the leading preventable cause of death in the United States and because it is the most widespread form of drug dependence in our society. More recently, however, psychosocial approaches have also been tested for their impact on alcohol and marijuana (Hawkins, Catalano, & Miller, 1992). Nonetheless, most of the available psychosocial prevention literature deals with cigarette smoking.

Psychological Inoculation

Some of the first psychosocial prevention strategies were a major departure from previous prevention efforts. Based on the belief that social and psychological factors influenced the initiation of cigarette smoking (Evans, 1976; Evans et al., 1978; Evans, Henderson, Hill, & Raines, 1979), these approaches were strongly influenced by "psychological inoculation," a concept of persuasive communications theory formulated by McGuire (1964, 1968). Psychological inoculation is a strategy that prepares the individual to resist social pressures to adopt health-compromising behaviors by exposing him or her to a weak dose of those same social pressures. This prevention strategy also incorporates two other innovative components: student feedback regarding actual schoolwide prevalence and health information concerning the immediate physiological effects of cigarette smoking.

Though the inoculation intervention did not produce significant reductions in smoking onset rates in the initial studies, this early work served as a model for many studies that followed (e.g., Luepker, Johnson, Murray,

& Pechacek, 1983; McAlister, Perry, & Maccoby, 1979; Telch, Killen, McAlister, Perry, & Maccoby, 1982). These studies developed and tested a variety of psychosocial approaches, but they all focused on increasing students' awareness of the various social influences to smoke cigarettes and on teaching specific skills for resisting those influences.

Resistance Skills Training

Resistance skills training stresses the importance of social influences that come from family, peers, and the mass media. These influences shape the adolescent's perceptions of what constitutes normal, acceptable, or even desirable behavior. As Bandura (1986) indicated, all human behavior is a product of the interaction between individual histories, the community, and the larger society.

These approaches generally teach students how to recognize, avoid, or cope with situations in which they will have a high likelihood of experiencing peer pressure to smoke, drink, or use drugs. Typically, this training includes teaching students the specific content of a model refusal message and how to deliver it in the most effective way. Students role-play and practice these skills in both classroom settings and after school. Many resistance skills training programs use peer leaders as program facilitators because peers frequently have higher source credibility with adolescents than adults have.

As with psychological inoculation approaches, there is an emphasis on combating the perception that substance use is widespread. In addition, these programs typically include a component designed to increase awareness of tobacco and alcoholic beverage advertisements and to teach counterarguments to the messages utilized by these commercial ads.

Considerable research conducted in recent years has documented the effectiveness of resistance skills training. These interventions generally have been shown, for example, to reduce the rate of smoking by 35% to 45%. Similar reductions have been reported for alcohol and marijuana use (e.g., McAlister, Perry, Killen, Slinkard, & Maccoby, 1980). In addition, some studies have demonstrated an impact on psychological correlates such as knowledge, attitudes, beliefs, and social resistance skills (Best et al., 1984).

For reasons that have been reviewed elsewhere (Orlandi, 1986), these studies have not focused on students who may be the most vulnerable to substance use. In one study, however, the resistance skills training program was found to be even more effective for students identified as being at high "social risk" (students whose friends, parents, and siblings smoke) than for other students in the sample, producing an 85% reduction in the proportion of nonsmokers becoming experimental smokers and a 100% reduction in the proportion becoming regular smokers (Best et al., 1984).

Personal and Social Skills Training

Broader based personal and social skills training has also been the focus of considerable research in recent years (Chassin, Presson, Sherman, & Edwards, 1992; Dusenbury et al., 1992; Perry, Pirie, Holder, Halper, & Dudovitz, 1990; Schinke et al., 1992). The objective of these programs is to teach a broad range of general skills for coping with life, in contrast to resistance skills training and its more specific focus on problem solving.

Each of these approaches is grounded in social-cognitive theory (Bandura, 1986) and problem-behavior theory (Jessor & Jessor, 1977). From this perspective, ATOD use and related problem behaviors are conceptualized as socially learned and as serving a function for the individual. As such, these behaviors, like other types of behavior, are learned through modeling and reinforcement, which are, in turn, influenced by personal psychological factors such as knowledge, attitudes, and beliefs.

A distinguishing characteristic of these programs is their emphasis on teaching an array of personal and social skills designed to be useful in a variety of life situations that may have little or nothing to do directly with substance use. For example, these approaches typically include components dealing with general problem-solving and decision-making skills (e.g., brainstorming and systematic decision-making techniques), general cognitive skills for resisting interpersonal or media influences (e.g., identifying persuasive advertising appeals and formulating counterarguments), skills for increasing self-control and self-esteem (e.g., self-instruction, self-reinforcement, goal setting, and principles of self-change), adaptive strategies for relieving stress and anxiety through the use of cognitive coping skills or behavioral relaxation techniques; general interpersonal skills (e.g., initiating social interactions, complimenting, and conversational skills), and general assertiveness skills (e.g., making requests, saying no, and expressing feelings and opinions). These skills are generally taught using a combination of instruction, demonstration, feedback, reinforcement, behavioral rehearsal, and extended practice through behavioral homework assignments.

In general, the studies reporting on the evaluation of personal and social skills training approaches to ATOD use prevention have uniformly demonstrated significant behavioral effects. In general, these studies have consistently demonstrated that such generic skills approaches can effect reductions in experimental smoking ranging from 42% to 75%. For example, Schinke and Gilchrist (1983) reported a reduction of 79% in the prevalence of experimental smoking. Data from two studies (Botvin & Eng, 1982; Botvin, Renick, & Baker, 1983) demonstrated effects ranging from 56% to 67%, measured as a reduction in the proportion of pretest nonsmokers becoming regular smokers at the 1-year follow-up without additional booster sessions. Another study reported an 87% reduction in the initiation of regular smoking for students who participated in the prevention program in Grade 7 and received additional booster sessions in Grade 8 (Botvin et al., 1983).

Some reviewers (e.g., Flay, 1985) have argued that the psychosocial prevention programs may merely have an impact on the transition from nonuse to experimental use and may not, in the final analysis, prevent or reduce more regular patterns of use. Evidence does exist, however, that these approaches produce initial reductions in the onset of experimental use, followed later by reductions in regular use (Botvin & Botvin, 1992; Tobler, 1992).

Methodological Issues

Despite the emphasis on rigorous design and evaluation methodology that characterizes psychosocial ATOD use prevention approaches, a number of reviews (Biglan & Ary, 1985; Botvin, 1986; Collins, 1992) have identified important methodological issues that deserve further consideration by prevention researchers. Many early studies testing psychosocial approaches, for example, have been criticized for shortcomings in the validity of self-report data, the appropriateness of research designs, the unit of assignment, the unit of analysis, the baseline equivalence or comparability of study groups, and the potential impact of attrition on internal and external validity.

However, in recent years studies have become progressively more rigorous. For example, studies now more typically collect physiological samples to validate self-report data. Even when these samples are not actually analyzed—a procedure commonly referred to as the "bogus pipeline"—the perception that they will be analyzed has been found to increase the validity of self-reported behavior. Other examples of methodological improvements include larger sample sizes, random assignment to study condition, baseline comparability, attention to intracluster correlation issues, and analyses of attrition patterns (Wallace & Bachman, 1993).

Program Providers

A variety of studies have demonstrated that psychosocial approaches to ATOD use prevention may be delivered effectively by different types of interventionists, including teachers (Botvin et al., 1983), older peer leaders (Botvin, Baker, Botvin, Filazzola, & Millman, 1984; Botvin & Eng, 1982; McAlister, Perry, & Maccoby, 1979; Perry, Killen, Telch, Slinkard, & Danaher, 1980), same-age peer leaders (Hurd et al., 1980; Luepker et al., 1983; Murray, Johnson, Luepker, Pechacek, & Jacobs, 1980), and project staff members (Schinke & Gilchrist, 1983). Nonetheless, most programs rely on classroom teachers to deliver intervention curricula (Botvin & Botvin, 1992). The obvious advantages of teachers are that they are readily available, are part of the school environment, and have teaching experience. As an alternative, some programs are implemented by outside experts such as physicians, nurses, and police officers. The rationale behind the use of nonschool personnel is that experts from the community have high credibility with students.

In the settings created by and for research projects, interventions have typically been implemented by project staff members. Such individuals generally have a strong commitment to the goals of the research, are highly trained, and often have prior teaching experience. Another advantage is that staff members help to ensure that the prevention program will be implemented according to the intervention protocol. This factor is generally referred to as implementation fidelity. A disadvantage of employing project staff is that they are not generally a regular part of the school environment. It is not unusual in such settings for school personnel concerned about "turf" issues to feel defensive and for this feeling to be manifested as low cooperation or even project sabotage in extreme cases. In addition, once the project is completed, these individuals will no longer be available to implement the program—a concern related to long-term program maintenance and institutionalization.

Finally, as with resistance skills training approaches, many psychosocial skills training programs have included peer leaders either as the primary providers or as adjuncts to the primary provider. The rationale behind the use of peer leaders is similar to that behind the use of outside experts. Peer leaders have a higher level of credibility with students than do teachers (Arkin, Roemhild, Johnson, Luepker, & Murray, 1981; Perry et al., 1980). Peer teaching has become recognized as a highly effective way for stimulating poorly motivated students (Vriend, 1969), and peer teaching teams have been used as a cost-efficient method of delivering more traditional health education instruction to large numbers of elementary school children (McRae & Nelson, 1971). Peer intervention in the form of counseling also has been successfully applied in several settings (Alwine, 1974; Hamburg & Varenhorst, 1972).

When a project is utilizing peer leaders, the selection process is critically important. It is typical, for example, for the students who are selected to be the most popular among the teachers and administration. However, such students may tend not to be well regarded by the high-risk students and consequently may actually have rather low credibility among an important segment of the target population. Nonetheless, it is important that the peer leaders be good role models (i.e., not smoke, drink, or use drugs; Perry et al., 1990).

Although there has been considerable support for the use of peer leaders, a number of disadvantages have been noted as well. For example, peer leaders do not generally have experience in teaching or in classroom management (Botvin & Eng, 1982). Moreover, peer leader programs, especially those in which the peer leaders have primary responsibility for conducting the program, require considerable time and effort in terms of training, coordination, and scheduling. In addition, the use of older peer leaders such as high school students may present logistical difficulties if their school is not physically near the school of the younger program participants. Furthermore, the results of one study suggest that although boys and girls may be equally affected by social influence programs when conducted by teachers, they may be differentially influenced by peer-led programs, with girls being influenced more by these programs than boys (Fisher, Armstrong, & de Kler, 1983).

A solution to many of these drawbacks that retains most of the benefits of utilizing peers might be to utilize a combination of both teachers and peer leaders (Ellickson, Bell, & McGuigan, 1993). Using this approach, teachers have primary responsibility for implementing the prevention program, thereby taking advantage of their teaching experience and classroom management skills. Peer leaders would assist teachers in program implementation, taking on specific formal responsibilities such as serving as discussion leaders, demonstrating refusal skills, and leading role-plays. In addition, peer leaders can serve in an important informal capacity as positive role models for the kinds of skills and behavior being taught in the program, particularly with respect to resisting peer influences promoting ATOD use.

Mass Media Approaches

It has long been recognized that the media are a powerful force in our society capable of shaping attitudes, beliefs, norms, and behavior. Analyses of the entertainment media have clearly indicated the pervasiveness of ATOD content in movies, television programs, radio programs, magazines, and music recordings (Winick & Winick, 1976). Adolescent readers of magazines, for example, find them to be replete with promotions for cigarettes and alcohol, as well as an ever-expanding array of proprietary drugs. Those watching television are similarly inundated with beer and pharmaceutical commercials.

A number of mass media promotions concerning ATOD use prevention and general issues related to health promotion have been developed and implemented. These campaigns often take the form of public service announcements that rely on information education and fear arousal strategies. A significant impediment for such campaigns is that television networks typically broadcast these announcements during times of low viewership when demand for commercial advertising time is lowest (Orlandi, Lieberman, & Schinke, 1989).

Effectiveness of Mass Media Approaches

Those mass media campaigns that have been evaluated have produced effects that at best can be described as inconsistent. Flay and Sobel (1983) reported that some campaigns have increased knowledge and changed attitudes in the desired direction, some have had no effects, and others have produced negative effects (i.e., have increased ATOD use). The finding that the overwhelming majority of mass media ATOD use prevention efforts have failed to change behavior is not surprising, considering that most public service announcements fail even to reach the intended audience.

A major exception was the counteradvertising campaign mounted against the tobacco industry in the late 1960s, through which there was approximately one example of counteradvertisement for every four or five cigarette ads. It has been frequently noted that the effectiveness of that particular mass media campaign was the most important factor in obtaining the cooperation of the tobacco industry to eliminate cigarette advertising from television (Dryfoos, 1993).

Despite the lack of empirically demonstrated effects, mass media campaigns represent a potentially powerful weapon in the war against ATOD use and related problems. To realize this potential, however, media interventions in the future must overcome the deficiencies of the past. It is axiomatic that mass media campaigns must reach their target audience if they are to achieve their intended effects—a factor termed *message penetration.* Clearly, therefore, public service announcements should be aired during "prime time" or other periods when viewership is high. In addition, such campaigns should downplay the use of information dissemination and fear arousal strategies and place greater emphasis on strategies designed to combat the powerful social influences to smoke, drink, or use drugs. Finally, rigorous evaluation research is needed to develop and refine prevention-oriented mass media campaigns (Orlandi, 1992).

Community-Based Approaches

The major emphasis of this chapter has been on school-based intervention technologies. This emphasis is justified because programs that target student populations constitute a substantial portion of the prevention efforts that have been initiated nationwide over the past several decades (Botvin & Botvin, 1992). However, community-based approaches, although far more difficult to evaluate, offer the potential of providing a broader supportive context for other prevention efforts carried out in smaller organizational settings such as schools (Orlandi et al., 1990).

Parent Groups

A rapidly growing force in ATOD use prevention in recent years is what has come to be called the Parents' Movement. This broader movement is actually a collection of smaller grassroots movements involving concerned parents from communities throughout the country (Zill, 1993). The main focus of these groups is to provide support for concerned parents and a mechanism for becoming educated about the problem of drug abuse. They also strive to increase the awareness of other parents throughout their communities and to serve as a catalyst for positive social change. One of the best known groups of this type is MADD (Mothers Against Drunk Driving).

Many of these local parent groups have been collected under the auspices of the National Federation of Parents for Drug-Free Youth, which was formed in 1980. The primary objective of this organization is to assist in the formation and support of local parent and youth groups. The organization also sponsors annual national conferences, distributes public service announcements, and lobbies state legislatures and the U.S. Congress.

Unfortunately, despite energy and enthusiasm of members, such organizations have difficulty in maintaining their memberships. Youth often report that their parents are not actively involved. It has been shown that very few parents are active within each local youth program.

Effectiveness of Parent Groups

Recent research has underscored the influence that parents can have on the ATOD use of their children (Cohen & Linton, 1995; Perry et al., 1990; Phares & Compas, 1992; Reilly, 1992; Santisteban, Szapocznik, & Rio, 1993). Although numerous claims have been made in the mass media concerning the effectiveness of parent groups in preventing substance abuse, no effort to evaluate their effectiveness objectively has been reported. One notable exception is a study conducted by Moskowitz (1985), which evaluated the effects of parent groups on adolescent substance use. In this study, two locations where parent groups had been active were selected for study. These sites were selected for the study specifically because assertions had been made that the parent groups operating out of these locations had been particularly successful in positively influencing adolescent ATOD use.

The parent groups involved at these sites were the Unified Parents of America (UPA) and the Naples Informed Parents (NIP). Considerable information was available concerning these parent groups because a previous study had focused on the organization and development of these groups (Manett, 1983). UPA had been credited with decreasing the use of alcohol and other drugs, truancy, and tardiness, as well as with increasing academic achievement test scores and participation in adult-sanctioned extracurricular activities. NIP also had been credited with contributing to a variety of positive changes related to ATOD use and academics.

As part of the evaluation, interviews were developed and administered to leaders of the parent groups and local school personnel. Available archival records were also examined for student academic achievement, absenteeism, vandalism, discipline problems, course enrollment, and ATOD use. Unfortunately, the analysis of available archival records could not adequately document or substantiate any of the changes in student behavior that had been reported by the parent groups. In addition, the interview data revealed that school personnel and parent group leaders had different perceptions of the contributions that parents had made to changes in school policy and student behavior. Moreover, it was impossible to separate what could have been parent group effects from other, concurrent community influences. Thus the task of objectively documenting the presence of any putative changes relating to ATOD use prevention turned out to be virtually impossible.

Local Youth Groups

A different approach to organizing local resources for ATOD use prevention has been adopted by the state of Nebraska, which has established a network of drug-free youth groups (Nelson-Simley & Erickson, 1995). Relying on a combination of alternative activities and ATOD education, this network has attempted to shift the normative beliefs of youth throughout the state by making it socially acceptable to be drug-free. In a 6-year evaluation of the program, over 4,500 youth reported that they were abstaining from alcohol (91%) and from tobacco (97%). Because more than a third of those surveyed met federal criteria for "high risk," it would appear that this approach may have potential for reaching youth who are more difficult to reach through traditional school-based approaches.

Ideally, approaches such as these that are effective in mobilizing youth to participate in out-of-school settings should be combined with the types of skills training approaches that have been shown to be effective in reducing ATOD use through the schools.

Comprehensive Community-Based Prevention

In general, community-based prevention efforts have tended to continue to rely on ATOD prevention approaches that have previously been shown to be ineffective (Orlandi et al., 1990). One excellent example, however, of a comprehensive community-based ATOD use prevention program is Project

STAR (Students Taught Awareness and Resistance), an ambitious program that involves the 15 contiguous communities making up the greater Kansas City metropolitan area.

The project has relied on matched funding from a private-sector business, a nonprofit foundation, and a federal agency, and it successfully integrates a community service project with a formal research project (Pentz, Cormack, Flay, Hansen, & Johnson, 1986). The intervention strategies are based a number of theoretical perspectives, including social learning theory (Bandura, 1977), Rothman's model of community organization (Rothman, Erlich, & Teresa, 1981), Green's system-centered education model (Green, 1985), the innovation-decision process model of Rogers (1983), and Watzlawick's model of planned change (Watzlawick, Weakland, & Fisch, 1974).

The core of the intervention is a school-based curriculum designed to teach resistance skills to middle- and junior-high school students. Over a 6-year period, there is a controlled expansion from the school-based initiative to include parent, media, and community components that involve community organization and health policy interventions. Pentz's (1986) model represents an integration of the major theoretical perspectives regarding ATOD use prevention and community organization and provides a practical step-by-step approach that may be followed by others interested in comprehensive community-based prevention.

The intervention is delivered through four program channels: school, family, media, and community organization. The three levels of intervention, based on the principles of social learning theory, are direct training of youth to promote the acquisition of drug resistance skills; training of teachers, parents, and other program interventionists; and ongoing booster sessions for both youth and program interventionists (Pentz, 1993).

This approach has been very successful on different levels. During the first 2 years of the project, the school-based component of the program was adopted by 100% of the schools in the Kansas City area and 95% of the teachers. The analysis of data collected from 50 participating junior high schools found that the rate of cigarette smoking among the students in the program was 14% as compared with 22% in a control group. Similarly, marijuana use was found to be 4% among the program students as compared with 8% in a control group. For alcohol use, only a modest difference was found, with 10% of the students in the program reporting drinking as compared with 13% in a control group (Pentz & Valente, 1993).

Summary

In an effort to prevent or reduce ATOD use and related problems in the United States, a variety of preventive technologies have been developed, and some of these have been evaluated. If measured in terms of their impact on ATOD-related behavior, most of these approaches either have not been adequately evaluated or have been found to be ineffective. Included in this group are approaches that disseminate factual information about substance use both with and without the use of fear arousal tactics or moral appeals, affective education, and alternative approaches. As our understanding of the factors promoting and maintaining ATOD use has expanded, it has become increasingly apparent that prevention approaches need to be multicomponent and comprehensive and that those based on narrower conceptual frameworks will invariably fail to address significant etiological factors adequately.

Though most of the traditional approaches reviewed here have been generally unsuccessful, several intervention technologies developed and tested in the past decade have proven to be far more promising. Much of the research over this time frame has been conducted with a focus on school-based interventions, but work on the development of comprehensive community-based approaches is also continuing. The most effective strategies identified to date address the psychosocial factors that appear to play the most important roles in promoting the initiation and maintenance of ATOD use.

There is a need to expand these successful psychosocial approaches and to develop comparable intervention models capable of delivery through various channels besides schools, including churches, youth centers, shopping malls, and other organizational settings; parents, siblings, and other family structures; and interactive videos, game-oriented software, the Internet, and other computer-based technologies. As with the approaches designed for implementation in school settings, the most cost-efficient development approaches will be grounded in carefully planned and rigorously designed research.

References

Alwine, G. (1974). If you need love, come to US: An overview of a peer counseling program in a senior high school. *Journal of School Health, 44,* 463-464.

Arkin, R. M., Roemhild, H. J., Johnson, C. A., Luepker, R. V., & Murray, D. M. (1981). The Minnesota smoking prevention program: A seventh grade health curriculum supplement. *Journal of School Health, 51,* 616-661.

Bandura, A. (1977). *Social learning theory.* Englewood Cliffs, NJ: Prentice Hall.

Bandura, A. (1986). *Social foundations of thought and action.* Englewood Cliffs, NJ: Prentice Hall.

Berberian, R. M., Gross, C., Lovejoy, J., & Paparella, S. (1976). The effectiveness of drug education programs: A critical review. *Health Education Monographs, 4,* 377-398.

Best, J. A., Flay, B. R., Towson, S. M. J., Ryan, L. B., Perry, C., Brown, K. S., Kersell, M. W., & d'Avernas, J. R. (1984). Smoking prevention and the concept of risk. *Journal of Applied Social Psychology, 14,* 257-273.

Biglan, A., & Ary, D. V. (1985). Current methodological issues in research on smoking prevention. In C. Bell & R. Battjes (Eds.), *Prevention research: Deterring drug abuse among children and adolescents* (NIDA Research Monograph No. 63, pp. 170-195). Washington, DC: Government Printing Office.

Botvin, G. J. (1982). Broadening the focus of smoking prevention strategies. In T. Coates, A. Petersen, & C. Perry (Eds.), *Promoting adolescent health: A dialogue on research and practice* (pp. 199-211). New York: Academic Press.

Botvin, G. J. (1986). Substance abuse prevention research: Recent developments and future directions. *Journal of School Health, 56,* 369-386.

Botvin, G. J., Baker, E., Botvin, E. M., Filazzola, A. D., & Millman, R. B. (1984). Alcohol abuse prevention through the development of personal and social competence: A pilot study. *Journal of Studies on Alcohol, 45,* 550-552.

Botvin, G. J., & Botvin, E. M. (1992). School-based and community-based prevention approaches. In J. H. Lowinson, P. Ruiz, & R. B. Millman (Eds.), *Substance abuse: A comprehensive textbook* (2nd ed., pp. 910-927). Baltimore: Williams & Wilkens.

Botvin, G. J., & Eng, A. (1982). The efficacy of a multicomponent approach to the prevention of cigarette smoking. *Preventive Medicine, 11,* 199-211.

Botvin, G. J., Renick, N., & Baker, E. (1983). The effects of scheduling format and booster sessions on a broad spectrum psychosocial approach to smoking prevention. *Journal of Behavioral Medicine, 6,* 359-379.

Brook, J. S., Brook, D. W., Gordon, A. S., Whiteman, M., & Cohen, P. (1990). The psychological etiology of adolescent drug use: A family interactional approach. *Genetic, Social and General Monographs, 116,* 111-267.

Chassin, L., Presson, C. C., Sherman, S. J., & Edwards, D. A. (1992). The natural history of cigarette smoking and young adult social roles. *Journal of Health and Social Behavior, 33,* 328-347.

Cohen, D. A., & Linton, K. L. (1995). Parent participation in an adolescent drug abuse prevention program. *Journal of Drug Education, 25,* 159-169.

Coie, J. D., Watt, N. F., West, S. G., Hawkins, J. D., Asarnow, J. R., Markman, H. J., Ramey, S. L., Shure, M. B., & Long, B. (1993). The science of prevention: A conceptual framework and some directions for a national research program. *American Psychologist, 48,* 1013-1022.

Collins, R. L. (1992). Methodological issues in conducting substance abuse research on ethnic minority populations. *Drugs and Society, 6,* 59-77.

Dorn, N., & Thompson, A. (1976). Evaluation of drug education in the longer term is not an optional extra. *Community Health, 7,* 154-161.

Dryfoos, J. G. (1993). Preventing substance use: Rethinking strategies. *American Journal of Public Health, 83,* 793-795.

Dusenbury, L., Kerner, J. F., Baker, E., Botvin, G. J., James-Ortiz, S., & Zauber, A. (1992). Predictors of smoking prevalence among New York Latino youth. *American Journal of Public Health, 82,* 55-58.

Ellickson, P. L., Bell, R. M., & McGuigan, K. (1993). Preventing adolescent drug use: Long term results of a junior high program. *American Journal of Public Health, 83,* 856-861.

Evans, R. I. (1976). Smoking in children: Developing a social psychological strategy of deterrence. *Preventive Medicine, 5,* 122-127.

Evans, R. I., Henderson, A. H., Hill, P. C., & Raines, B. E. (1979). Current psychological, social and educational programs in control and prevention of smoking: A critical methodological review. *Atherosclerosis Reviews, 6,* 203-245.

Evans, R. I., Rozelle, R. M., Mittlemark, M. B., Hansen, W. B., Bane, A. L., & Havis, J. (1978). Deterring the onset of smoking in children: Knowledge of immediate physiological effects and coping with peer pressure, media pressure, and parent modeling. *Journal of Applied Social Psychology, 8,* 126-135.

Fisher, D. A., Armstrong, B. K., & de Kler, N. H. (1983, October). *A randomized-controlled trial of education for prevention of smoking in 12-year-old children.* Paper presented at the Fifth World Conference on Smoking and Health, Winnipeg, Canada.

Flay, B. R. (1985). Psychosocial approaches to smoking prevention: A review of findings. *Health Psychology, 4,* 449-488.

Flay, B., & Sobel, J. (1983). The role of mass media in preventing adolescent substance abuse. In T. Glynn, C. Luekefeld, & J. Ludford (Eds.), *Preventing adolescent drug abuse: Intervention strategies* (NIDA Research Monograph No. 47, pp. 5-35). Washington, DC: Government Printing Office.

Gorman, D. M. (1995). The effectiveness of DARE and other drug use prevention programs. *American Journal of Public Health, 85,* 873-874.

Green, L. W. (1985). *Toward a healthy community: Organizing events for community health promotion.* Washington, DC: Government Printing Office.

Hamburg, B. A., & Varenhorst, B. B. (1972). Peer counseling in the secondary schools: A community mental health project for youth. *American Journal of Orthopsychiatry, 42,* 566-581.

Hawkins, J. D., Catalano, R. F., & Miller, J. Y. (1992). Risk and protective factors for alcohol and other drug problems in adolescence and early adulthood: Implications for substance abuse prevention. *Psychological Bulletin, 112,* 64-105.

Hurd, P., Johnson, C. A., Pechacek, T., Best, C. P., Jacobs, D., & Luepker, R. (1980). Prevention of cigarette smoking in 7th grade students. *Journal of Behavioral Medicine, 3,* 15-28.

Jessor, R., & Jessor, S. L. (1977). *Problem behavior and psychosocial development: A longitudinal study of youth.* New York: Academic Press.

Kim, S. (1988). *A short- and long-term evaluation of "Here's Looking at You."* II. *Journal of Drug Education, 18,* 235-242

Luepker, R. V., Johnson, C. A., Murray, D. M., & Pechacek, T. F. (1983). Prevention of cigarette smoking: Three year follow-up of educational programs for youth. *Journal of Behavioral Medicine, 6,* 53-61.

Manett, M. (1983). *Parents, peers and pot II: Parents in action* (DHHS Publication No. ADM 83-1290). Washington, DC: Government Printing Office.

Mason, M. L. (1973). Drug education effects. *Dissertation Abstracts, 34*(4-B), 418.

McAlister, A., Perry, C. L., Killen, J., Slinkard, L. A., & Maccoby, N. (1980) Pilot study of smoking, alcohol, and drug abuse prevention. *American Journal of Public Health, 70,* 719-721.

McAlister, A., Perry, C., & Maccoby, N. (1979). Adolescent smoking: Onset and prevention. *Pediatrics, 63,* 650-658.

McGuire, W. J. (1964). Inducing resistance to persuasion: Some contemporary approaches. *Advances in Experimental Social Psychology, 1,* 192-227.

McGuire, W. J. (1968). The nature of attitudes and attitude change. In B. Lindzey & E. Aronson (Eds.), *Handbook of social psychology* (pp. 136-314). Reading, MA: Addison-Wesley.

McRae, C. F., & Nelson, D. M. (1971). Youth to youth communication on smoking and health. *Journal of School Health, 41,* 445-447.

Moskowitz, J. M. (1985). Evaluating the effects of parent groups on the correlates of adolescent substance abuse. *Journal of Psychoactive Drugs, 17,* 173-178.

Murray, D. M., Johnson, C. A., Luepker, R. V., Pechacek, T. F., & Jacobs, D. R. (1980, November). *Issues in smoking prevention research.* Paper presented at the annual meeting of the American Psychological Association, Montreal, Canada.

Nelson-Simley, K., & Erickson, L. (1995). The Nebraska "Network of Drug-Free Youth" program. *Journal of School Health, 65*(2), 49-53.

Orlandi, M. A. (1986). Community-based substance abuse prevention: A multicultural perspective. *Journal of School Health, 56*(9), 394-401.

Orlandi, M. A. (1992). The challenge of evaluating community-based prevention programs: A cross-cultural perspective. In M. A. Orlandi, R. Weston, & L. Epstein (Eds.), *A guide for alcohol and other drug abuse prevention practitioners working with racial/ethnic communities* (pp. 92-97). Washington, DC: Office for Substance Abuse Prevention, Division of Community Prevention and Training.

Orlandi, M. A., Landers, C., Weston, R., & Haley, N. (1990). Diffusion of health promotion innovations. In K. Glanz, F. M. Lewis, & B. K. Rimer (Eds.), *Health behavior and health education: Theory, research and practice* (pp. 288-313). San Francisco: Jossey-Bass.

Orlandi, M. A., Lieberman, L. R., & Schinke, S. P. (1989). The effects of alcohol and tobacco advertising on adolescents. *Drugs and Society, 3,* 77-97.

Pentz, M. A. (1986). Community organizations and school liaisons: How to get programs started. *Journal of School Health, 56,* 382-388.

Pentz, M. A. (1993). Comparative effects of community-based drug abuse prevention. In J. S. Baer, G. A. Marlatt, & R. J. McMahon (Eds.), *Addictive behaviors across the lifespan: Prevention, treatment, and policy issues* (pp. 69-87). Newbury Park, CA: Sage.

Pentz, M. A., Cormack, C., Flay, B., Hansen, W., & Johnson, C. A. (1986). Balancing program and research integrity in community drug abuse prevention: Project STAR approach. *Journal of School Health, 56*(9), 389-393.

Pentz, M. A., & Valente, T. (1993). Project STAR: A substance abuse prevention campaign in Kansas City. In T. E. Backer, E. Rogers, M. Rogers, & R. Denniston (Eds.), *Impact of organizations on mass media health behavior campaigns* (pp. 37-66). Newbury Park, CA: Sage.

Perry, C. L., Killen, J., Telch, M., Slinkard, L. A., & Danaher, B. G. (1980). Modifying smoking behavior of teenagers: A school-based intervention. *American Journal of Public Health, 70,* 772-775.

Perry, C. L., Pirie, P., Holder, W., Halper, A., & Dudovitz, B. (1990). Parent involvement in cigarette smoking prevention: Two pilot evaluations of the "Unpuffables Program." *Journal of School Health, 60,* 443-447.

Phares, V., & Compas, B. (1992). The role of fathers in child and adolescent psychopathology: Make room for daddy. *Psychological Bulletin, 111,* 387-412.

Reilly, D. M. (1992). Drug-abusing families: Intrafamilial dynamics and brief triphasic treatment. In E. Kaufman & P. Kaufman (Eds.), *Family therapy of drug and alcohol abuse* (pp. 105-119). Boston: Allyn & Bacon.

Rogers, E. M. (1983). *The diffusion of innovations.* New York: Macmillan.

Rothman, J., Erlich, J. L., & Teresa, J. G. (1981). *Changing organizations and community programs.* Beverly Hills, CA: Sage.

Santisteban, D. A., Szapocznik, J., & Rio, A. T. (1993). Family therapy for Hispanic substance abusing youth: An empirical approach to substance abuse prevention. In R. S. Mayer, B. L. Kail, & T. D. Watts (Eds.), *Hispanic substance abuse* (pp. 157-173). Springfield, IL: Charles C Thomas.

Schaps, E., Bartolo, R. D., Moskowitz, J., Palley, C. S., & Churgin, S. (1981). A review of 127 drug abuse prevention program evaluations. *Journal of Drug Issues, 12,* 17-43.

Schinke, S. P., & Gilchrist, L. D. (1983). Primary prevention of tobacco smoking. *Journal of School Health, 53*(7), 416-419.

Schinke, S., Orlandi, M., Vaccaro, D., Espinoza, R., McAlister, A., & Botvin, G. (1992). Substance use among Hispanic and non-Hispanic adolescents. *Addictive Behaviors, 17,* 117-124.

Swisher, J. D. (1979). Prevention issues. In R. I. Dupont, A. Goldstein, & J. O'Donnell (Eds.), *Handbook on drug abuse* (pp. 49-62). Washington, DC: Government Printing Office.

Swisher, J. D., Crawford, J. L., Goldstein, R., & Yura, M. (1971). Drug education: Pushing or preventing? *Peabody Journal of Education, 49,* 68-75.

Swisher, J. D., & Hoffman, A. (1975). Information: The irrelevant variable in drug education. In B. W. Corder, R. A. Smith, & J. D. Swisher (Eds.), *Drug abuse prevention: Perspectives and approaches for educators* (pp. 49-62). Dubuque, IA: William C. Brown.

Telch, M. J., Killen, J. D., McAlister, A. L., Perry, C. L., & Maccoby, N. (1982). Long-term follow-up of a pilot project on smoking prevention with adolescents. *Journal of Behavioral Medicine, 5,* 1-8.

Tobler, N. S. (1992). Drug prevention programs can work: Research findings. *Journal of Addictive Diseases, 11,* 1-28.

Vriend, T. (1969). High-performing inner-city adolescents assist low-performing peers in counseling groups. *Personnel Guidance Journal, 48,* 897-904.

Wallace, J. M., & Bachman, J. G. (1993). Validity of self-reports in student based studies on minority populations: Issues and concerns. In M. R. De La Rosa & J. L. R. Adredos (Eds.), *Drug abuse among minority youth: Advances in research and methodology* (Research Monograph No. 130, pp. 167-200). Rockville, MD: National Institute on Drug Abuse.

Watzlawick, F., Weakland, J. H., & Fisch, R. (1974). *Change: Principles of problem formation and problem resolution.* New York: Norton.

Winick, C., & Winick, M. P. (1976). Drug education and a content of mass media dealing with "dangerous drugs" and alcohol. In R. E. Osteman (Ed.), *Communication research and drug education* (Vol. 4, pp. 102-117). London: Sage.

Zigler, E., Tanssig, C., & Black, K. (1992). Early childhood intervention. *American Psychologist, 47,* 997-1006.

Zill, N. (1993). The changing realities of family life. *Aspen Institute Quarterly, 5,* 27-51.

5

DARE (Drug Abuse Resistance Education)

Very Popular but Not Very Effective

Richard R. Clayton
Carl G. Leukefeld
Nancy Grant Harrington
Anne Cattarello

The purpose of this chapter is to review and examine what is known about the most widely distributed school-based drug abuse prevention program in the world, DARE (Drug Abuse Resistance Education). It is likely that you know about DARE; you have seen the T-shirts, the bumper stickers, floats in Independence Day parades, DARE cars, and the hundreds of other ways that this program has been marketed. Perhaps you yourself were in a class or school that received the DARE curriculum in the fifth or sixth grade.

DARE is a social phenomenon (Wysong, 1993). In the 1983-84 school year, it was delivered to about 8,000 elementary school students in Los Angeles. Today, DARE is found in more than one half of all school districts in the United States and reaches at least 25 million students each year

AUTHORS' NOTE: This study was funded by Grant No. DA-05312 from the National Institute on Drug Abuse to the Center for Prevention Research, University of Kentucky.

(Ennett, Tobler, Ringwalt, & Flewelling, 1994). Although the numbers are difficult to confirm, it is estimated that $750 million is spent on DARE each year in the United States. DARE can also be found in Australia, Canada, Mexico, New Zealand, Norway, and Sweden.

The DARE Program

DARE began in Los Angeles in 1983-84 as a school-based drug prevention program. The curriculum is a result of the joint efforts of the Los Angeles Police Department and the Los Angeles Unified School District, one of the country's largest.

Unlike most other school-based prevention programs, which are taught by teachers, DARE is taught by uniformed police officers who must undergo 80 hours of rigorous training before they can teach the program (Falco, 1989).

The stated purpose of DARE is to "prevent substance abuse among school children." The principal way it seeks to achieve this goal is to teach students the skills for recognizing and resisting social pressures to experiment with tobacco, alcohol, and other drugs. The 17 DARE lessons also focus on enhancing students' self-esteem, decision making, coping, assertiveness, and communication skills and on teaching positive alternatives to substance use. The curriculum and basic goals and structure of the DARE program have remained essentially the same since its beginnings. However, in 1992-94, additional lessons were added to place greater emphasis on the prevention of tobacco use and a new and enhanced focus was placed on violence prevention and conflict resolution. In addition, the actual classroom style became more "interactive" rather than one-directional from officer to student. The revisions were phased in during 1993-94, and beginning January 1, 1995, all DARE officers were required to use the "new" program.

The original DARE program was targeted at students in the fifth or sixth grade, preferably the grade immediately prior to entering junior high or middle school. Now there are DARE programs for kindergarten through third-grade students, middle-school students, and high school students (Kochis, 1995).

Being at the Right Place at the Right Time

National political interest in the drug problem was focused in 1986 with President Reagan's "War on Drugs" address to the nation. This led to broad support from both the Democratic and Republican parties and the passage of the Anti-Drug Abuse Act of 1986 (Falco, 1989). In both the Bush and the Clinton administrations, there was increasing recognition of the complexity of the problem and the requirements that law enforcement/supply reduction and prevention-treatment/demand reduction efforts be coordinated. The Office of National Drug Control Policy (ONDCP) is responsible for this coordination and has placed increasingly strong emphasis on prevention and drug education programs. In fact, federal spending for all "educational" prevention activities rose from $230 million in 1988 to $660 million in 1995.

DARE was at the right place at the right time, with just the right types of political support to become what the Justice Department called the "long term solution to the drug problem." In fact, the congressional testimony of Los Angeles Police Chief Daryl Gates and support from powerful members of Congress and President Bush led in 1990 to an amendment to the 1986 Drug Free Schools and Communities Act. This amendment mandated federal funding for DARE. The Drug Free Schools Act divided money given to the states into two parts: 70% of the money went to the departments of education in the states, and 30% went to the governor. The amendment required that 10% of the governor's portion be used to fund programs such as Project Drug Abuse Resistance Education (DARE). In fact, DARE was the only school-based prevention program singled out for mandated funding.

Congressional and other support for DARE continued into the mid-1990s, when it was again singled out for federal funding through a renewed commitment in Congress to what was now called the "Safe and Drug Free Schools and Communities Act."

DARE: More Than Just a Drug Prevention Program

One of the reasons DARE has been so successful in spreading across the country is organizational. DARE America is a private, nonprofit corporation organized in 1987 with a goal of getting the program into all states and

communities, developing and supporting a national DARE instructor training program, and getting funding nationally.

Training

The Bureau of Justice Assistance (BJA) within the Department of Justice
started funding DARE in 1986 with a BJA grant of $140,000. In the late
1980s, BJA funded five regional DARE training centers. As part of the
funding agreement, BJA appoints 5 of the 15 members of the DARE training
center policy advisory board.

Additional Funding and Support

DARE America has been successful in attracting major corporate sponsors such as Bayliner, Herbalife, Kentucky Fried Chicken, Kimberly-Clark,
McDonalds, Packard Bell, Security Pacific National Bank, and Warner
Brothers. At the local and state level, there are thousands of large and small
firms contributing to the program.

Inconsistency: DARE's Popularity and Its Effectiveness

The principal purpose of DARE is to reduce substance abuse among
school children. About the only way to determine if DARE has achieved
success (i.e., "works") is to conduct research on students who receive DARE
and those who do not receive DARE. Both the experimental group (received
DARE) and the control group should be examined prior to the start of the
prevention effort and followed for 1 to 5 years to see if differences persist.
DARE is the most widely research-evaluated school-based prevention program in the United States. There have been at least 15 evaluation studies
conducted (Ennett et al., 1994), several of which followed DARE and
non-DARE students for up to 4 or 5 years (Clayton, Cattarello, & Johnstone,
1996). Although the results from various studies differ somewhat, all studies
are consistent in finding that DARE does not have long-term effects on drug
use (Kochis, 1995). It does seem to have some effects on knowledge and
attitudes toward drugs, but even these effects diminish over time. In fact, two
long-term follow-up studies show that after 3 or more years, students who
received DARE do not even have more positive attitudes toward the police

than students who did not receive DARE (Clayton et al., 1996; Wysong, Aniskiewicz, & Wright, 1994).

Why Is DARE So Popular if It Is Not Effective?

This is an important question because it reveals so much about the United States and its approach to social problems (Aniskiewicz & Wysong, 1990).

Police

DARE is popular among police for two reasons. First, it puts police officers into community institutions previously "off limits" to them. Before the advent of DARE, there was a widespread and deep-seated mistrust of police officers by school officials. In fact, police were seen by many community members and organizations as generally less educated and brutish. By entering school systems to teach DARE, police can change these stereotypes. Second, it allows police officers to do things that are seen as "positive." In most police departments prior to the mid-1980s, absolutely the worst assignment was what was then called "community relations." No police officer wanted that assignment. Now police officers are standing in line for an opportunity to be a DARE officer. Police officers perceive a different response to them from the public if they are involved with DARE. In fact, it could be said that DARE has had a major effect on the relationship between police departments and other community-based organizations. Police are now active players in a wide variety of positive community projects and initiatives.

Parents

DARE is popular among parents for at least two reasons. First, they are extremely concerned about drug abuse and violence, and most feel helpless in dealing with either. Therefore, if there is a police officer in the school teaching the DARE program, it might protect their child from being victimized by violent predators or by drug dealers. Second, most Americans have a naive and false sense of confidence in the power of "education." It is the panacea brought out to "solve" all our problems: If people just know the "facts," they will make rational choices. The DARE officer represents authority, and parents have faith that children will listen to and heed the advice of an authority. Besides, the prevailing orientation to drugs in this society is primarily concerned with legality/illegality—a law enforcement perspective. The DARE officer represents the prevailing perspective held by parents.

Teachers

DARE is also quite popular among teachers, and for two very good reasons. First, teachers, just like the parents, perceive the school to be a safer place when DARE officers are in the school. Second, the DARE officer teaches the drug prevention curriculum, which means that the teachers do not have to teach the lessons. In fact, although the teachers are required to be "in the classroom" during the drug prevention lessons, they get a respite from their work, a break of sorts. This second reason is very important as an unintended consequence of how far and how quickly DARE has diffused across the country. At present, no colleges of education require preparation of teachers to deliver substance abuse prevention curricula. Even so, a significant proportion of fifth- and sixth-grade teachers in the United States could probably teach the DARE curriculum because they have seen and heard it taught one or more times. If the education establishment had been called on to provide 80 hours of training to teach a drug prevention curriculum such as DARE, it would have cost billions of dollars. Instead, such a curriculum has been provided at no cost to the education establishment in the course of the spread of DARE across America.

Administrators

School administrators, the principals and superintendents, seem to like DARE because it provides a sense of extra security at the school, it provides a respite for the teachers which makes them happy, it is generally very popular among parents and gets them more involved with the school than would otherwise be likely, and it links the school with another important institution of the community, the police department. A number of principals regularly request that the DARE officer be in the school on Mondays because attendance is noticeably higher when the DARE officer is in the school (Clayton, Cattarello, Day, & Walden, 1991).

The "Feel-Good" Approach to Drug Prevention

Someone might wonder: If everybody likes DARE and it makes students, teachers, administrators, parents, police, and politicians "feel good" because something is being done about drug abuse, why should we be worried by lack of evidence that it delays the onset or inhibits the continuance of drug use by adolescents? The answer to this question is quite simple and has three parts. First, publicly funded programs should be accountable for what they achieve. If they do not achieve their stated goal (in this instance, a reduction in drug use), how can further expenditure of public funds be justified? Second, other similar programs consistently show some effects in the desired direction, although the effects are not huge (Botvin, Dusenbury, Botvin, & Diaz, 1995). Why should the American public pay for a program that has proven to be ineffective when programs that have proven to be successful exist? Third, a principal reason for evaluation research is to examine the effectiveness of public programming that may seem sound on the surface but is unsound in practice. The evidence for the lack of sustained effectiveness of DARE is strong, consistent, and impressive.

Why, then, the continued strong support of DARE? The answer to this question must be: Because it makes all the important groups (parents, teachers, administrators, police, politicians) "feel good." It is sad to say, but an overwhelming majority of people in the United States have a rather naive view of the world and how to solve social problems such as drug use and abuse by adolescents. DARE seems to reflect most of these naive notions and in some ways to exploit them.

Drug use is *not* a simple phenomenon. It will not be solved by simple slogans and bumper stickers and T-shirts and a bunch of people believing that DARE is "the" answer to drug abuse in America. If anyone really and truly believes this is true, we have some swamp land in Florida we would like for them to buy.

The "scientific" research on the effectiveness of DARE is clear. DARE does not produce sustained effects on drug use or on even attitudes toward police (Clayton et al., 1996). Furthermore, the most recent data suggest that drug use (marijuana, inhalants, LSD, stimulants, cigarettes) began to rise significantly among 8th, 10th, and 12th graders beginning in 1992 and continuing through 1994. The cohorts in which drug use began to rise for the first time since 1979 would have been 6th graders in 1990, 8th graders in 1992, and 10th graders in 1994. If we assumed that DARE had spread all across America by 1990, these would be the students who would have been most affected by the diffusion of DARE.

To be fair, DARE could not be expected to produce miracles and wipe out drug use among adolescents entirely. Many forces in society promote drug use or dilute efforts to fight drug use among adolescents. However, DARE could be expected to produce some reduction in drug use, or at the very least positive and sustained effects on attitudes toward drug use by adolescents. Instead, as has been shown, there are *no* sustained effects from the DARE program on attitudes or behavior. In fact, it is probably naive to think that any *universal* (one size fitting all students) type of school-based, curriculum-driven drug prevention program could exert enough influence to counter the forces driving youth toward experimentation with various drugs. These types of programs are simply not powerful enough, do not provide enough exposures to the intervention, and may not even directly address the primary causes of drug use by youth. For example, one entire lesson in the DARE curriculum is designed to heighten self-esteem. However, the extensive research literature on the relationship between self-esteem and drug use among adolescents indicates very little correlation between drug use and self-esteem. Therefore, even if the lesson helped to improve self-esteem for some of the students, that improvement would probably not be translated into a lower probability of drug use. So although DARE is very popular, it is not very effective. Therefore we as a nation should be ready to accept that fact and deal with its implications if we *really* want to have an effect on drug use among youth.

References

Aniskiewicz, R., & Wysong, E. (1990). Evaluating DARE: Drug education and the multiple meanings of success. *Policy Studies Review, 9,* 727-747.

Botvin, G. J., Dusenbury, L., Botvin, E. M., & Diaz, T. (1995). Long term follow-up results of a randomized drug abuse trial in a white middle class population. *Journal of the American Medical Association, 273,* 1106-1112.

Clayton, R. R., Cattarello, L., Day, E., & Walden, K. P. (1991). Persuasive communication and drug prevention: An evaluation of the DARE program. In H. Sypher, L. Donohew, & W. Bukoski (Eds.), *Persuasive communication and drug abuse prevention.* Hillsdale, NJ: Lawrence Erlbaum.

Clayton, R. R., Cattarello, A. M., & Johnstone, B. M. (in press). The effectiveness of Drug Abuse Resistance Education (Project DARE): Five year follow-up results. *Preventive Medicine.*

Ennett, S., Tobler, N., Ringwalt, C., & Flewelling, R. (1994). How effective is Drug Abuse Resistance Education? A meta-analysis of Project DARE outcome evaluations. *American Journal of Public Health, 84,* 1394-1401.

Falco, M. (1989). *Winning the drug war: A national strategy.* New York: Priority.

Kochis, D. S. (1995). The effectiveness of Project DARE: Does it work? *Journal of Alcohol and Drug Education, 40,* 40-47.

Wysong, E. (1993, October). *The frontier of drug education: D.A.R.E. as a social movement.* Paper presented at the annual meeting of the Indiana Academy of Social Sciences, Hanover College, Hanover, IN.

Wysong, E., Aniskiewicz, R., & Wright, D. (1994). Truth and DARE: Tracking drug education to graduation and as symbolic politics. *Social Problems, 41,* 448-473.

6

Religious Belief and the Initiation and Prevention of Drug Use Among Youth

Duane C. McBride
Patricia B. Mutch
Dale D. Chitwood

Train up a child in the way he should go: and when he is old, he will not depart from it.—*Proverbs* 22:6.

As a behavioral phenomenon, chronic drug use receives considerable public attention. Researchers, clinicians, and policy makers recognize that the etiology of drug use is extraordinarily complex and multicausal. Research and clinical literature is rich in theoretical models and extensive in the number of variables that have been evaluated as factors associated with drug use. Research and clinical conclusions have historically focused on

1. The role of genetics in substance use (Crabbe & Goldman, 1992)
2. How neural transmission facilitates drug effect, tolerance, and addiction (Bodor, 1995)
3. Drug use as a coping mechanism to deal with chronic or situational depression and personality disorders (Cooper, Russell, Skinner, Frone, & Mudar, 1992)

4. Social and economic structure as a facilitative and direct cause of drug use (Agnew & White, 1992)

5. Parental and peer relationships as protecting from or causing drug use (Brook, Whiteman, & Finch, 1993)

6. The subcultural and social role of addiction as a meaningful social existence (Stephens, 1991)

Some excellent integrative theoretical models have attempted to bring together these various disciplinary perspectives. Although the literature contains a variety of theoretical models of drug use, these models generally do not include a major empirical variable consistently found to be related to drug use: religious belief. Religiosity is typically seen merely as indicative of conventional relationships or attitudes rather than as a direct causative factor in alcohol and drug use abstinence or moderation. This perspective was well expressed by Hirschi and Stark (1969), who, in the analysis of data from a large-scale delinquency study, found no statistical relationship between religious involvement and delinquency. They therefore concluded that in an increasingly secular era, religion was irrelevant to the understanding of and, by implication, the prevention of delinquency. Later, however, Stark (1984) became convinced that this conclusion was incorrect. He suggested that modern scholars often have strongly secular attitudes and thus have difficulty understanding the conceptual, attitudinal, and behavioral power of religion in modern society.

Research data consistently show at least a moderately strong inverse relationship between religious values and drug use (e.g., see Hadaway, Elifson, & Petersen, 1984). The socializing impact of the monotheistic religions (Christianity, Judaism, and Islam) in general society continues to strongly affect societal attitudes toward drug use and intoxication. Religious organizations have been highly involved in initiating programs to prevent and/or treat drug use problems; their efforts range from educational materials used in prevention programs to street-level outreach aimed at helping chronic drug users attain and maintain abstinence. Treatment programs operated by religious organizations vary widely. They may resemble standard drug treatment programs operated by secular treatment groups in their use of standard psychological intervention techniques; they may be ministries that give traditional 12-step programs specific theological underpinnings, or they may rely totally on the power of God to convert drug users and miraculously free them from their addictions (Moss, 1995).

Empirical and conceptual findings as well as emerging religious-based prevention and treatment efforts suggest that it is important to further examine the role of religion in (a) the etiology and cultural understanding of drug use and (b) drug use treatment and prevention. Such a focus is important both for a more complete understanding of the drug use phenomenon and for planning comprehensive treatment and intervention services.

It is the purpose of this chapter to

1. Examine briefly selected religious perspectives on alcohol and drug use and chemically altered states of consciousness
2. Review selected literature on the empirical relationship between religious values and drug use
3. Examine data on reasons for alcohol and drug abstinence among college students in two colleges operated by a proscriptive Christian denomination

Religion and Altered States of Consciousness

Anthropological literature documents that chemically altered states of consciousness have been a part of religious expression and experience throughout human history. Such practices have involved the use of psychoactive mushrooms, peyote, coca, alcohol, concentrated tobacco, or other psychoactive drugs (e.g., see Aberle, 1966). Within many cultural traditions, it has been thought that such altered states place one in direct communication with the gods, and allow the gods to communicate directly with human beings to express divine will. In these traditions, the use of psychoactive chemicals is a transcendent experience, placing one beyond the ordinary into the realm of the gods. Researchers have noted that in times of stress, poverty, or other forms of deprivation, chemically altered states of consciousness might become particularly valued because they take the individual away from an intolerable situation into a realm of consciousness beyond the horror of the moment (Bourguignon, 1973). Scholars have also noted that an element of the 1970s drug revolution focused on the religious meaning of drugs, particularly the effects of LSD and certain mushrooms. The 1970s argument essentially held that the use of drugs to expand consciousness was intrinsically an attempt to reach beyond daily experience of a mechanistic and materialistic world toward transcendent religious experience (for a discussion of the issues of modern drug-induced religious experience, see Bakalar, 1985).

Altered States of Consciousness and the Monotheistic Religions

The monotheistic religions (Judaism, Christianity, and Islam) often had components that emphasized the importance of altered states of consciousness in worship and in the understanding of divine will. However, they generally strongly opposed chemically altered states of consciousness within religious experience (Bourguignon, 1973). The mainstream adherents of these theological traditions did not believe that chemically altered states enhanced religious experience or put believers into a closer, more direct relationship with God. Indeed, monotheism tends to be strongly skeptical of the positive religious meaning of alcohol and drug use and has generally expressed great concern about the effects of substance use.

Apart from their opposition to the religious enhancement value of chemicals, however, the three monotheistic traditions vary considerably in their theological views and daily life religious practices of adherents regarding alcohol and other drug use. Islam has had the most consistent position. Since its origins, Islam has continually argued that the use of alcohol and all other intoxicating substances has been forbidden by Allah. In contrast, although small elements of Christianity have often argued for drug and alcohol abstinence, the vast majority of Christians consume alcohol. Church theologians and scholars generally conclude that the Christian New Testament advocates not abstinence but some level of restraint in alcohol use. In practice, Christianity has frequently been tolerant of a high level of alcohol use. Judaism is often seen as the moderate tradition within the monotheistic triad.

Judaism and Alcohol and Drugs

The Jewish faith has emphasized moderation in the use of alcohol and has opposed other forms of recreational drug use (except tobacco). The Torah consistently expresses concern about the effects of alcohol on an individual's life, human relationships, and relationship with God. There also appears to be considerable concern that alcohol, and by extension other psychoactive drugs, may prevent the user from being able to enter into the presence of God by interfering with the user's ability to perform correctly the appropriate sacred rituals required by God (Leviticus 10:1-10). In addition, the Torah offers many examples and warnings about alcohol as a direct cause of behavior abhorrent to God, including murder and incest (Genesis 19:30-38).

As Alder (1991) said, "The abandonment of societal norms in drunkenness, while meeting a primordial urge, is antithetical to all that Jewish tradition stands for" (p. 14). However, the Torah and the Talmud fall far short of advocating total absence from alcohol; they rather emphasize, and some have argued that they even require, the use of alcohol in very moderate and controlled settings (Novak, 1984). Orthodox Jewish daily practice appears to have integrated alcohol use into religious, family, and cultural rituals in ways that are seen as enhancing the value of those rituals and yet strongly controlling the use of alcohol and minimizing its negative effects. As Alder (1991) also noted, "The power of wine, when drunk in moderation, to stimulate and symbolize joy, has long been recognized and employed by Jewish tradition" (p. 60). For example, wine is used in traditional Jewish homes to welcome the Sabbath and other holy days (Alder, 1991). Thus alcohol use has traditionally been contained within very controlled religious and family settings. The research literature clearly indicates that Jews have lower rates of alcohol abuse and alcoholism than the general population (Carlucci, Genova, Rubackin, Rubackin, & Dayson, 1993).

The Orthodox position on the emerging drug epidemic of the 1970s was presented in an article in *Tradition: A Journal of Orthodox Thought*. In that article, Soloveichik (1972) argued that drug use violated basic principles of the Torah. He stated that the Torah stressed an absolute distinction between right and wrong and emphasized *tznuit*: purity, meekness, and dignity. Purity involved adhering to what was eternal and avoiding what caused deterioration, meekness involved an awareness of God and of being created in the image of God, and dignity involved behaving appropriately in purity and meekness. According to Soloveichik,

> The use of drugs is conducive toward the total deterioration (impurity) and emasculation of the human personality, depriving it of every vestige of freedom (the capacity for dignity and for being aware of God and that one is created in His image). This fact makes the use of drugs an extremely impure and immodest act. (pp. 55-56)

Soloveichik argued that Torah *tznuit* required one to strive toward perfection of character and avoid what was harmful to health. In the same journal, Brayer

(1968), examining the claim that modern drug use may expand religious consciousness, stated that in Judaism, mystical religious experience came from within and was aroused by fervent prayer when the purified soul encountered the Holy, not when the chemically altered impure being attempted to encounter Holiness (pp. 38-39).

Christianity and Alcohol and Drugs

Christianity offers a more complex view of chemically altered states of consciousness. Historically, Christian scholars and apologists have tended to accept the traditional Jewish view of alcohol and drugs. That is, they have urged believers to avoid what is most harmful and to exercise moderation in what is good. However, in practice, different forms of Christianity have held very dissimilar attitudes toward alcohol or other types of drug use. Generally, the church fathers did not advocate abstinence from alcohol use but rather advocated moderation. In the first few centuries of the Christian era, although drunkenness was condemned, the use of alcohol was not a significant religious issue. Fermented wine was an integral part of the most basic Christian ritual: the Eucharist. In addition, as many writers have noted, Christ's first miracle was turning water into wine (see Story, 1991), and the apostle Paul advocated the use of wine for stomach problems (1 Timothy 5:23). Although relatively isolated ascetic monastic groups might at least for a time give up alcohol, the mainstream Christian view of alcohol use was well described by Kortrey (quoted in *Christian Educational Materials,* 1983, pp. 14-15):

> The witness of the Old Testament and the example of Jesus declare in various ways that the fermented grape or grain are to be seen as part of God's creation intended for the joy of human life on earth. . . . Jesus came eating and drinking. . . . Unlike John the Baptist, Jesus pursued a lifestyle that included drinking wine as a way of celebrating the coming of [God's] kingdom.

However, Kortrey also noted that Christian churches, on the basis of Romans 13:13 and 1 Corinthians 5:11, consistently opposed drunkenness.

Although mainstream Christian tradition has always been comfortable with alcohol consumption, throughout the history of Christianity, reform movements have often focused on the mission of bringing sobriety to drunken Christians, particularly drunken clergy. The pietistic elements of the

Christian reform movements from the 17th through the early 20th century particularly focused on avoiding or controlling alcohol use (Jones, 1962-1963). In early colonial history (1726), the Reverend Cotton Mather published a "Serious Address to Those Who Unnecessarily Frequent the Tavern" (Cherrington, 1920, p. 65). But the Puritans for the most part advocated merely temperate use of alcohol. The Methodists, under their leader John Wesley, were to play perhaps the largest role in the development of the American abstinence movement.

In 1789, John Wesley delivered a series of sermons emphatically declaring that total alcohol abstinence was required of his followers (Cherrington, 1920, p. 66). By the early 1800s, many (if not most) Protestant churches, including the Methodists, the Presbyterians, the Society of Friends, the Seventh-Day Baptists, and even the Universalists, had officially adopted a policy calling for their members to refrain from intoxicating beverages and being engaged in any alcohol-related business (Cherrington, 1920). These reformers strongly argued that the use of alcohol harmed the body (seen as the temple of God), interfered with the believer's ability to communicate with God, destroyed the family, and generally displeased God.

From this individual level of concern with church members, church leaders soon moved to a broader concern for general society. By the end of the second decade of the 19th century, church members were very active in the formation of local, state, and national temperance societies. The first official pronouncement of the executive committee of the newly organized American Temperance Society clearly indicated that the temperance movement was going to go well beyond the community of believers. It was aimed at the perfection of society!

> The American Society for the Promotion of Temperance has, after devout and deliberate attention to the subject, resolved in the strength of the Lord, and with a view to the account which they must render to Him for the influence they exert in the world, to make a vigorous, united and persevering effort, to produce a change of public sentiment and practice, with regard to the use of intoxicating liquors. (Clark, 1847, p. 21)

Although theologically diverse, ranging from the socially conservative Methodists to the socially progressive Universalists, churches were united in their belief that human beings could only be religiously and socially improved if they did not use intoxicants and if alcohol were totally eliminated from society. Newly developing American churches such as the Latter Day Saints and the Seventh-day Adventists, though theologically distinct and distant from mainstream Protestant churches, enthusiastically joined the temperance movement. (It is interesting to note that as centrally organized bodies, only these two churches officially still regard the use of alcohol as a matter of church discipline; see, for example, the Seventh-day Adventist Church Manual, 1995). Further, the churches involved in the temperance movement all shared a strong emphasis on the need for believers to return to an early form of Christianity and Christian society. Several groups urged their followers to prepare for the imminent return of Christ by overcoming sins of the flesh (such as alcohol) and having a perfect living temple (a healthy body). Those who did not emphasize the Apocalypse tended to focus even more strongly on the perfectibility of the individual in society. Many came to believe that alcohol use was destroying society and preventing 19th-century American society from evolving into the perfect Christian nation (for an excellent history of the then-successful prohibition movement, see Krout, 1925).

Though it is beyond the scope of this chapter, it is important to note that the temperance movement and the burgeoning women's movement of the late 19th century were intertwined. The 19th-century women's rights movement came to view liquor trafficking and drunkenness as an integral part of the oppression of women. Many suffragist leaders believed that prohibition was part of the total social reform package that would free women, grant them the vote, and protect the financial security and safety of their families. The Women's Christian Temperance Union (WCTU) provided considerable local and national political and leadership opportunities for women. Suffragist leaders such as Susan B. Anthony supported the work begun by female temperance leaders such as Carrie Nation (see Krout, 1925, pp. 214-216).

The culmination of the centuries-long temperance movement in the United States was the passage and ratification of the 18th Amendment to the U.S. Constitution on January 16, 1919. As Krout (1925) implied, the 18th Amendment was an expression of the conservative and progressive Christian view of the perfectibility of the individual and society and of the absolute necessity of eliminating alcohol if human beings were to be improved (for a recent discussion of the temperance movement, see Schmidt, 1995). To a significant extent, modern society is still influenced by these views. The more conservative Christian churches, which also advocate alcohol abstinence, are the fastest-growing denominations; many communities still maintain some types of alcohol prohibition on specific days (often Sundays) or severely restrict alcohol use in other ways; and many counties are still dry, even in states where alcohol is actually produced.

The mainstream Christian view of drugs other than alcohol has tended to be moderate. With a few exceptions, Christian theology and religious practice have accepted drugs as a legitimate part of medical practice. Even in the midst of the recreational drug revolution, Cassens (1970), in a Lutheran publication, noted that "as Christians we recognize that drugs are a part of God's ongoing creative activity. . . . As with the rest of creation, drugs can be thought of as being a good thing that can be used by man as a gift from God for his physical and emotional benefit" (p. 124). Perhaps this kind of tolerant Christian attitude was a source, in 19th-century America, of the widespread social acceptability of a whole pharmacopeia of drugs (including opiates, cocaine, and barbiturates) that were freely sold on the streets and through major merchandising catalogues (see Inciardi, 1992). As David Musto (1973) noted of that era, "Opiates and cocaine became popular—if unrecognized—items in the everyday life of Americans" (p. 3).

The same types of conservative and progressive Christian forces that were involved in the alcohol prohibition movement were also very involved in broader social reform movements that included opposition to the free-market distribution of a wide variety of drugs, including opiates and cocaine. Christian groups involved in the antinarcotics movement emphasized the societal destructiveness and physical harmfulness of narcotic patent medicines (Hobson, 1928; McBride & McCoy, 1993).

One of the first manifestations of the reform movement was the passage of the Pure Food and Drug Act in 1906 (P.L. 59-384, 34 Stat. 768). This act required the listing of ingredients in readily available over-the-counter drugs. As a grassroots response to the national reform movement, many states began severely limiting the distribution of drugs. The culmination of the social reform directed at opiate use was the passage of the Harrison Narcotics Act in 1914 (P.L. 63-223, 38 Stat. 768). In a manner similar to their involvement in the national alcohol prohibition movement, conservative and progressive Christian groups were very involved in these grassroots movements and in providing local, state, and national support bases. More recently, at a less visibly organized level, anecdotal evidence suggests that individual Christians have been very involved in community drug prevention and education and in policy discussions arguing for strong drug abuse policies and against drug legalization and commercialization.

Islam and Alcohol and Drugs

For many centuries, Western Christianity and Islam have had minimal routine daily social interaction. Most of the interaction has been and continues to be characterized by considerable hostility. However, migration patterns over the last few decades have resulted in a considerable influx of individuals from predominantly Muslim cultures into the United States. In addition, an indigenous Muslim movement has emerged in the African American community.

Perhaps the initial Muslim perspective is entering public discourse through the Nation of Islam. In October 1995, the Nation of Islam organized a "Million Man March" on Washington, D.C. Speakers from the Nation of Islam consistently called for an end to drug and alcohol use in the African American community, linking the use of these substances to racial subordination and many other problems in the African American community (for descriptions of this event, see Holmes, 1995; Rolland, 1995). As the Nation of Islam becomes a larger player in the political and social policy discussions in the United States, its views on substance abuse will probably become a larger part of the discourse on national substance use policy.

From its earliest days, Islam has been very critical of Christianity's tolerance for and even advocacy of alcohol use. Historically and currently, Muslims often criticize Christians for their acceptance of drunkenness. Whereas Judaism incorporates alcohol use into religious ritual and Christianity generally accepts alcohol use in daily life (even seeing it as a gift of God), the prophet Mohammed condemned alcohol and other intoxicating substances in unequivocal language at the very beginning of his movement. In a famous *Hadith* (saying of the prophet), Mohammed said:

> Surely Allah has cursed al-khamr [alcohol and other intoxicating substances] and cursed the one who brews it and the one for whom it is brewed, the one who drinks it and the one who serves it, the one who carries it and the one for whom it is carried, the one who buys and the one who profits from its price. (Katheer, 1970, p. 636)

The words of the Koran are also clear:

> They ask you (O Muhammad) concerning alcoholic drink and gambling. Say: "In them is a great sin, and (some) benefit for men, but the sin of them is greater then their benefit" (Surah 2:219).

O you who believe! Intoxicants (all kinds of alcoholic drinks), gambling, *Al-Ansab,* and *Al-Azlam* (arrows for seeking luck or decision) are an abomination of Satan's handiwork. So avoid (strictly all) that (abomination) in order that you may be successful. (Surah 5:90)

Although there have been documented lapses in abstinence policy (Hitti, 1967), Islam in its various theological manifestations has continued to espouse a strong abstinence position.

Islamic scholars have offered a variety of explanations for the prohibition against alcohol and other intoxicating substances. It has been argued that the Prophet viewed alcohol as the primary cause of hatred, violence, and other evils that kept pre-Islamic society weak, divided, and cursed by Allah (Badri, 1976; Sakr, 1975). The Koran also indicates that alcohol could interfere with the correct, prayerful worship of Allah: "O you who believe! Approach not prayer when you are in a drunken state until you know (the meaning) of what you utter. . . ." (Surah 4:43). Another Surah indicates that strong drink causes believers to forget Allah (Surah 5:90-91). Badri (1976) argued that a changed religious heart and submission to Allah removes the desire to drink or become intoxicated and that abstinence is evidence of a changed heart and life as well as an indication of total submission. Overall, Islam views alcohol use as well as the use of other intoxicating substances as the cause of gross immorality, as preventing the true worship of God, and as evidence of rebellion against God.

The Empirical Relationship Between Drug Use and Religious Values and Involvement

As discussed at the beginning of this chapter, in the late 1960s, the view emerged that in a strongly secular era, religiosity was simply not related to delinquent behavior. Religion was therefore not a useful theoretical, empirical, or policy tool for understanding or preventing delinquency (Hirschi & Stark, 1969). Within a few years after the publication of Hirschi and Stark's article, evidence was already accumulating that denominational membership and religiosity (frequency of attendance and participation) were consistently related to lower rates of alcohol and drug use (as well as to less deviant behavior in general). One of the first replications of Hirschi and Stark's classic study was by Burkett and White (1974). They found that although religiosity was not related to offenses against property or persons, there was a moderately strong inverse relationship between religiosity and the use of marijuana and alcohol. Others suggested that the effect of religion might be most powerful in those communities where the general culture was more religious—in the "Bible Belt" South, for example (Higgins & Albrecht, 1977). However, others, such as Tittle and Welch (1983), found that religiosity was inversely related to deviant behavior even in communities characterized as amoral and disorganized. By 1984, these and other studies convinced Stark that religion did indeed have a powerful effect on human behavior and that there was a need to examine further how religion operated to affect behavior (Stark, 1984). Research in the last decade has focused primarily on the nature of the relationship between religiosity and deviant behavior. What are the contexts that best explain the relationship, and what are the theoretical models that help us understand the relationship?

Studies that have tried to disentangle the elements of religiosity have tended to conclude that saliency (the importance of religious participation), personal devotions, and orthodoxy (the extent to which adherents accept and internalize the religious organization's traditional beliefs) are the elements most strongly related to lower alcohol and drug use rates (Hadaway et al., 1984). Dudley, Mutch, and Cruise (1987) further illustrated these findings in a study that focused on factors related to alcohol and drug abstinence in a proscriptive denomination (the Seventh-day Adventist Church). These researchers found that personal prayer and family worship were the variables most strongly related to alcohol abstinence. These and similar studies strongly suggest that religiosity operates to affect alcohol and drug use, primarily through the most personal religious devotions and beliefs.

Sociologists have long recognized that religious groups are strongly moral communities that generally provide their adherents with clear ethical guidelines for daily living (Weber, 1996). Researchers appear to have concluded that religion operates as a strong social control mechanism through general socialization in which youth are taught morally based beliefs, norms, attitudes, and ethical guidelines favorable to alcohol and drug abstinence or moderation. Scholars have particularly focused on religion's emphasis on the body as the temple of God, the need to live a morally pure life, and the importance of a relationship with God. Alcohol, drugs, and chemically altered states of consciousness in general are seen as obstacles to all of the preceding religious requirements (for example, see Bainton, 1958; Dudley et al., 1987; Price, 1975).

These socialized attitudes are reinforced through peer and reference group identification. Cochran, Beeghley, and Bock (1992) have convincingly argued that religious groups are classic examples of reference groups because they generally involve voluntary, sustained interaction with relatively clear criteria for group participation and membership. Further, religious groups are seen as often affecting other human interactions, such as the choice of spouse and friends, that further strengthen the role of the religious group as reference group (see Cochran et al., 1992). Overall, the research literature consistently shows that religious groups, through their socialization processes and reference and peer group influences, are and can be powerful parts of substance abuse prevention and intervention.

Reasons for Abstinence in a Conservative Christian Young Adult Population

An important question in research on the role of religion in alcohol and drug use involves the relative effect of religion compared to other variables that have been found to be related to alcohol and drug use. In addition to the influence of religious variables, the same variables that influence youth in general society to abstain from drugs probably also affect religious youth. To examine how variables found to influence youthful drug use decisions in general society affect religious youth, a survey was conducted in a population of college students who attended two schools operated by the Seventh-day Adventist Church.

Historically, the Seventh-day Adventist Church has held a strong abstinence position ("Statement II," 1993). Adventists teach that there is a strong relationship between a healthy body and a healthy spiritual life and that the body is the temple of God (Jarnes, 1990). These theological views have resulted in Adventists operating a large health care system, being involved in major public health efforts, operating health food companies, and being study subjects in various types of epidemiological research examining the effect of tobacco, alcohol, and diet on morbidity and mortality. However, as researchers have found, Adventist culture has been affected by general cultural substance use behavior patterns. Epidemiologists have found that about 15% to 20% of Adventist high school students at Adventist schools drink on an annual basis and that about 25% to 30% of students at Adventist colleges drink on an annual basis. These data indicate that alcohol is certainly available on these parochial school campuses and that students are probably confronted with opportunities to use and make decisions to use or not use (Dudley et al., 1987; McBride, Mutch, Dudley, Julian, & Beaven, 1989; Mutch, 1989). In an attempt to understand decisions not to use alcohol or drugs, we surveyed 1,865 students at two Seventh-Day Adventist Church-operated colleges. The survey focused on a wide variety of variables that the literature suggested were related to decisions not to use alcohol or drugs. These were

1. Concern for health
2. Concern for academic standing
3. Concern for future occupation/profession
4. Fear of parents' reaction
5. Not wanting to disappoint parents
6. Commitment to follow Christ
7. Control over one's life
8. Abstaining friends
9. Potential damage to future children
10. Expense of drugs
11. Fear of law/authority

Research literature shows that these variables have been found to be correlated with abstinence or cessation decisions. These variables also reflect a variety of theoretical traditions that include learning theory and social control theory. The respondents were asked to indicate, using a 4-point scale, to what extent the variables would or did influence them to abstain from alcohol or drugs (see Table 6.1).

Reasons for Abstinence

Overall, in the population of college students surveyed, the belief of harmfulness to health of drugs was cited as the primary reason for not using alcohol or drugs. Over 87% of the students indicated that the harmfulness of alcohol and drugs did or would influence their decision not to use. Being in control of one's life was the second most frequently listed reason for not using substances (84.3%). Basic religious commitment came in third, with just over 73% of the respondents indicating that a commitment to following Christ influenced their alcohol and drug use decisions. Concerns about the

Table 6.1 Reasons for Abstinence

Reason	% Citing
Concern for health	87.4
Being in control of one's life	84.3
Commitment to follow Christ	73.1
Concern for future occupation/profession	68.2
Concern for academic standing	61.9
Damage to future children	60.0
Did not want to disappoint parents	50.5
Fear of law/authority	35.6
Fear of parental reaction	35.2
Friends do not use	31.7
Drugs cost too much	38.1

future consequences of drug and alcohol use were also important. Concerns about the effects of substances on academic achievement, future employment, or future children were cited by over 60% of the respondents as influencing their abstinence decisions. Concern for maintaining good parental relationships was important to half of the respondents. Fear-based reasons for abstinence, however, influenced only about a third of the respondents. It is interesting to note that in these populations, the influence of abstaining peers was relatively weak, with less than a third indicating that this would influence their use decisions. Overall, better than two thirds of the respondents gave three motivational reasons for alcohol and drug abstinence: health concerns, controlling one's life, and religious commitment. These college students, the large majority of whom were living apart from their parents, indicated that their desire for establishing an independent—in control— healthy life within the framework of their own personal beliefs was the most likely motivation for abstinence.

Differences by Ethnicity

The data reported in Table 6.2 indicate that on the majority of the variables examined, there were no significant differences by ethnicity. Generally, Hispanics, African Americans, and white non-Hispanics did not differ on the extent to which these variables affected their abstinence decisions. However, the data in Table 6.2 indicate that there were statistically significant differences by ethnic group on 5 of the 11 examined reasons for abstinence. In all

Table 6.2 Ethnicity and Reasons for Abstinence

Reasons	Hispanic	Black	White	Other
Concern for health	87.3%	91.8%	86.5%	80.0%
Being in control of one's life	87.2	88.1	83.9	82.3
Commitment to follow Christ**	84.8	85.2	70.2	71.6
Concern for future occupation/prof.	72.7	76.2	66.0	74.7
Concern for academic standing	70.1	67.1	68.2	64.7
Damage to future children*	69.9	66.2	57.7	63.1
Did not want to disappoint parents*	56.3	61.0	46.9	56.5
Fear of law/authority**	44.3	48.3	32.6	34.7
Fear of parental reaction**	34.3	47.9	31.5	42.0
Friends do not use	39.7	28.6	30.6	32.3
Drugs cost too much	49.3	38.6	37.1	35.8

*$p < .05$. **$p < .01$.

cases, whites were less likely than Hispanics or African Americans to view these reasons as related to abstinence decisions. For example, over 84% of Hispanics and African Americans reported that a commitment to following Christ had an influence on abstinence decisions, whereas only about 70% of whites reported such an influence. African American students were more likely to be influenced by parents in their abstinence decisions than were whites or Hispanics, and whites were also less likely than Hispanics or African Americans to be influenced in their abstinence decisions by fear of effects on future children. Finally, African American and Hispanic students were significantly more likely than white students to report fear of the law or authorities as having an influence on their abstinence decisions.

A Note on Gender Differences

There were only two significant differences in perceived effect of abstinence reasons by gender: not wanting to disappoint parents and concern for damage to future children. In both cases, females were significantly more likely than males to perceive these two reasons for abstinence as likely to be influential. About 46% of males said that not wanting to disappoint parents would influence their decisions to abstain from alcohol or drugs, compared to 54% of the females. Sixty-six percent of female students reported that concerns about damage to future children would influence their use decisions, compared to 54% of males.

Discussion

The data presented here from students at two colleges affiliated with a conservative church that advocates abstinence from alcohol and other drugs showed that a higher proportion of respondents perceived physical harmfulness as having a stronger influence on their abstinence decisions than any other variable. All three monotheistic religions emphasize the harmfulness of drug use, particularly harmfulness to the body, to character development, and to a complete relationship with God. It is to avoid this harmfulness that adherents are admonished to avoid alcohol and drugs or to be moderate in the use of alcohol.

In examining the reasons that adolescents do not use drugs, many researchers have concluded that perceived harmfulness is an important variable. In this current era of health promotion, researchers and clinicians are finding that concerns about health and the perceived harmfulness of alcohol and drugs are increasingly powerful motivations for abstinence. Empirically, Stacy, Bentler, and Newcomb (1991) found that particularly for males, the perceived harmfulness of drugs had a stronger relationship to drug nonuse than any other reason for abstinence. Other researchers, such as Duncan (1988) and Sarvela and McClendon (1988), found, in very diverse populations, that perceived physical and mental health consequences were strong predictors of abstinence and cessation. In addition, in a large, complex study of alcohol abstinence, DiClemente, Carbonair, Rosario, and Montgomery (1994) found that perceived physical harm was related to abstinence. The traditional religious emphasis on avoiding the harmful may play a role in youth decisions to avoid or limit substance use in general society.

It is also important to point out that a very high proportion of the surveyed students attending these church-affiliated colleges also indicated that a basic commitment to following Christ had an influence on decisions for abstinence. This was particularly true for minority groups and is consistent with research data that indicate a higher degree of religiosity among minorities. These data imply that religious commitment may be more of a factor in abstinence decisions for Hispanic and African American youth than for whites. In addition, there is evidence that religious-based intervention may be particularly applicable to minority communities. Research on a large national population of street drug users found that over a quarter of Hispanic and African American street drug users perceived religion as an influence in their lives, compared to only 13% of white street drug users (McBride et al., 1994).

Summary and Conclusions

This chapter examined the role of religion in the prevention of alcohol and drug use in contemporary society by briefly examining the theological and philosophical underpinnings of religious views, reviewing selected empirical literature on religiosity and drug use, and examining data from two colleges operated by an officially abstinent church.

Judaism, conservative Christianity, and Islam emphasize the importance of righteous character development, the believer's responsibility to maintain a healthy body, and the necessity of a right relationship with God. In all three religions, substance use and chemically altered states of consciousness do or may interfere with this. In all three traditions, substance abuse is seen as immoral—as a sin. In particular, the emphasis in religious tradition on the body as the temple of God may have influenced general societal views on health.

Data were also presented showing that specific religious commitment may be a powerful component of abstinence decisions among religious youth, particularly minority religious youth. These data further suggest that churches, synagogues, and mosques could play an important role in emphasizing religious commitment to the youth in their congregations as a means of preventing drug abuse. Particularly, it appears that the religious meaning of a healthy lifestyle and commitment to religious beliefs are related to abstinence decisions. Given the data on the extent of religiosity in minority communities, religious organizations may have a particularly significant role to play in prevention in those communities.

Recently, those in the substance abuse prevention and treatment fields have come to recognize the role of communities of religious faith in prevention and treatment. For example, the Center for Substance Abuse Treatment (CSAT) has published material advocating the involvement of religious groups in prevention. CSAT has focused on elements of religious belief viewed as particularly effective in prevention. Specifically, the agency has advocated that clergy focus on substance abuse as violating the body as a temple of God and that clergy advocate religious belief, not drugs, as a solution for hopelessness (Mitchell, 1994).

Further, religious values have been seen as an integral part of treatment and recovery. It has been argued that religious views are involved in perceiving drug addiction as a chronic recurring condition that requires frequent forgiveness and a new beginning and the need for a higher power to aid in the recovery process (Muffler, Langrod, & Larson, 1992). There is also literature suggesting that religious organizations are already playing a significant role in substance use education that could perhaps be integrated into broader community programs. For example, Lorch (1987) found in a survey of clergy that the majority of pastors believed that churches should be involved in substance abuse prevention and that the majority, in fact, already had youth education and prevention programs. Increasingly, from government agencies to community programs, there is a recognition of the power of religious beliefs and values in the prevention and treatment of substance abuse and the need to integrate those beliefs into comprehensive community-based prevention or intervention programs.

References

Aberle, D. F. (1966). *The peyote religion among the Navaho*. Chicago: Aldine.

Agnew, R., & White, H. R. (1992). An Empirical test of general strain theory. *Criminology, 30*, 475-499.

Alder, D. (1991, Winter). Drinking on Purim: When to say when. *Judaism: A Quarterly Journal, 40*, 6-15.

Badri, M. B. (1976). *Islam and alcoholism*. American Trust.

Bainton, R. H. (1958). Total abstinence and biblical principles. *Christianity Today, 2*, 3-6.

Bakalar, J. B. (1985). Social and intellectual attitudes toward drug-induced religious experience. *Journal of Humanistic Psychology, 25*, 45-66.

Bodor, N. (1995). Targeting drugs to the brain by sequential metabolism. In R. S. Rapaka & H. Sorer (Eds.), *Discovery of novel opioid medications* (NIDA Research Monograph No. 147, pp. 1-32). Washington, DC: Government Printing Office.

Bourguignon, E. (1973). *Religion, altered states of consciousness, and social change*. Columbus: Ohio State University Press.

Brayer, M. M. (1968, Summer). LSD: A Jewish view. *Tradition: A Journal of Orthodox Thought, 10*, 31-41.

Brook, J. S., Whiteman, M., & Finch, S. (1993). Role of mutual attachment in drug use: A longitudinal study. *Journal of the American Academy of Child and Adolescent Psychiatry, 32*, 982-989.

Burkett, S. R., & White, M. (1974). Hellfire and delinquency: Another look. *Journal for the Scientific Study of Religion, 13*, 455-462.

Carlucci, K., Genova, J., Rubackin, F., Rubackin, R., & Dayson, W. A. (1993). Effects of sex, religion, and amount of alcohol consumption on self-reported drinking-related problem behaviors. *Psychological Reports, 72*, 983-987.

Cassens, J. (1970). *Drugs and drug abuse.* St Louis: Concordia.

Cherrington, E. H. (1920). *The evolution of prohibition in the United States of America.* Westerville, OH: American Press.

Christian education materials for youth and families: Alcohol and drugs. (1983). Minneapolis: Hazelden.

Clark, J. K. (1847). *The present position and claims of the temperance.* New York: Enterprise.

Cochran, J. K., Beeghley, L., & Bock, E. W. (1992). The influence of religious stability and homogamy on the relationship between religiosity and alcohol use among Protestants. *Journal for the Scientific Study of Religion, 31,* 441-456.

Cooper, J. L., Russell, M., Skinner, J. B., Frone, M. R., & Mudar, P. (1992). Stress and alcohol use: Moderating effects of gender, coping and alcohol expectancies. *Journal of Abnormal Psychology, 101,* 139-153.

Crabbe, J. C., & Goldman, D. (1992). Alcoholism: A complex genetic disease. *Alcohol Health and Research World, 16,* 297-303.

DiClemente, C. C., Carbonair, J. P., Rosario, P., & Montgomery, G. (1994). The Alcohol Abstinence Self-Efficacy Scale. *Journal of Studies on Alcohol, 55,* 141-148.

Dudley, R. L., Mutch, P. B., & Cruise, R. S. (1987). Religious factors and drug usage among Seventh-Day Adventist youth in North America. *Journal for the Scientific Study of Religion, 26,* 218-233.

Duncan, D. F. (1988). Reasons for discontinuing hashish use in a group of central European athletes. *Journal of Drug Education, 18,* 49-53.

General Conference of Seventh-day Adventists. (1995). *Seventh-day Adventist Church Manual.* Washington, DC: Author.

Hadaway, C. K., Elifson, K. W., & Petersen, D. M. (1984). Religious involvement and drug use among urban adolescents. *Journal for the Scientific Study of Religion, 23,* 109-128.

Higgins, P. C., & Albrecht, G. L. (1977). Hellfire and delinquency revisited. *Social Forces, 55,* 952-958.

Hirschi, T., & Stark, R. (1969). Hellfire and delinquency. *Social Problems, 17,* 202-213.

Hitti, P. (1967). *History of the Arabs.* New York: Macmillan.

Hobson, R. P. (1928). The struggle of mankind against its deadliest foe. *Narcotic Education, 1,* 51-54.

Holmes, S. A. (1995, October 17). For hundreds of thousands, a heartfelt joining of hands. *New York Times,* p. A1.

Inciardi, J. A. (1992). *The war on drugs II.* Mountain View, CA: Mayfield.

Jarnes, D. C. (1990). Religion promotes health. *Ministry, 63,* 22.

Jones, B. C. (1962-1963). Prohibition and Christianity, 1920-1933. *Journal of Religious Thought, 19,* 39-57.

Katheer, I. (1970). *Tafseer Al-Quran Al-Zeem* (Vol. 2). Beirut: Dar Al-Fikr.

Krout, J. A. (1925). *The origins of prohibition.* New York: Russell & Russell.

Lorch, B. R. (1987). Church youth alcohol and drug education programs. *Journal of Religion and Health, 26,* 106-114.

McBride, D. C., & McCoy, C. B. (1993). The drugs-crime relationship: an analytical framework. *Prison Journal, 73,* 257-278.

McBride, D. C., McCoy, C. B., Chitwood, D. D., Inciardi, J. A., Hernandez, E. L., & Mutch, P. M. (1994). Religious institutions as sources of AIDS information for street injection drug users. *Review of Religious Research, 35,* 324-334.

McBride, D. C., Mutch, P. M., Dudley, R. L., Julian, A. G., & Beaven, W. H. (1989, June 1). Adventists, drugs, and a changing church. *Adventist Review, 166,* 12-14.

Mitchell, C. D. (1994). *Alcohol, tobacco, and other drug abuse: Challenges and responses for ministry.* Washington, DC: Center for Substance Abuse Treatment.

Moss, A. L. (1995, July). *How to be an effective witness to the drug culture.* Workshop presented at the North American Christian Convention, Indianapolis.

Muffler, J., Langrod, J. G., & Larson, D. (1992). There is a balm in Gilead: Religion and substance abuse treatment. In J. Lowinson, P. Ruiz, & R. B. Millman (Eds.), *Substance abuse: A comprehensive textbook.* Baltimore: Williams & Wilkins.

Musto, D. F. (1973). *The American disease.* New Haven, CT: Yale University Press.

Mutch, P. B. (1989, June 1). Penetrating the denial zone. *Adventist Review, 166,* 14-15.

Novak, D. (1984). Alcohol and drug abuse in the perspective of Jewish tradition. *Judaism, 33,* 220-232.

Price, T. E. (1975). The Bible speaks on alcohol. *Engage/Social Action, 3,* 39-42.

Rolland, I. M. (1995). Inheriting the earth: Louis Farrakhan and the Nation of Islam. *Vital Speeches, 61,* 376-180.

Sakr, A. H. (1975, October-November). *Alcohol in Islam.* Paper presented at the 8th annual convention of the Islamic Medical Association of the United States and Canada, Washington, DC.

Sarvela, P. D., & McClendon, E. J. (1988). Indicators of rural youth drug use. *Journal of Youth and Adolescence, 17,* 335-347.

Schmidt, L. (1995). A battle not man's but God's: Origins of the American temperance crusade in the struggle for religious authority. *Journal of Studies on Alcohol, 56,* 110-121.

Soloveichik, A. (1972, Fall). Torah Tzniut versus new morality and drugs. *Tradition: A Journal of Orthodox Thought, 13,* 52-58.

Stacy, A. W., Bentler, P. M., & Newcomb, M. D. (1991). Cognitive motivation and drug use: A 9-year longitudinal study. *Journal of Abnormal Psychology, 100,* 502-515.

Stark, R. (1984). Religion and conformity: Reaffirming a sociology of religion. *Sociological Analysis, 45,* 273-282.

Statement II: Historic stand for temperance. (1993). *Ministry, 66,* 23-24.

Stephens, R. C. (1991). *The street addict role.* Albany: State University of New York Press.

Story, C. K. (1991). The mental attitude of Jesus at Bethany: John 11:33, 38. *New Testament Studies, 37,* 51-66.

The Noble Qur'ān. (1994). Riyadh, Kingdom of Saudi Arabia: Maktaba Dar-us-Salam. (Muhammed Tagî-ud-dîn Al-Hilâlî and Muhammed Muhsin Khân, Trans.)

Tittle, C. R., & Welch, M. R. (1983). Religiosity and deviance: Toward a contingency theory of constraining effects. *Social Forces, 61,* 653-682.

Weber, M. (1996). *The Protestant ethic and the spirit of capitalism* (T. Parsons, Trans.). Los Angeles: Roxbury.

PART 3
Treatment Initiatives

7

Juvenile Health Service Centers

An Exciting Opportunity to Intervene With Drug-Involved and Other High-Risk Youth

Richard Dembo
James E. Rivers

Both violent crime and drug abuse have been increasing among U.S. youth in recent years, and the two are often directly associated. Drugs and violent crime are related in a variety of ways: territorial and exchange disputes and robberies of supplies among those who are participants in drug distribution and dealing, robberies with violence by drug abusers to obtain drug purchase money, and perpetration of or victimization by anger- and/or paranoia-driven violence resulting from drug-impaired self-control or judgment (Goldstein, 1985). Equally important is the probability that both violent crime and drug abuse stem from common sociological roots.

Most estimates of criminal acts and drug use among youth are probably conservative, especially those that are projections based on various surveys of the general or in-school populations. "High-risk" youth (i.e., those already involved in the justice system, those who are "eligible" but haven't yet been

AUTHORS' NOTE: Although listed in alphabetical order, each author was an equal contributor to the preparation of this chapter. We would like to thank Ms. Camille Chin-Sue for proofing an earlier version of this chapter.

apprehended, and those on the verge of criminal involvement) are often underrepresented in such surveys. Alcohol and other drug use (particularly marijuana/hashish and cocaine) rates among such youth have been found to be far higher than the rates reported by a comparable age group in national household surveys (Dembo, Williams, Berry, et al., 1990). Recent data from the National Institute of Justice's (NIJ) Drug Use Forecasting (DUF) program showed drug use among male juvenile arrestees/detainees that ranged from 18% in Portland to 54% in Denver (NIJ, 1994).

Violent and other high-risk youth, including those who are substance abusers, enter local and state juvenile justice systems, where they absorb huge portions of public health, welfare, and safety resources. The drain on such resources is worsening, both because the proportion of youth who are offenders is increasing and because increasing numbers of aging repeat offenders with more severe problems requiring higher-cost responses are involved in various correctional systems (Institute for Health Policy, 1993).

Youths entering juvenile justice systems often have serious multiple personal and family problems. Among the problems most consistently reported by researchers are physical abuse (Dembo, Dertke, Borders, Washburn, & Schmeidler, 1988), sexual victimization (Dembo et al., 1989; Mouzakitis, 1981), emotional/psychological functioning (Dembo, Williams, La Voie, et al., 1990; Teplin & Swartz, 1989), educational functioning (Dembo, Williams, Schmeidler, & Howitt, 1991) and alcohol and other drug use (Dembo, Williams, Wish, & Schmeidler, 1990; U.S. Department of Justice, 1983a, 1983b). Many of these youths' difficulties can be traced to family alcohol/other drug use, mental health, or crime problems that began at an early age (Dembo, Williams, Wothke, Schmeidler, & Brown, 1992; Garbarino & Gilliam, 1980). Further, Dembo, Williams, Schmeidler, and Wothke (1993) found that large proportions of juveniles involved in the juvenile justice system had experienced adverse behavioral and psychological effects from their substance use.

Minority and inner-city youth are being socialized in communities and families that are often economically and socially stressed. The psychosocial strain suffered by these youth often increases their risk for future drug use and delinquency/crime (Nurco, Balter, & Kinlock, 1994) and impedes their development as socially responsible and productive adults (Le Blanc, 1990).

Increasingly it is being realized that juveniles who are likely to be victims or perpetrators of violent crime because of drug abuse also are in mortal danger from a biological threat. Drug-using youths are at elevated risk for being infected by or transmitting the human immunodeficiency virus (HIV) via injecting drugs or crack-cocaine-driven sexual activity involving multiple partners (Rivers, 1989a, 1989b). Wish, O'Neil, Crawford, and Baldau (1992) identified persons having contact with the justice system as an important HIV/AIDS risk-reduction target group. Inciardi and his colleagues (Inciardi, Pottieger, Forney, Chitwood, & McBride, 1991; Inciardi & Pottieger, 1991) noted that minorities and inner-city youths in general are particularly at risk for drug-related HIV infection. Rivers' (1993) review of policy and the research literature highlights the exceptional HIV risk intervention opportunities represented by substance abusers who are under the control of the justice system.

One result of these dynamics is a national juvenile justice system truly in crisis, a situation that will continue, if not worsen, unless some fundamental changes are made in perspectives and basic operating procedures. The goals must be to identify the multiple problems of high-risk youths as early as possible and to address those needs with interventions of evaluated effectiveness that use a holistic perspective.

The barriers to such efforts are challenging and even daunting. Juvenile justice systems and associated programs in most jurisdictions are sanction oriented; their structures and procedures often result as much from cumulative political and historical forces and service program fads as from purposeful design. Most U.S. juvenile justice jurisdictions also are crisis oriented, working with inadequate fiscal, physical, and personnel resources. Rarely are these systems the products of deliberative thinking grounded in knowledge based on empirical data or guided by an understanding of the developmental perspectives that help to explain the initiation and maintenance of troubled youthful behavior. Guidry (1991) noted that juvenile justice agencies typically have an episodic interest in troubled youth. Interest is focused on the judicially imposed consequences of illegal behavior, with court-imposed intervention coming only after repeated court appearances. At that point, many youths have developed a long list of failures in informal or loosely structured programs, developed serious problems at school, and established a pattern of delinquent behavior, including drug use.

Reaching these youths in early adolescence provides an excellent opportunity to involve them in health and human service intervention programs before their problems become more serious. Existing resources should be redirected and additional resources provided to assess these youths thoroughly and provide needed services to them and their families at the earliest (ideally the first) point of contact with the juvenile justice system in a balanced strategy that still strives to rehabilitate youthful repeat offenders (Klitzner, Fisher, Stewart, & Gilbert, 1991). Early intervention can reduce the probability that they will continue criminal and high health-risk behavior into adulthood, thus helping to reduce the enormous cost to society of crime, drug abuse, and mental illness (Dembo, Williams, Schmeidler, & Christensen, 1993; Institute for Health Policy, 1993; Klitzner et al., 1991; Rice, Kelman, Miller, & Dunmeyer, 1990). Unfortunately, few jurisdictions apparently have the vision, the political will, or the resources to identify and intervene effectively with high-risk youths at or before their first contact with the juvenile justice system.

This chapter is based on experiences at the Hillsborough County (Tampa, Florida) Juvenile Assessment Center (HCJAC), which has been recognized as a national leader in addressing the issues just noted. The conceptualization and implementation of the HCJAC are outlined to provide a context relevant to the model's generalizability/portability, a matter of immediate relevance because the Tampa model quickly has become a prototype being promoted for wide implementation in Florida and in other states. The operation of the HCJAC is outlined. In addition, an enhanced health-oriented version of this model is proposed that would enable juvenile assessment centers (JACs) to serve as epidemiological monitoring stations and as bases for implementing new targeted prevention and early intervention programs into the surrounding community. A concluding cautionary note is sounded regarding prospects for broader implementation of even the current JAC model.

Conceptualization, Planning, and Implementation of the HCJAC

The HCJAC officially began operations January 4, 1993, with major funding supplied under federal programs originated by the Anti-Drug Abuse Act of 1988. As with most innovations, myriad factors, numerous groups, and key individuals were involved in the conceptualization, planning, and implementation of the HCJAC. Major catalysts in the development of the HCJAC were the Hillsborough County Anti-Drug Alliance, the Hillsborough County Sheriff's Office, and the Hillsborough County School Board.

Hillsborough County has an Anti-Drug Alliance that advises the county commissioners on drug abuse issues. The Anti-Drug Alliance includes representatives from a variety of agencies, including law enforcement, substance abuse service providers, and the State Department of Health and Rehabilitative Services. The Alliance provided a vehicle and forum for the establishment of the HCJAC. Dr. Richard Dembo, former vice chair of the Alliance and an experienced university researcher in the area of juvenile delinquency and drug abuse, provided leadership based on knowledge of the pertinent literature and years of personal and service program experience in the field. Mr. Richard Brown, Director of Planning and Evaluation for the Agency for Community Services, Inc., a local service provider, initially proposed the JAC concept, and guided its implentation.

Because many youths entering the juvenile justice system have serious multiple problems, basic clinical and social work theory and practice dictated that comprehensive information be collected on their service needs so that appropriate interventions could be applied (or developed). The HCJAC planners knew that adequate health screening/assessment services are absent in most communities and that large percentages of troubled youths do not connect with existing health and human service delivery programs (Pickens, Leukefeld, & Schuster, 1991; Thornberry, Tolnay, Flanagan, & Glynn, 1991).

During the course of months of self-education, consensus building, development of trust and rapport, and other aspects of team building, the planning group decided to initiate operations in a carefully staggered fashion. Consequently the HCJAC began operations in January 1993 by opening its Truancy Intake Center. Youths who were picked up for truancy by Tampa Police Department (TPD) officers or Hillsborough County Sheriff's Office deputies began to be brought to the truancy center for evaluation and services. Four months later, the HCJAC delinquency component opened, with processing initially being limited to youths arrested on felony or weapons misdemeanor charges. During the following year, the HCJAC completed its "learning curve" and "shakeout" period and progressed to routine operations; it accumulated a base of experience from which it could confidently project dynamic caseload capacity, and it established a performance record that assured key stakeholders that the program could be expanded. Thus, in April 1994, the HCJAC began to accept youths arrested on other misdemeanor charges.

The HCJAC as a Prototype

Recognizing that there were significant gaps in problem identification, assessment, referral, and access to services by youth at high risk of drug abuse and associated health consequences, as well as delinquent behavior, the Florida legislature began providing funds to support the establishment of JACs throughout the state. During a special session of the Florida legislature in June 1993, $1.2 million was appropriated to support the development of three additional JACs. The following year, the Florida lawmakers passed a new Juvenile Justice Bill that, among other things, provided $2 million to help establish eight more JAC programs. Legislative language included the stated intent to establish JAC facilities in all Florida metropolitan areas. To date, Orlando and Ft. Lauderdale have opened JACs under this initiative, and a Miami JAC is scheduled to open in 1996. JAC programs are in various stages of being established in Pensacola, West Palm Beach, Sarasota, Ft. Myers, Tallahassee, and St. Petersburg. JACs based on the HCJAC model also are being established throughout the state of Kansas.

In various communities, as key stakeholders assemble to plan the local JAC program, variations on the HCJAC model are emerging. In most cases, however, the basic elements and functions of the model include centralized location of relevant agencies to permit the efficient completion of required legal and social service interventions for at-risk youths and their families; screening, diagnosis, and, if indicated, linkage of arrested and other high-risk juveniles with community-based service providers; case management of juveniles assigned to justice system diversion programs; and tracking (usually limited to the purpose of determining referral disposition).

Hillsborough County Juvenile Assessment Center Operations

The following description applies specifically to arrested youths who are delivered to the Tampa JAC facility by law enforcement personnel. (The HCJAC has other programs, such as those targeting school truants, in which the juveniles are not under arrest when they are delivered to the facility.)

Arrested youths are delivered to the HCJAC premises by law enforcement personnel via a "sallyport" (definition: a gate in a fortification designed for sorties). On entering the HCJAC, an exchange of official forms occurs between the arresting officer, sheriff's deputies operating the HCJAC's secure wing, and State Department of Juvenile Justice (DJJ) staff. Within minutes, the arresting officer is free to return to his or her assigned duties. Once law enforcement and DJJ personnel have completed their admission tasks (see Figure 7.1), the juveniles are further processed by DJJ detention intake and HCJAC assessor personnel.

The HCJAC facility is coordinated by a Tampa-based private not-for-profit substance abuse treatment agency, the Agency for Community Treatment Services (ACTS), Inc. The HCJAC is co-located with the treatment agency's 20-bed adolescent detoxification and stabilization program, which has full-time nursing staff and medical, psychological, and psychiatric backup services. The staff who provide these core treatment services, as well as those who perform assessment and case management services, are available 24 hours a day. This physical consolidation of services contributes greatly to operational efficiency and cost savings (e.g., reduced transportation costs, cross-trained staff serving as multiposition backups).

JAC assessors complete preliminary screening of arrested youths and, if indicated, refer juveniles to specific services, such as Treatment Alternatives to Street Crime (TASC) and Delinquency (Psychological) Assessment Team (DAT) services. All procedures are designed and delivered in conformity with pertinent state law. The outcomes of the referral process are tracked (referral and referral outcome; Dembo & Brown, 1994). JAC assessors also obtain identifying information (e.g., social security number) and the names and locations of significant others, permitting tracking of the youths once they leave the HCJAC and/or community-based service programs.

The HCJAC relies heavily on its exceptionally comprehensive information system (IS; see Rivers, 1994). This IS has three integrated subsystems: (a) preliminary screening data, (b) in-depth assessment data, and (c) referral and referral outcome data (Dembo & Brown, 1994). The IS reflects the components of the HCJAC's operational activities, which are modeled after the National Institute on Drug Abuse Adolescent Assessment/Referral System (NIDA/AARS; Rahdert, 1991). A flowchart of youths' progression through the HCJAC preliminary screening and in-depth assessment processes and the information collected at each point appears in Figure 7.1.

Arrested youths delivered to the HCJAC for screening submit to breathalyzer and EMIT\reg urine testing for other drugs; these tests are performed on site. The HCJAC tests for cannabis (marijuana), cocaine, barbiturates, amphetamines, opiates, and PCP. All youths processed at the center undergo a preliminary screening process using the NIDA Problem Oriented Screening

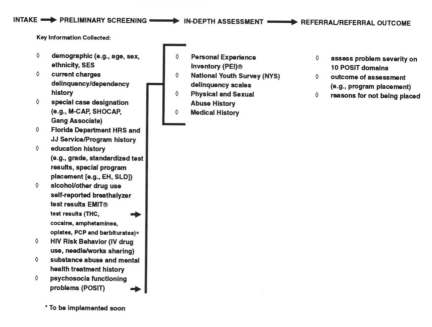

INTAKE ➤ PRELIMINARY SCREENING ➤ IN-DEPTH ASSESSMENT ➤ REFERRAL/REFERRAL OUTCOME

Key Information Collected:

◊ demographic (e.g., age, sex, ethnicity, SES
◊ current charges delinquency/dependency history
◊ special case designation (e.g., M-CAP, SHOCAP, Gang Associate)
◊ Florida Department HRS and JJ Service/Program history
◊ education history (e.g., grade, standardized test results, special program placement [e.g., EH, SLD])
◊ alcohol/other drug use self-reported breathalyzer test results EMIT® test results (THC, cocaine, amphetamines, opiates, PCP and barbiturates)* ➤
◊ HIV Risk Behavior (IV drug use, needle/works sharing)
◊ substance abuse and mental health treatment history
◊ psychosocia functioning problems (POSIT) ➤

◊ Personal Experience Inventory (PEI)®
◊ National Youth Survey (NYS) delinquency scales
◊ Physical and Sexual Abuse History
◊ Medical History

◊ assess problem severity on 10 POSIT domains
◊ outcome of assessment (e.g., program placement)
◊ reasons for not being placed

* To be implemented soon

Figure 7.1. Processing Through the Juvenile Assessment Center
SOURCE: Juvenile Assessment Center Research Project Unit. Copyright, USF, 1994

Instrument for Teenagers (POSIT) to identify potential problems in any of 10 psychosocial functioning areas. The reliability and discriminant and predictive validity of the POSIT have been established (Dembo et al., 1995). Responses to the POSIT are computer scored. The results, based on cut-off scores and red flag items recommended by the AARS manual together with breathalyzer or urine test findings (positive for alcohol or other drug use), are used to determine whether to proceed with more in-depth assessments. The HCJAC experience reveals that a significant proportion of served youth have recently used an illicit drug (e.g., 38% of arrested youths processed at the center during March 1995 were EMIT\reg-positive for marijuana and 5% were positive for cocaine) or were experiencing potential problems in one or more areas probed by the POSIT.

Again as recommended by the AARS manual, the in-depth assessment protocol includes the Personal Experience Inventory (PEI; Winters & Henley, 1989) and the National Youth Survey Delinquency Scale (Elliott, Ageton, Huizinga, Knowles, & Canter, 1983). This delinquency protocol provides information on general theft crimes, crimes against persons, index offenses, drug sales, and total delinquency. Further, information is collected on the youths' sexual victimization (on the basis of work of Finkelhor, 1979), physical abuse (on the basis of work of Straus, 1979), and medical histories. Screening and assessment information from the HCJAC to date indicates that the mental health or substance abuse service needs of arrested juveniles have been significantly unattended or unmet.

As indicated earlier, HCJAC operational procedures begin with justice system tasks. On delivery by an arresting officer, the juvenile is immediately fingerprinted and photographed. Florida DJJ detention intake staff complete a Detention Risk Assessment Instrument on the youth (Dembo et al., 1994). A file on the youth is opened or reopened on the HCJAC information system. Demographic and current arrest information are entered into the computer by assessors who have received data entry training. On-line computer communication with the DJJ Client Information System at agency headquarters in the state capitol allows paper copies of any delinquency and abuse histories to be printed at the HCJAC. Similarly, HCJAC staff have computer terminal access to county school systems' specified information on youths' educational history.

On the basis of current charges and arrest history, Florida DJJ delinquency intake staff determine whether the youth should be placed in secure detention or home detention or released to the supervision of a parent, guardian, or responsible relative. Youths released from the HCJAC to their parents, guardians, or other relatives are scheduled, if necessary, for an appointment to receive in-depth assessments by TASC or DAT staff located at the HCJAC. Youths meeting state-determined detention criteria are transported immediately, regardless of time of day, to the local regional Juvenile Detention Center by a van operated by HCJAC operations staff. These youths have in-depth assessments completed by counselors from another local service provider that is contracted by detention center administrators to operate a triage-screening unit there.

If the assessed youth is already under DJJ supervision, his or her DJJ counselor will be notified of the new arrest. If the youth is not currently under the supervision of DJJ but is arrested on felony or weapon misdemeanor charges, he or she will be assigned a DJJ counselor. If the youth is arrested on other misdemeanor charges and is not detention eligible, he or she will be assigned to case management staff located at the HCJAC.

The major purpose of the JAC misdemeanor case management unit is to review the arrest histories and current charges of youths arrested on misdemeanor offenses to determine their eligibility for involvement in a nonjudicial diversion program: the Juvenile Alternative Services Program (JASP) or arbitration. Admission of guilt is required for a youth to be accepted in either diversion program. JASP is a 60-day program that provides immediate sanctions to misdemeanor offenders. It has a number of program components: community work service (in which youths are assigned to complete a number of community service hours), victim restitution (in which youths make monetary or other reimbursement to the victim), and counseling services (which provides short-term individual, adolescent group, and family counseling). The arbitration program involves a trained arbitrator (not a judge) hearing the case against a youth and obtaining relevant information from the youth, the victim, and arresting officer. On the basis of this information, the arbitrator decides on sanctions against the youth. These sanctions can include community service hours, participating in a counseling program, paying restitution, or a combination of these sanctions.

The parents/guardians of a misdemeanor youth are called to pick him or her up at the JAC the same day he or she is processed and to meet with the youth's case manager. The case manager informs the youth's parents/guardians of the legal issues surrounding their child, the results of the youth's preliminary screening, and their recommendation to arbitration or JASP. The case manager is also expected to inform the parents/guardians about their child's specific service needs.

Youths meeting the criteria for arbitration or JASP are recommended to one of these programs by the misdemeanor case managers. Such recommendations are forwarded to the state attorney's office, where they are usually approved. Youths placed in the arbitration or JASP program are carried on the caseloads of JAC misdemeanor case managers until they successfully complete the program to which they are assigned. If they fail to complete the program, the misdemeanor case manager makes a recommendation to the state attorney's office to reinstate them in the program, place them in another program, or file a delinquency petition against them. If a delinquency petition is filed, the misdemeanor case manager transfers the case to a DJJ case manager.

A Recommended Enhanced JAC Model

The HCJAC has recast the front end of the juvenile justice system in Hillsborough County, increased coordination among various stakeholder agencies, and resulted in improved efficiency in the processing of arrested youths. Some of its key developers recognize that the HCJAC model is basically a "second-generation" facility and that there needs to be a new-generation model of the JAC that is essentially a juvenile health service center (JHSC). Such JHSCs would more creatively identify and effectively respond to the multiple problems of high-risk youth and their families and would more efficiently coordinate and integrate substance abuse, other mental health, medical, and social services. Related contributions would involve improving existing or developing new service linkage and delivery strategies by analyzing client sociocultural and service delivery factors, with the goal of improving client access and service delivery/utilization.

Addressing the needs of ethnic minority and other poorly served groups constitutes a critical service delivery need. Black and Hispanic families have lower substance abuse, mental health, social, and medical service utilization rates (program entry, engagement, and duration) than Anglo families. A number of sociodemographic factors are associated with lower service utilization rates—Black, Latino, or other ethnic minority status; female head of household; maternal education less than 12 years; teen motherhood; and transportation problems—but these attributes may be less causal than another variable with which they all are correlated: lower median income. Being poor makes people reliant on unavailable or inaccessible, often inadequately funded, public services (Arcia, Keyes, Gallagher, & Herrick, 1993). Other factors that contribute to lowered service utilization rates are cultural insensitivity among service providers and language differences (Espada, 1979).

Related research on mental health service utilization has consistently found service process and delivery factors (e.g., having contact with more than one service provider and not involving parents and other family members in diagnostic sessions and in treatment; Tolan, Ryan, & Jaffe, 1988; Sirles, 1990) to be related to failure to enter or remain in treatment. Innovative strategies are needed to address this situation.

A number of planning, design, and development steps are needed to implement the envisioned JHSCs: (a) performing a comprehensive analysis of juvenile health and social service needs and of service availability and utilization in the community; (b) applying these findings to current operations, including existing JACs; and (c) utilizing the information derived from these first two activities to design and implement interventions that target specific high-risk groups in the surrounding community. As a final step, if resources and expertise permit, these interventions should be evaluated for effectiveness and cost-efficiency (benefits/costs or, less feasibly, cost-effectiveness). The following discussion briefly addresses each of these steps.

Analysis of Local Juvenile Health and Social Service Needs

Juvenile substance abuse and related health service needs can be estimated by examining indirect indicator data such as those from the general population census. If an indicator data approach is taken, more direct indicators of substance abuse and associated service needs are preferred. The following is a selective listing of substance abuse indicator databases:

1. *Social indicator data* include such measures as percentage of population below the poverty line, percentage living in renter-occupied dwellings occupied by one person, and percentage with less than a high school education. These data can be extracted from census reports by census areas or zip code and by age/gender categories, when appropriate, for calculation of more refined population-at-risk rates.

2. *Educational indicator data,* obtainable from school system databases, include such measures as retention-in-grade, absentee, and dropout rates.

3. *Health indicator data,* available from state or county health departments, can provide such important information as rates of teen pregnancy, suicide, reported sexual or physical abuse, child neglect, and mental health problems (e.g., mental health service use rates).

4. *Criminal justice data* are typically matters of public record and include information such as arrests for drug law violations. Many local law enforcement agencies have programs to identify specific areas within the community where extensive drug dealing is occurring that they are willing to share with responsible planning efforts.

5. *Hospital emergency department data* can be captured that reflect drug-related problems. Communities that do not already participate in the Drug Abuse Warning Network (DAWN) system can develop an independent system based on the model. DAWN emergency department reports include drug use, route of administration, demographic, and residential zip code data.

6. *Other morbidity data,* often in geo-coded breakdowns, are available from county or state health departments: for example, sexually transmitted diseases (gonorrhea, primary and secondary syphilis, nongonococcal urethritis, and herpes), hepatitis B, tuberculosis, AIDS, births to teenagers, low birthweight babies, and births in which the mother had no first-trimester prenatal care.

7. Even *mortality data,* which typically reflect few juvenile deaths, can supply information on drug-induced or drug-related and/or violent deaths that help to characterize specific sections of the community as ecologically "risky"

for juveniles. (See Rivers, 1992, for a further discussion of indicator data methods.)

Coordinated indicator databases such as those just noted can be used to identify and classify geographic areas as being at relatively lower or higher "risk." Subsets of indicator data can be selected and displayed graphically via Geographic Information Systems (GIS) computer software, as well as in tabular form.

GIS packages have become powerful new resources in needs assessment analysis and service planning because of recent developments in computer technology, affordable software, and the proliferation of spatially referenced data (Ripple, 1989). These packages typically have five basic data subsystems: (a) input and editing, (b) management, (c) query and retrieval, (d) analysis/modeling/synthesis, and (e) display and output (Aronoff, 1989; Pharr, 1991). They have other defining features, such as the ability to display geo-referenced data (e.g., a longitudinally and latitudinally referenced point, such as a street address), to bring into display simultaneously multiple data sets in correct spatial relationship to their original and other applicable overlay maps, and to add or subtract detail easily and iteratively (e.g., roads, public transportation routes; Albert, 1994).

Indicator data and GIS software can help identify demographically and geographically defined subpopulations most in need of general types of juvenile intervention services. But another critical issue must be addressed concurrently with the database development process, or at least before the planning process can apply the indicator data analysis results. This issue involves public policy (justice system, health, and social services), political processes, and multiple agency budgets, though it may appear to the layperson to be a straightforward and simple task. *The issue initially involves specifying currently who is providing what services to whom and where.* Target populations for existing individual programs need to be specified by demographic characteristics, by specific risk factors, and by geographic catchment or service area. Each existing intervention program needs to be identified by its primary goals and/or the specific outcomes being sought.

Once the above-noted processes have been completed, specific target populations and geographic areas can be examined for unmet service needs, defined as differences between indications of need and reported current service availability. Considerable flexibility and creativity are possible in this comparative process, with high potential for reaching compromise or consensus decisions. Composite indicators and iterative processes can be used, involving different combinations of variables, "cutting points," definitions of rates, and methods of comparative rankings. The goal is to develop an implementable intervention plan that is both politically acceptable and empirically based.

Applying Service-Needs Analysis to an Operational/Management Review

The above-outlined service-needs analysis can be approached from various perspectives. From the standpoint of planning for a juvenile health services center, a recommended strategy would be to examine records on juveniles who have recently been processed through the local justice system, JAC, or comparable agency/service function.

The findings from the needs analysis can be compared and contrasted to juvenile justice system data to fine-tune or help develop specific internal procedures, processes, and programs. Such applied analysis can inform changes in JAC/justice system program management, structure, and staff; operation, referral, and agency coordination activities; assessment/data collection; and program monitoring. A few examples of operational areas in which impact from such analysis could be anticipated are agency participation (the kinds of agencies participating on site—e.g., health department, representatives from the state attorney's office, the public defender, and the court clerk), expanded case management services (e.g., to include truant youths; McCoy, Dodds, Rivers, & McCoy, 1992), staff task assignments, training (e.g., cultural competence) and cross training, and overall organizational structure.

Screening and assessment functions likely to be affected by coordinated community service-needs assessment and juvenile justice system analysis include

1. An emphasis on prevention and engagement by hiring JHSC-based community outreach workers to engage "at-risk" youth (i.e., unarrested youth or recently arrested youth who were not placed in a detention center) in needed services (McCoy, Rivers, & Chitwood, 1993) and by having outreach workers from local service provider agencies available on site on a rotating basis to engage youths needing their services

2. Systematic analysis and refinement of the criteria for referring youths to specific services, including asking additional questions regarding substance use, mental health and medical history, and specific program experiences, as

well as attitudes toward and motivation or readiness for treatment (DeLeon, personal communication, March 11, 1994)

3. An emphasis on youths' health needs by providing nutritional and general health education and information, screening, and counseling to reduce the risk of infection by HIV or other sexually transmitted diseases (McCoy, Rivers, & Khoury, 1993)

JHSCs can be expected to have a positive impact in other areas. Additional areas likely to experience improvements as a result of a well-conceived and implemented JHSC (i.e., one based on theory, research findings, and specific local community service-needs assessment and systems analysis processes) include client-tracking capabilities, evaluations of the psychometric qualities of key instruments used in preliminary screening and in-depth assessments, and coordination among various collaborating agencies (e.g., law enforcement, court, and corrections representatives; substance use, primary health, and mental health treatment providers; state juvenile health agency representatives; and school system personnel).

Further, juvenile justice system (JAC or comparable) data can be examined for sociodemographic information, presenting drug use, other problems (e.g., educational, mental health), and other health-related factors to ascertain differences by types of referral agencies, service providers, and providers' geographic area (catchment areas or areas near facility locations). These data will help to specify groups, problems, providers, and services, as well as geographic areas that need more fine-grained analysis using not only indicator and JAC information system data but focus groups, on-site observations, and other primary data collection efforts (e.g., interviews, surveys, screening instruments).

Developing Individual Interventions Within the Plan to "Fill the Gaps"

The above-discussed analyses will suggest populations, services, locations, and perceived service barriers (Metsch et al., 1995) to be targeted for interventions. These suggested populations will be derived by comparatively analyzing the indicator, census, service agency, and juvenile justice population data in geographical context and presenting the results to groups of community stakeholders in focus groups to obtain input and commitment. A key objective of these meetings will be to set priorities based on consensus or level of importance, using participant ratings from focus groups of the most relevant stakeholders, including JAC personnel and community service providers.

Using the results from this process, administrators and program developers (with the participation of researchers) can design specific intervention strategies (e.g., to improve accessibility, accommodation, and/or acceptability of services or to provide in-home care) for identified problem areas that are feasible (e.g., from political, budgetary, or zoning perspectives). By including program evaluation research specialists in the needs assessment, systems analysis, priority-setting, and intervention design processes, prospects are maximized that implementation, operations monitoring, and outcome analyses will be designed and conducted that are both "doable" and address questions that are pertinent to major stakeholders. These deeply involved investigators can also serve as coinvestigators with health services researchers who specialize in health economics and cost-efficiency analysis. Cost-efficiency analysis includes both benefits/cost analysis (cost per unit of program outcome) and cost-effectiveness analysis (comparative net costs of two or more programming alternatives). Such investigations usually are quite difficult and often very expensive to complete, but they ultimately may prove necessary to justify the development and implementation of efforts as ambitious as the JHSCs.

Periodically (annually or biannually), the JHSC program and its components should be revisited by a broad-based policy steering committee or similar group to advise whether additional changes are needed and, if so, how best to proceed. These advisors should have updated information on operations, community service needs, measures of satisfaction, and other comments from surveys of various stakeholder groups (e.g., clients, service agencies). Such surveys should be designed to determine respondents' level of knowledge of the activities and services provided by the JHSC; their experience with various aspects of the JHSC program; their assessments of the cultural relevance, helpfulness, quality, and usefulness of JHSC activities and program components; the perceived impact of JHSC operations on the juvenile substance abuse problem and juvenile crime; areas and activities recommended for change; and additional services that are felt to be needed. In addition to their use in informing the advisory group, these repeated surveys would document temporal trends in perceptions of the JHSC by the various sampled audiences. These changes could then be correlated with objective indicators and measures of changes in served youths' health and other service needs, juvenile crime, and levels/patterns of substance abuse.

From a slightly different perspective, the data collected and analyzed for service-planning purposes can also serve "sentinel," "surveillance," and epidemiologic functions. The data collection and analysis processes attendant on JHSC planning and routine operations could document the availability and use of new substances, new drug use combinations, new use patterns (e.g., circumstances, motivations, methods of use), and related health/safety issues (e.g., overdoses, trauma from vehicular or other locomotion accidents such as falls, and neurological or physiological damage from use). By carefully collecting, analyzing, interpreting, and disseminating such information, the envisioned JHSC could expand its role to become a program of tremendous social importance on the front lines of health promotion, crime reduction, and improvements in the quality of life for the youth and the community it serves.

Postscript

In contrast to the sanguine and even visionary discussion just presented, there currently are real questions regarding whether adequate political support and resources will be made available for the effective operation of existing and planned juvenile prevention and early intervention programs in general and JACs in particular. These questions result from the continuing, and even increasingly, punitive perspective of an apparent majority of federal and state lawmakers who are perceived to reflect a "get-tough" public attitude toward juvenile offenders.

One indication of this growing punitive, antirehabilitative attitude among federal legislators is their activities relating to the Local Crime Prevention Block Grant (Title III, Subtitle B) program within the Violent Crime Control and Law Enforcement Act of 1994. As enacted, this law authorized almost $76 billion per fiscal year from 1996 through 1999 in formula grants to be awarded to local governments via the states. The distribution scheme within states is simply based on the proportion of statewide violent crimes reported by the local jurisdiction. Local governments must agree to establish trust funds in which to deposit their grant dollars and *may* provide subgrants to private nonprofit entities and community-based organizations to implement projects. Fourteen specific types of projects may be carried out under this block grant program, including education, training, research, prevention, treatment, and rehabilitation services that are intended to prevent juvenile violence (Violent Crime Control and Law Enforcement Act of 1994). Although this law was hailed by prevention advocates, the newly elected conservative majority within Congress is in the process of drastically paring if not eliminating its prevention/rehabilitation-oriented elements.

As another example, Florida crime rates dropped in 1993 in most categories: Burglaries, robberies, and murders hit a 14-year low. Yet the fear of crime continues to dominate office seekers' election strategies, a situation that was described by Ted Chiricos, a state-capitol university criminologist, as "very cynical, if not disingenuous. There's nothing happening that would justify the extreme outcry of what I would call a moral panic" (quoted in Leen, 1994, p. 18A). He and many others feel that the media and the public have grossly overreacted to a few high-profile 1993 violent crimes against tourists. Others believe that these brazen crimes simply provided a focus for the free-floating fear and rage of crime-weary citizens, and still other analysts point to the real increase in gun-involved juvenile crime as a major reason for public calls for tougher responses to violent juvenile crime (Leen, 1994).

Consequently, the new Florida Department of Juvenile Justice, which assumed most of the authority and responsibility for dealing with juveniles who came into contact with the justice system, has slackened its efforts to provide funding for the development and operation of JACs. A related effort, under the administrative umbrella of Florida's Department of Health and Rehabilitative Services, promoted the establishment of Adolescent Receiving Facilities (ARFs) that could detain juveniles while extensive diagnostic assessments of their substance abuse and related service needs were conducted. This program has languished for want of adequate funding. Thoughtful planners in a few localities immediately recognized the logic of colocating or closely coordinating the operations of developing JACs and ARFs, but there seems to be no formal coordination of these efforts on the state level.

Experienced observers have recognized the similarities between many functions performed under the JAC model and those historically performed by local juvenile Treatment Alternatives to Street Crime (TASC) units. Indeed, a few jurisdictions in Florida that have existing juvenile TASC units are "folding" the staff and functions into JAC plans and operations. But there are indications in some jurisdictions that local governmental entities currently operating TASC-like juvenile functions may have "turf issues" with JACs that are being planned.

In some jurisdictions, TASC has been accepted grudgingly by judges who view the clinically based decisions regarding placement, treatment retention, sanctions, and completion by TASC and treatment program staff as infringements on judicial authority. Some analysts have interpreted the recent popularity of "treatment drug courts" as being based in part on dissatisfaction among judges (and some prosecutors) with shared decision making regarding defendants' cases (Inciardi, McBride, & Rivers, 1995). Florida has been in the vanguard in establishing treatment drug courts. In fact, the Florida legislature has authorized the development of such courts in every jurisdiction of the state; many jurisdictions have already developed them. To date, however, none have been created within juvenile divisions. Critics of drug courts as radical and unwarranted departures from traditional functions were urged by Tauber (1994) to consider them a return to

[a] time when judges ran their own calendars and were responsible for their courts' operations, defendants had to answer directly and immediately to the judge for their conduct, and cases moved slowly and purposefully through the judicial system, rather than relying on sentencing guidelines, mandatory minimums and negotiated pleas to speed up the court process. (p. 28)

Tauber probably expressed the sentiments of most judges when he characterized jurists as being

in a unique position to exert effective leadership in the promotion of coordinated drug control efforts, both within the criminal justice system and their local communities. Judges have the political influence, the ties to government agencies, the moral authority, the perceived fairness and impartiality, and the expertise and focus necessary to bring leadership to coordinated anti-drug efforts. Traditionally, judges have played the passive role of objective, impartial referee, only reluctantly stepping beyond the boundaries of their own courtroom. However, where the fair and effective administration of justice is threatened (as in this case by an exploding drug problem), the court has the responsibility to come forward and become a leader and active participant in the organization, design and implementation of coordinated criminal justice and community-wide drug control efforts. (p. 77)

The relevance of the treatment drug court "movement" in the present context is the example it provides for current efforts to develop coordinated action involving the justice and health/social service communities. In any given jurisdiction, the "local legal culture"—those shared expectations, practices, and informal rules of behavior of judges and attorneys (see Church, Carlson, Lee, & Tan, 1978), as well as the past and present working relationships among community-based service providers and between them and the courts—forms a cluster of intangible factors that are important for the prospects of successful development, implementation, operation, and institutionalization of a JAC.

In summary, JACs modeled after the HCJAC can probably expect to struggle in most jurisdictions to obtain cooperation and funding. The improvements in screening, diagnostic assessment, early intervention, placement, case management, and tracking that are possible under this model may be destined to become an unrealized potential if adequate resources are not forthcoming for JAC operations and for community-based services to which JACs can refer juveniles. It is hoped that some jurisdictions with vision and political courage will find ways to implement and support JACs as well as evaluation research that provides empirical evidence of their efficacy. We sincerely believe that the enhanced JHSC model we describe is a design that deserves to be implemented and evaluated. Without efforts such as the JACs and JHSCs, the prospects for reducing the human tragedy and reversing the indefensible social policy represented by our current juvenile justice system are dim.

References

Albert, D. (1994). Geographic information systems. In T. C. Ricketts, A. Savitz, W. M. Gesler, & D. N. Osborne (Eds.), *Geographic methods for health services research* (pp. 201-206). New York: University Press of America.

Arcia, E., Keyes, L., Gallagher, J. J., & Herrick, H. (1993). National portrait of sociodemographic factors associated with underutilization of services: Relevance to early intervention. *Journal of Early Intervention, 17*, 283-297.

Aronoff, S. (1989). *Geographic information systems: A management perspective.* Ottawa: WDL.

Church, T., Carlson, A., Lee, J. L., & Tan, T. (1978). *Justice delayed: The pace of litigation in urban trial courts.* Williamsburg, VA: National Center for State Courts.

Dembo, R., & Brown, R. (1994). The Hillsborough County Juvenile Assessment Center. *Journal of Child and Adolescent Substance Abuse, 3,* 25-43.

Dembo, R., Dertke, M., Borders, S., Washburn, M., & Schmeidler, J. (1988). The relationship between physical and sexual abuse and tobacco, alcohol and illicit drug use among youths in a juvenile detention center. *International Journal of the Addictions, 23,* 351-378.

Dembo, R., Schmeidler, J., Borden, P., Turner, G., Chin Sue, C., & Manning, D. (1995). Examination of the reliability of the Problem Oriented Screening Instrument for Teenagers (POSIT) among youths entering a juvenile assessment center. *International Journal of the Addictions, 3,* 69-93.

Dembo, R., Turner, G., Chin Sue, C., Schmeidler, J., Borden, P., & Manning, D. (1994). An assessment of the Florida Department of Health and Rehabilitative Services Detention Risk Assessment Instrument on youths screened and processed at the Hillsborough County Juvenile Assessment Center. *Journal of Child and Adolescent Substance Abuse, 4,* 45-77.

Dembo, R., Williams, L., Berry, E., Getreu, A., Washburn, M., Wish, E. D., & Schmeidler, J. (1990). Examination of the relationships among drug use, emotional/psychological problems and crime among youths entering a juvenile detention center. *International Journal of the Addictions, 25,* 1301-1340.

Dembo, R., Williams, L., La Voie, L., Berry, E., Getreu, A., Wish, E. D., Schmeidler, J., & Washburn, M. (1989). Physical abuse, sexual victimization and illicit drug use: Replication of a structural analysis among a new sample of high risk youths. *Violence and Victims, 4,* 121-138.

Dembo, R., Williams, L., La Voie, L., Getreu, A., Berry, E., Genung, L., Schmeidler, J., Wish, E. D., & Kern, J. (1990). A longitudinal study of the relationships among alcohol use, marijuana/hashish use, cocaine use and emotional/psychological functioning problems in a cohort of high risk youths. *International Journal of the Addictions, 25,* 1341-1382.

Dembo, R., Williams, L., Schmeidler, J., & Christensen, C. (1993). Recidivism in a cohort of juvenile detainees: A 3-1/2 year follow-up. *International Journal of the Addictions, 28,* 631-657.

Dembo, R., Williams, L., Schmeidler, J., & Howitt, D. (1991). *Troubled lifestyles: High-risk youth in Florida.* Washington, DC: U.S. Department of Education, Office of the Assistant Secretary for Educational Research and Improvement.

Dembo, R., Williams, L., Schmeidler, J., & Wothke, W. (1993). A longitudinal study of the predictors of the adverse effects of alcohol and marijuana/hashish use among a cohort of high risk youths. *International Journal of the Addictions, 28,* 1045-1085.

Dembo, R., Williams, L., Wish, E. D., & Schmeidler, J. (1990). *Urine testing of detained juveniles to identify high-risk youth.* Washington, DC: U.S. Department of Justice.

Dembo, R., Williams, L., Wothke, W., Schmeidler, J., & Brown, C. H. (1992). The role of family factors, physical abuse and sexual victimization experiences in high risk youths' alcohol and other drug use and delinquency: A longitudinal model. *Violence and Victims, 7,* 245-266.

Elliott, D. S., Ageton, S. S., Huizinga, D., Knowles, B. A., & Canter, R. J. (1983). *The prevalence and incidence of delinquent behavior: 1976-1980.* Boulder, CO: Behavioral Research Institute.

Espada, F. (1979). The drug abuse industry and the "minority" communities: Time for change. In R. L. Dupont, A. Goldstein, & J. O'Donnell (Eds.), *Handbook on drug abuse.* Washington, DC: Government Printing Office.

Finkelhor, D. (1979). *Sexually victimized children.* New York: Free Press.

Garbarino, J., & Gilliam, G. (1980). *Understanding abusive families.* Lexington, MA: Lexington.

Goldstein, P. J. (1985). The drugs/violence nexus: A tripartite conceptual framework. *Journal of Drug Issues, 15,* 493-506.

Guidry, J. (1991, June 18). Cloak of evil not worn by adults alone. *Tampa Tribune.*

Inciardi, J., McBride, D., & Rivers, J. (1995). *Drug control and the courts.* Newbury Park, CA: Sage.

Inciardi, J. A., & Pottieger, A. E. (1991). Kids, crack, and crime. *Journal of Drug Issues, 21,* 257-270.

Inciardi, J. A., Pottieger, A. E., Forney, M. A., Chitwood, D. D., & McBride, D. C. (1991). Prostitution, IV drug use, and sex-for-crack exchanges among serious delinquents: Risks for HIV infection. *Criminology, 29,* 221-235.

Institute for Health Policy. (1993). *Substance abuse: The nation's number one health problem.* Waltham, MA: Author.

Klitzner, M., Fisher, D., Stewart, K., & Gilbert, S. (1991). *Report to the Robert Wood Johnson Foundation on strategies for early intervention with children and youth to avoid abuse of addictive substances.* Bethesda, MD: Pacific Institute for Research and Evaluation.

Le Blanc, M. (1990, September). *Family dynamics, adolescent delinquency and adult criminality.* Paper presented at the Society for Life History Research Conference, Keystone, CO.

Leen, J. (1994, October 30). Florida's crime issue: Rhetoric versus reality. *Miami Herald,* pp. 1A, 18A.

McCoy, H. V., Dodds, S., Rivers, J., & McCoy, C. (1992). Case management services for HIV-seropositive IDUs. In R. S. Ashery (Ed.), *Progress and issues in case management* (NIDA Research Monograph No. 127, pp. 181-207). Rockville, MD: National Institute on Drug Abuse.

McCoy, C., Rivers, J., & Chitwood, D. (1993). Community outreach for injection drug users and the need for cocaine treatment. In F. Tims & C. Leukefeld (Eds.), *Cocaine treatment: Research and clinical perspectives* (NIDA Research Monograph No. 135, pp. 190-202). Washington, DC: National Institute on Drug Abuse.

McCoy, C., Rivers, J., & Khoury, E. (1993). An emerging public health model for reducing AIDS-related risk behavior among injecting drug users and their sexual partners. In D. G. Fisher & R. Needle (Eds.), *AIDS and community-based drug intervention programs: Evaluation and outreach* (pp. 143-159). Binghamton, NY: Hawthorn.

Metsch, L., Rivers, J., Miller, M., Bohs, R., McCoy, C. B., Morrow, C. J., Bandstra, E. S., & Gissen, M. (1995). Implementation of a women and children's residential drug treatment program: Barriers and resolutions. *Journal of Psychoactive Drugs, 27,* 73-83.

Mouzakitis, C. W. (1981). Inquiry into the problem of child abuse and juvenile delinquency. In R. J. Hunner & Y. E. Walker (Eds.), *Exploring the relationship between child abuse and delinquency* (pp. 220-239). Montclair, NJ: Allenheld, Osmun.

National Institute of Justice. (1994). *Drug use forecasting, 1993 annual report on juvenile arrestees/detainees: Drugs and crime in America's cities.* Washington, DC: Author.

Nurco, D. N., Balter, M. B., & Kinlock, T. (1994). Vulnerability to narcotic addiction. *Journal of Drug Issues, 24,* 293-314.

Pharr, D. M. (Ed.). (1991). *Introduction to Geographic Information Systems Workshop.* Wilmington, NC: Urban and Regional Information Systems Association.

Pickens, R. W., Leukefeld, C. G., & Schuster, C. R. (Eds.). (1991). *Improving drug abuse treatment.* Rockville, MD: National Institute on Drug Abuse.

Pontell, H. N., & Welsh, W. N. (1994). Incarceration as a deviant form of social control: Jail overcrowding in California. *Crime and Delinquency, 40*(1), 18-36.

Rahdert, E. (Ed.). (1991). *The adolescent assessment/referral system manual.* Rockville, MD: National Institute on Drug Abuse.

Rice, D. P., Kelman, S., Miller, L. S., & Dunmeyer, S. (1990). *The economic costs of alcohol and drug abuse and mental illness.* San Francisco: University of California, San Francisco, Institute for Health and Aging.

Ripple, W. J. (Ed.). (1989). *Fundamentals of Geographic Information Systems: A compendium.* Bethesda, MD: American Society for Photogrammetry and Remote Sensing and the American Congress on Surveying and Mapping.

Rivers, J. (1989a). Drug use and criminal activity among Miami youth involved in the crack-cocaine business. In *Proceedings of the Florida Epidemiology Work Group* (pp. 47-58). Tallahassee, FL: Florida Department of Health and Rehabilitative Services.

Rivers, J. (1989b, October). *Youthful drug use and HIV infection prevention.* Paper presented at HIV and Adolescents: Miami Invitational Meeting, National Institute on Child Health and Human Development, National Institute on Drug Abuse, National Institute on Mental Health, and Society for Adolescent Medicine, Miami.

Rivers, J. (1992, February). *The use of substance abuse indicator data in a cooperative agreement HIV risk reduction project.* Paper presented to the NIDA Monitoring Subcommittee, Cooperative Agreement Risk Evaluation Project, Rockville, MD.

Rivers, J. (1993). Substance abuse and HIV among criminal justice populations: Overview from a program evaluation perspective. In J. A. Inciardi (Ed.), *Drug treatment and criminal justice* (pp. 228-246). Newbury Park, CA: Sage.

Rivers, J. (1994, May). Target cities: Implications for an integrated MIS for mental health and substance abuse treatment. Paper presented at the Linking Forces Conference, Center for Substance Abuse Treatment, Children's Council, and Interagency Council, Miami.

Sirles, E. A. (1990). Dropout from intake, diagnostics, and treatment. *Community Mental Health Journal, 26,* 345-360.

Straus, M. A. (1979). Measuring intrafamily conflict and violence: The Conflict Tactics (CT) Scales. *Journal of Marriage and the Family, 41,* 75-88.

Tauber, J. S. (1994, February). Drug courts: Treating drug-using offenders through sanctions, incentives. *Corrections Today,* pp. 28-30, 32-33, 76-77.

Teplin, L. A., & Swartz, J. (1989). Screening for severe mental disorder in jails: The development of a referral decision scale. *Law and Human Behavior, 13,* 1-18.

Thornberry, T. P., Tolnay, S. E., Flanagan, T. J., & Glynn, P. (1991). *Children in custody 1987: A comparison of public and private juvenile custody facilities.* Washington, DC: U.S. Department of Justice, Office of Juvenile Justice and Delinquency Prevention.

Tolan, P., Ryan, K., & Jaffe, C. (1988). Adolescents' mental health service use and provider, process, and recipient characteristics. *Journal of Clinical Child Psychology, 17,* 229-236.

U.S. Department of Justice. (1983a). *Prisoners and alcohol* (NCJ-86223). Washington, DC: Bureau of Justice Statistics Bulletin.

U.S. Department of Justice. (1983b). *Prisoners and drugs* (NCJ-87575). Washington, DC: Bureau of Justice Statistics Bulletin.

Violent Crime Control and Law Enforcement Act, 42 U.S.C. \sec 30201-30208 (1994).

Winters, K. C., & Henley, G. A. (1989). *Personal Experience Inventory manual.* Los Angeles: Western Psychological Services.

Wish, E. D., O'Neil, J. A., Crawford, C. A., & Baldau, V. (1992). Lost opportunity to combat AIDS: Drug users in the criminal justice system—an update. In T. Mieczkowski (Ed.), *Drugs, crime and social policy* (pp. 278-298). Boston: Allyn & Bacon.

8

Issues and Intervention

Substance Abuse Treatment for Adolescents
Using a Modified Therapeutic Community Model

Sally J. Stevens
Naya Arbiter
Rod Mullen
Bridget Murphy

The percentage of America's youth who use drugs has been increasing over the past several years. This upward trend in drug use is documented not only for marijuana use but for harder drugs as well. Research results of the National Institute on Drug Abuse (NIDA) 1994 Monitoring the Future study show that for the third year in a row, a statistically significant increase in marijuana and cocaine use was substantiated in annual use by 8th-grade students. Among 8th graders, 25.7% reported illicit drug use at some point in their lives. When inhalants such as gasoline or glue were included, the percentage rose to 35.1%. Increases in drug use by 10th and 12th graders were also evidenced (Swan, 1995). Access by teens to alcohol and other drugs (AOD) is easy; 78% of teens have easy access to alcohol, 80% of older teens have easy access to marijuana, and 54% of older teens have easy access to cocaine and heroin.

Adolescents' attitude toward drug use is becoming more accepting. The NIDA survey showed a decline in the percentage of students who think that using marijuana, cocaine, or crack cocaine is harmful. For instance, in 1991, 62.8% of 8th-grade students perceived trying crack cocaine once or twice as risky. In 1994, this percentage decreased to 54.4%. In addition, there was a drop in the number of 8th-, 10th-, and 12th-grade students who said that trying marijuana once or twice, smoking marijuana occasionally, or even smoking marijuana regularly is harmful to one's health.

Although adolescents' attitude toward drug use may be more accepting, results from a survey conducted by the Center on Addiction and Substance Abuse (CASA) showed that 32% of the 400 adolescents surveyed named drugs as the greatest problem that they faced on a daily basis. The adolescents surveyed named crime and violence (13%) as their next biggest problem ("Teens Rate Drugs," 1995). Results from a poll of 504 boys and girls aged 8 to 12 years indicated that 92% thought that people using drugs caused violence (McClain, 1994). Although the estimates of the number of violent crimes committed by drug users vary, there is little argument that drugs and violence go hand in hand. The National Center for Juvenile Justice reported that the number of murders committed by youths under the age of 18 increased by 85% from 1986 to 1991; sexual offenses rose 9% in a 1-year period, 1990 to 1991 (Ingrassia, Annin, Biddle, & Miller, 1993). Every 15 seconds, an American teen is victimized by a violent crime. The staggering rise in violent crimes committed by juveniles and experienced by juveniles can in part be attributed to the increase in drug use and involvement in the drug culture, the availability and use of guns, an increased level of violence and child abuse within the neighborhood and the home, and the lack of job opportunities and economic empowerment.

The number of street crimes committed by adolescents increased with the onset of the crack cocaine epidemic. Because of the relatively low cost of a "rock," young people could more readily afford the drug. However, the highly addictive nature of crack cocaine also led young people to seek out more of the drug. Without a source of income, adolescent drug users turned to crime and drug dealing as avenues for obtaining money and drugs. With more involvement in criminal activities and the drug trade, the demand for weapons, particularly guns, increased. Guns were needed not only for committing crimes such as robbery and burglary but for protection from those who might want to steal one's money or drugs.

A survey of 1,600 male students in 10 inner-city high schools found that 22% of the students owned at least one gun. Of the youths that owned guns, 82% owned a semiautomatic handgun, 68% a revolver, 45% a shotgun, 41% a sawed-off shotgun, 36% a target hunting rifle, 27% a military-style rifle, 18% a single-shot handgun, and 18% owned a homemade handgun. As might be expected, the percent of gun owners among teens who use drugs is higher than it is among those who do not use drugs. Interviews with youths ages 11 to 17 indicate that guns are easy to get and are viewed as a necessity in many schools and neighborhoods. In some cities, teenagers talk about their guns as if they were baseball cards—and trade them almost as frequently (McClain & Gaynor, 1994).

Nearly 1 million teenagers are victims of violent crimes each year. The number of teenagers and younger children killed annually by firearms rose by 59% between 1986 and 1991. Arrests of juveniles for murders increased by 128% between 1983 and 1992 (Moyers, 1995). Violence occurs more frequently in poor, urban areas, areas often occupied by minority ethnic groups, including Hispanics and African Americans. Black youth are six times more likely to be homicide victims than are white youth.

Domestic violence accounts for much of the violent crime committed. It is estimated that 35% to 45% of all U.S. homicides in 1995 stemmed from domestic violence. Jaffe, Wilson, and Wolfe (1986) reported that exposure to marital violence is related to greater frequency of child behavior problems. Furthermore, research sponsored by the National Institute on Justice found that childhood abuse increased the odds of future delinquency and adult criminality overall by 40% (Widom, 1992). Children who witness violence also have elevated levels of dysfunctional and violent behavior.

Strong correlations have been uncovered linking violence with psychoactive substances, including alcohol (Roth, 1994). Children who grow up in homes in which violence and drug use are daily activities are at tremendous risk for becoming drug-using, violent adults. The Tucson forensic psychologist Todd Flynn, as quoted in the *Tucson Citizen,* stated, "The most violent kids I see witness violence and are subjected to violence in the home. They have parents without any motivation or ability to spend time with them, who use a blend of drugs, and don't help them learn anything" (McClain & Gaynor, 1994, p. 13).

Although the incidence of drug use and violence among American teenagers is high, the rates vary by race, class, educational achievement, job status, and geographic location (urban, suburban, or rural). Thus, although concern exists for the spread of drug use and violence *throughout* society, additional concern exists for youths growing up in high-density, underprivileged, poverty-stricken areas of the country. Children and adolescents are disproportionately represented among the poor in America. One in every three children in New York City under the age of 19 lives at or below the poverty line (Green, 1993). Also, a disproportionate number of youths living in poverty are minority youths. Whereas Latino and African American families are disproportionately represented in urban areas such as New York, in Arizona 53% of the youths living at or below the poverty line are Native Americans. To these people, the American dream of hard work, job security, safety, and family does not exist. Consequently the drug trade is often alluring. As Currie (1993) pointed out, the decay of economic opportunities combined with an exaltation of consumer values has made the urban drug culture especially attractive and difficult to dislodge. Constricted economic opportunities have weakened the indigenous institutions and traditions of poor communities, and this weakening has helped make possible the rise of a violent and materialistic street culture.

There has been considerable debate concerning how to intervene with drug-involved youth, particularly those who are also involved in criminal activities, violence, and gangs. Some advocate stricter laws, longer juvenile sentences, or even trying juveniles as young as 13 in adult courts. Others advocate treatment—not only drug treatment but the provision of extensive services, including family therapy, job training, academic training, and relapse prevention. Whether removing the youth from the home is more effective than providing intensive treatment services within the home has also been debated. Although research data on residential versus nonresidential treatment are scarce, both models have demonstrated some success with this population. One promising model of treatment for drug-, violence-, and gang-involved youth is that of the therapeutic community (TC). The TC model of treatment originated with adult heroin addicts in the 1950s. More recently, adolescent TCs have been established in many parts of the country. Adolescent TCs tend to enroll youths whose drug involvement, criminal behavior, and family situations are such that removal from the home is considered a necessary intervention. In addition, many adolescent TCs are set up as "diversion" from adolescent detention centers. Young men and women are given a choice either to complete detention center time or to enroll in treatment or are simply stipulated to treatment by a judge.

In Arizona, Amity, a nonprofit drug treatment, prevention, and research TC, operated several adolescent TCs for youths who were drug involved. Almost all of the youth were involved in criminal behavior, and many were gang members. For the purpose of this chapter, descriptive data collected on participants who entered one of Amity's adolescent TCs in 1993 are provided below. This information includes data from Amity's Pioneer Ranch (PR), an adolescent boys' TC located on an 80-acre ranch northeast of Phoenix, Arizona; Amity's Adobe Mountain (AM) TC, an adolescent boys' TC located at the Adobe Mountain Juvenile Detention Center in Phoenix, Arizona; and Amity's Las Rosas (LR) ranch, an adolescent girls' TC located on a 23-acre ranch outside of Tucson, Arizona. Referrals to all three Amity TCs were almost exclusively from the Arizona Department of Corrections, although there was one private placement at Pioneer Ranch and there were two private placements at Las Rosas.

It is interesting to note that the percentage of Hispanics at Amity's incarcerated TC was much higher (AM = 56%) than at the noninstitutional TCs (PR = 36%; LR = 32%). Moreover, the number of African Americans referred to any of the three TCs was very low (PR = 3%; AM = 8%; LR = 10%) in comparison to the overall number of eligible incarcerated youths (Table 8.1).

Age of first police contact (Table 8.2) and the number of times in detention centers (Table 8.3) were similar across TCs, with the overall mean age of first police contact being 11.0 years. The overall mean number of times in a detention center was 8.1.

All of the participants were polydrug users. There were no substantial differences between boys' and girls' drug use. One difference evidenced, however, was between the number of heroin and crack cocaine users who were referred to the nonincarcerated TC. Eighty-eight percent of those in the incarcerated Adobe Mountain TC had used crack cocaine, compared to 39% of those referred on to the nonincarcerated (PR and LR) TCs. Alternatively, only 2% of those participating in the incarcerated Adobe Mountain TC setting reported using heroin, compared to 20% at PR and 25% at LR (Table 8.4).

Substantial differences existed between boys and girls with regard to family environment and experiences (Table 8.5). More girls reported (a) having a mother with an AOD problem (LR = 63% vs. PR = 59% and AM = 49%), (b) having a father with an AOD problem (LR = 75% vs. PR = 62% and AM = 59%), (c) having been in a physical fight with a parent (LR = 71%

Table 8.1 Ethnic Background (%)

	White	Hispanic	African American	Native American	Asian American
Pioneer Ranch (*n* = 59)	44	36	3	17	0
Adobe Mountain (*n* = 36)	25	56	8	11	0
Las Rosas (*n* = 31)	39	32	10	16	3

Table 8.2 Age of First Police Contact (Years)

	Mean	Mode	Range
Pioneer Ranch (*n* = 59)	11.0	11	2-16
Adobe Mountain (*n* = 36)	10.7	10 & 13	3-15
Las Rosas (*n* = 31)	11.4	10	2-16

Table 8.3 Number of Times in Detention Centers

	Mean	Mode	Range
Pioneer Ranch (*n* = 59)	8.3	2	0-40
Adobe Mountain (*n* = 36)	6.9	4	1-30
Las Rosas (*n* = 31)	9.0	3	0-50

vs. PR = 37% and AM = 31%), (d) having been physically abused (LR = 55% vs. PR = 26% and AM = 21%), and (e) having been sexually abused (LR = 73% vs. PR = 17% and AM = 7%). Given these data, it is not surprising that more girls reported having attempted suicide (LR = 55% vs. PR = 30% and AM = 14%) and that more girls reported having run away from home (LR = 84% vs. PR = 71% and AM = 56%; see Table 8.6).

Finally, most of these drug-involved youth were also involved in delinquent acts (Table 8.7). Although differences between boys and girls and between TC placements were in evidence, it appears that the girls were just as involved in delinquency as boys. More girls than boys reported (a) having stolen a vehicle (LR = 63% vs. PR = 56% and AM = 53%) and (b) having attacked someone with the intent to injure seriously (LR = 63% vs. PR =

Table 8.4 Drug Use (% Who Have Used)

	Pioneer Ranch (n = 59)	Adobe Mountain (n = 36)	Las Rosas (n = 31)
Alcohol	89	100	100
Marijuana	98	98	98
Cocaine	70	58	58
Crack	39	88	39
Inhalants	60	67	57
Amphetamines	58	40	50
Hallucinogens	67	50	53
Heroin	20	2	25

Table 8.5 Home Environment (%)

	Pioneer Ranch (n = 59)	Adobe Mountain (n = 36)	Las Rosas (n = 31)
Family member ever arrested	78	75	65
Mothers have AOD problem	59	49	63
Fathers have AOD problem	62	59	73
Ever have physical fight w/a parent	37	31	71
Ever physically abused	26	21	55
Ever sexually abused	17	7	73
Ever attempted suicide	30	14	55

Table 8.6 Runaway Behavior

	%	Mean[a]	Mode	Range
Pioneer Ranch (n = 59)	71	4	0	0-20
Adobe Mountain (n = 36)	56	6	3	0-20
Las Rosas (n = 31)	84	10	3	0-50

a. Mean is calculated for the population of youths who have run away at least once.

61% and AM = 47%). More boys reported (a) having carried a hidden weapon (PR = 78% and AM = 82% vs. LR = 63%) and (b) having been in a gang fight (PR = 47% and AM = 65% vs. LR = 36%).

Table 8.7 Delinquency Scale (%)

	Pioneer Ranch (n = 36)			Adobe Mountain (n = 17)			Las Rosas (n = 8)		
	%	Range of Times Act Committed	Mean Age at 1st Time	%	Range of Times Act Committed	Mean Age at 1st Time	%	Range of Times Act Committed	Mean Age at 1st Time
Stole vehicle	56	1-50	14.3	53	1-50	13.3	63	1-60	15.0
Carried hidden weapon	78	1-365	13.6	82	1-365	13.4	63	1-50	14.8
Attacked with intent to injure seriously	61	1-50	13.8	47	1-8	13.1	63	1-5	14.6
Took part in gang fight	47	1-152	14.4	65	1-65	13.8	36	2-7	14.0

NOTE: Data collection using this scale began later. Consequently the sample size is smaller.

Because of these youths' involvement with the police, the number of times they were placed in detention centers, their extensive AOD involvement, their home environment, and their delinquency tendencies, they were stipulated to Amity's long-term residential program, which employs a TC model of treatment.

Many elements in the TC contribute to a distinctive model of treatment. Traditionally, TCs are residential, with the proposed length of stay between 15 and 18 months. According to De Leon (1985), treatment in traditional TCs is broken down into three stages, with the initial stage (0 to 100 days) focusing on assessment of individual needs and orientation and assimilation into the TC. The second phase (4 to 12 months) challenges individuals to do more personal work and to become more psychologically aware and socialized. During the third phase (13 to 18 months), individuals strengthen their skills for autonomous decision making and prepare for reentry into the wider community.

Proponents of the TC model insist that drug use is a symptom of the person's disorder, not the essence of the disorder. A global change in lifestyle is the goal of treatment, not just a reduction or cessation of drug use. The model is one of "self-help"; consequently staff take a limited role. Residents are expected to live publicly; self-disclosure is viewed as essential for one's own recovery process and the recovery process of other community members. The TC is viewed as a microcosm of the wider community and is therefore considered the primary teacher. The majority of the primary treatment staff in traditional TCs are recovering addicts themselves. Because of the staff's background of addiction and their positive change in values and lifestyle, the staff serve as role models for the residents. Interaction with biological family members who often use drugs themselves is limited. Instead, those living in the TC are considered "family" (Stevens, Arbiter, & McGrath, in press).

Services provided at the TC are generally comprehensive, with little need for collaboration with outside agencies. There is an organized structure to each day, with morning and evening meetings anchoring the majority of the activities for the day. Mimicking the wider community, residents engage in a spectrum of activities, including academic education, work/jobs on the property, social events, and exercise, as well as various types of therapeutic groups.

At Amity's adolescent TCs, the traditional TC model has been modified to fit the specific needs of adolescents. Underlying Amity's adolescent TC model is the assumption that most of the teenagers referred to the program come from dysfunctional homes in which family life was chaotic. Many have experienced traumatic events during their childhood. Some may have been physically or sexually abused. Although these adolescents may be "streetwise," many are psychologically and emotionally delayed. Treatment, therefore, involves not only addressing their AOD problem but also examining and resolving a number of issues, in accordance with the assumption that substance abuse is a symptom of a more global disorder.

In working with psychologically and emotionally delayed youth, Amity's treatment philosophy is based on Miller's hypothesis regarding rage and pain. Miller (1983) asserted that repressed rage and pain experienced in childhood must be expressed as it was experienced in childhood. If repressed emotions are not expressed and directed to the source, the individual will continue to be out of control and will act self-destructively and/or compulsively to hurt others. Therefore, although skill building is important, it is essential that underlying psychogenetic material be resolved (Mullen, Arbiter, & Glider, 1991).

With resolution of underlying psychogenetic material being of primary importance, much of the structure of the day and content of the therapeutic curriculum involves the articulation and resolution of emotionally and psychologically charged issues. Following the traditional TC "stage" model, much of this work is done in the second stage, after the individual has been assimilated into the TC and prior to focusing on reentry into the wider community. A variety of groups and retreats are facilitated. Although "peer-facilitated" groups are common in adult TCs, they are not appropriate for adolescents. Mature and understanding leadership, the leadership of a senior staff member, is particularly important for making encounter groups safe for adolescents to discuss sensitive personal matters. Therefore, although the treatment model remains one of self-help, participation, facilitation, and leadership provided by staff are much more prominent in Amity's adolescent TCs.

Perhaps the bulk of deep psychological work is accomplished during participation in retreats. At Amity's adolescent TCs, retreats last from 3 to 4 days and are scheduled several times a year. Retreats are often looked on as an emotional adventure. Although there may be as many as 30 participants, the larger group is divided into groups of 8 to 10 adolescents, each with two staff leaders. Retreats are highly structured, with a specific schedule of activities, including teaching sessions, art activities, field trips, exercise, encounter groups, psychodrama, and ceremonies. The retreat curriculum is built around a specific theme, such as family dynamics, violence, pride and prejudice, sexuality, or relationships. Spending concentrated time together in a small, psychologically safe setting, the adolescents are able to address sensitive issues. Frequently, these retreats are the settings in which adolescents feel safest to talk about their most painful and difficult experiences.

The home life of many of the adolescents lacked a sense of organization and structure and was devoid of ritual and ceremony that are often common in a healthy environment. Because the TC is viewed as a microcosm of the wider community, it is important that these elements be present. Simple rituals such as the morning meeting, formal dining, the end-of-the-day ceremony, the evening meeting, and the bedtime story give a sense of organization, wholeness, and substance to lives that have been devoid of such formality and repetitiveness. Along with this, the day-to-day structure of formal education and work/jobs intended to build skills for use on reentry into the wider community offers security and a sense of stability that have been lacking in most of these adolescents' lives. The educational curriculum provides not only basic GED preparation but also teaching of skills related to day-to-day living, such as communication and negotiating skills; sex and health education, including HIV prevention; bank accounting; and transportation issues. Work in the TC has two benefits. First, prevocational skills, such as getting to the job on time, learning to get along with coworkers, and responding appropriately to supervisors' directives, are learned. In addition, job skills that increase adolescents' job opportunities on discharge from the program are acquired. Second, the work/job assignment allows for bonding with other coworkers, a sense of responsibility and ownership, and an opportunity to be involved in what has become an adult activity.

Part of the structured activities includes a recreation-exercise program. It is thought that discipline and teamwork can best be taught through physical activities because adolescents' attention span tends to be short for cognitive tasks, particularly at the beginning of the program. Frequently, when adolescents first enter the TC, they have "written off" physical exercise and physical activities as not part of their self-image. At best, the young men engage in weight lifting or basketball. Within a month of participation in Amity's recreation program, almost all of the teenagers admit that they enjoy at least some of the exercise activities. Two reasons seem to account for this change in attitude toward recreation. First, Amity offers a variety of activities in which the youths can engage. These include horseback riding, fishing, hiking, packing with llamas, mountaineering, rock climbing, baseball, basketball, swimming, jogging, and aerobics. Second, the staff do not just "referee" these activities but rather participate along with the residents. The teenagers seem truly to enjoy being part of a team with staff or competing against staff in a healthy, fun activity.

Unlike traditional adult TCs, in which the biological family is required to take a limited role, most adolescent TCs attempt to engage the family as soon as possible. This is also true of Amity's adolescent TCs. Phone contact, family orientations, family picnics, family groups, family therapy sessions, and family workshops are all part of the regularly scheduled activities. Unfortunately, in many cases the family of origin does not have a functioning, non-drug-using parent who can be involved and supportive of positive behavioral change on the part of the adolescent. Occasionally, a relative, sibling, foster parent, or involved neighbor may be the significant other who becomes involved in the family activities. For those adolescents who are to be reunited with their family members, the period of transition includes a more intensive training for family members willing to participate. Family members go through relapse prevention strategies with the adolescents so that they can identify high-risk situations and relapse triggers. For those adolescents not returning to the family, an emphasis is placed on developing supportive relationship with others in the community, whether peers, former graduates, or staff members (Mullen et al., 1991).

Unfortunately, transition back into the wider community is a difficult challenge. Often the environment, family, and social network are not supportive of the positive changes made by the adolescent. Too often, staff at the TC must concentrate on the new incoming individuals, and those who are transitioned back into the wider community do not receive enough supportive services to continue their positive change of lifestyle. Amity provides aftercare groups and recreational activities for all adolescents who have completed residential treatment. Adolescents are contacted by staff on a regular basis and encouraged to attend not only the aftercare groups and recreational activities but also Amity's Saturday Night Open House, Community Circle, and other gatherings. In addition, a transitional house was set up and maintained for six to eight adolescents. Although outcome data were not formally obtained, anecdotal data from both Pioneer Ranch and Las Rosas suggest that over 80% of the adolescents remained AOD-free at 6 months post discharge. Regrettably, this percentage progressively decreased thereafter, with many experiencing relapse within a 2-year period. Interestingly, however, some of the relapsing individuals have come back around and are again living sober and productive lives.

In summary, the TC model of treatment provides an excellent intervention for youth who are drug involved. This model, given its residential aspect, extensive length, and intensive therapy, is well suited for adolescents who are not only AOD users but also involved in criminal activity and gangs and who come from families that are dysfunctional and unsupportive of positive change. The traditional adult model needs some modifications to fit the specific needs of adolescents. These modifications include more staff involvement, more structure and organization, a more comprehensive family program, and a more intensive transition period from residential treatment to the wider community. Like adults, however, adolescents need appropriate recovering role models, ceremony and rituals, education, job training, recreation and exercise, therapeutic groups, and retreat settings in which deep psychological work can be accomplished. Structured interviews with participants suggest that adolescents welcome emotional challenge as long as they feel safe and trust those with whom they are working. Once assimilated into the TC, almost all of the participants request to be included in retreats and look forward to them with anticipation and excitement. Many report that the retreat experience was an important component of their treatment process.

Within the treatment field, there is recognition that the transition from the TC back into the wider community must be more extensive and that aftercare services must be more intensive so that these youths can continue to lead productive, responsible, drug-free lives. Although the TC provides an excellent setting to habilitate youth, the temptations and pressures of their familial and social network on reentry to the wider community are often overwhelming, especially for individuals who are still making the difficult transition into adulthood. Perhaps the TC model needs to be further modified so that the third stage of treatment is extended to include supervised independent living in the wider community. Funding this component up front would allow for more intensive services at the critical juncture of transition.

Longitudinal data on those who participate in TC treatment as adolescents are lacking. Although nonscientific follow-up data from the Amity TCs suggest that most adolescents remain AOD-free for at least 6 months, many of them eventually relapse. Interestingly, many do seek treatment soon after their relapse. It appears that the adolescents who had been in Amity's adolescent TC and who relapsed sought treatment relatively sooner than those who had not been in Amity's adolescent TC or any other long-term adolescent residential treatment program. Treatment entry data from Amity's adult program indicate that those who had participated in long-term treatment as adolescents and subsequently relapsed reentered treatment at a younger age, with fewer total years of AOD use, than those who did not have exposure to treatment as juveniles. Maybe it should not always be terribly disappointing to hear that relapse occurs, or perhaps exposure to treatment as adolescents enables individuals who do relapse to seek treatment sooner, ending the cycle of drugs, violence, and destruction of lives sooner than what might have been possible without the exposure to treatment as juveniles. Consequently it is suggested that longitudinal data need to be collected to clarify fully the true effects of adolescent interventions and treatment.

References

Currie, E. (1993). *Reckoning: Drugs, the cities, and the American future.* New York: Hill & Wang.

De Leon, G. (1985). The therapeutic community: Status and evaluation. *International Journal of Addictions, 20,* 823-844.

Green, M. B. (1993). Chronic exposure to violence and poverty: Interventions that work for youth. *Crime and Delinquency, 39,* 106-124.

Ingrassia, M., Annin, P., Biddle, N. A., & Miller, S. (July 19, 1993). Life means nothing: Is adolescent brutality on the rise? *Newsweek,* pp. 16-17.

Jaffe, P., Wilson, S., & Wolfe, D. (1986). Promoting changes in attitudes and understanding of conflict resolution among child witnesses of family violence. *Canadian Journal of Behavioral Sciences, 18,* 356-366.

McClain, C. (1994, October 31). A grim hit parade. *Tucson Citizen,* pp. 25-28.

McClain, C., & Gaynor, G. (1994, October 31). Making a bad kid. *Tucson Citizen,* pp. 12-13.

Miller, A. (1983). *For your own good: Hidden cruelty in child-rearing and the roots of violence.* New York: Farrar Straus Giroux.

Moyers, B. (1995, January 8). There is so much that we can do. *Parade,* pp. 4-6.

Mullen, R., Arbiter, N., & Glider, P. (1991). A comprehensive therapeutic community approach for chronic substance-abusing juvenile offenders: The Amity model. In T. L. Armstrong (Ed.), *Intensive interventions with high risk youths: Promising approaches in juvenile probation and parole* (pp. 211-243). Monsey, NY: Criminal Justice Press.

Roth, J. A. (1994, February). Psychoactive substance and violence. *National Institute of Justice, Research in Brief,* pp. 1-8.

Stevens, S. J., Arbiter, N., & McGrath, R. (in press). Women and children: Therapeutic community substance abuse treatment. In G. De Leon (Ed.), *Community as method: Modified therapeutic communities for special populations in special settings.* New York: Greenwood.

Swan, N. (1995). Marijuana, other drug use among teens continues to rise. *NIDA Notes, 10*(2), 8-9.

Teen rate drugs biggest problem in their lives. (1995). *Substance Abuse Report, 26*(15), 3.

Widom, C. S. (1992, October). The cycle of violence. *National Institute of Justice, Research in Brief,* pp. 1-6.

PART 4

International
Perspectives

9

Drug Use, HIV Risks, and Prevention/Intervention Strategies Among Street Youths in Rio De Janeiro, Brazil

Hilary L. Surratt
James A. Inciardi

> It is the duty of the family, society, and the State to ensure children and adolescents, with absolute priority, the right to life, health, food, education, leisure, professional training, culture, dignity, respect, freedom and family and community life, in addition to safeguarding them against all forms of negligence, discrimination, exploitation, violence, cruelty and oppression.—Article 227 of the Brazilian Constitution of 1988

Despite the protections and rights guaranteed by the Constitution of 1988, millions of children in the largest South American nation continue to live in conditions of abject poverty and misery. Brazil ranks near the bottom of the hemisphere in terms of standard of living, health status, and social indicators. Approximately 59 million people, 41% of Brazil's total population, are under age 18, and 35 million children are living in families earning less than $50 per person a month (Raphael & Berkman, 1992). Almost half of all Brazilian families live below the poverty line (88% of the minimum wage), and almost a third are below the indigency line (53% of the minimum wage).[1] Some 20% of Brazil's population is illiterate, and 35% of children between ages 7 and 15 are not enrolled in school. In addition, with the exception of Haiti and Guatemala, malnutrition is more prevalent in Brazil than in any other Latin American or Caribbean nation (Raphael & Berkman, 1992). According to official government statistics, 1,000 children die from hunger and malnutrition each day in Brazil. Moreover, Brazil's infant mortality rate in 1993 was 63 per 1,000 live births, one of the highest in Latin America, exceeded only by Peru (88) and Bolivia (98). In the poorest regions of the country and in impoverished areas near industrial centers, 10% of children are expected to die before they reach 5 years of age (Martins, 1993).

These discouraging statistics documenting the destitution of millions of Brazilians become even more troubling when one considers that Brazil has a higher per capita GNP—$2,540—than any other Latin American country except Uruguay. Brazil is a relatively wealthy country and possesses the 10th largest economy in the world, but the distribution of resources within its population is highly skewed. For example, one study reported a staggering amount of land concentration in Brazil, with 43% of the total land area owned by 1% of the population (Raphael & Berkman, 1992). Moreover, the top 20% of Brazil's population earns on average 26 times as much as the bottom 20%, whereas in the United States that variation is 9 to 1 (Michaels, 1993).

The striking economic disparity that exists between different segments of Brazilian society has its roots in regional inequalities and racial discrimination. During Brazil's "Economic Miracle" of the 1970s, government funds and foreign loans flowed into the industries of the south, resulting in improved standards of living and employment opportunities in that area of the country. In the agricultural northern regions, however, the poverty rate increased 9% over this same time period (Raphael & Berkman, 1992). Further, the aim of the Brazilian government to achieve "economic growth at all costs" led to a decrease in spending for health care, social programs, and educational initiatives. As a result, the proportion of malnourished children under age 5 increased from 13.7% in the late 1970s to 30.7% by the end of the 1980s.

With respect to economic disparity and racial inequality, Brazil is thought to have the largest black population of any country outside of Africa, with about 70 million people, or 46% of the total population, being Afro-Brazilians (International Child Resource Institute, 1994). Blacks in Brazil are typically overrepresented in the lowest income levels and represent the majority of the underemployed (International Child Resource Institute, 1994). Several studies have documented that incomes of white Brazilians are, on average, twice that of black Brazilians (International Child Resource Institute, 1994; Raphael & Berkman, 1992). In addition, a World Bank study found that almost 30% of Afro-Brazilian children live in households with incomes at the lowest wage levels (Tilak, 1989).

An important consequence of regional and racial economic inequalities in Brazil has been a massive influx of migrants from rural to urban areas. Over the past 20 years, urban areas in Brazil have absorbed over 29 million migrants seeking employment and a better life for themselves and their families. Others were evicted from their land by mining projects or cattle raising (International Child Resource Institute, 1994). This influx of migrants created a seemingly inexhaustible pool of unskilled laborers in Brazil's large cities. Moreover, the infrastructure of Brazilian cities has increasingly been unable to expand to meet the demands for health care, education, and jobs. As a result, slum dwellings, unemployment, hunger, and violence have risen dramatically. Today, 75% of the people in Brazil reside in cities, and among them are 52 million boys and girls under age 19 (Eisenstein, 1992).

The southeastern region of Brazil, where Rio de Janeiro is situated, is the most heavily populated section of the country. It is estimated that in metropolitan Rio alone there are 800,000 children living in extreme poverty. And it is this destitution that drives children to the streets in an attempt to survive.

The New Face of Child Labor

Throughout Latin America, street children represent the new face of child labor: youths working in the urban informal sector. Their occupations range from shining shoes or selling cigarettes, flowers, newspapers, or chewing gum to hauling garbage or engaging in drug trafficking, petty theft, street robberies, or prostitution.

The existence of street children in the large metropolitan areas of Brazil is not particularly new. The international media began to document the plight of large numbers of Brazilian street children as early as the 1970s. Despite the significant media attention focused on these children over the past 15 to 20 years, however, much remains unknown about their daily lives and activities. In fact, even approximating the true size of the population of street children has proven difficult. Estimates of the number of street children in Brazil have ranged from 7 to 17 million, but more informed assessments suggest that between 7 and 8 million children aged 5 to 18 live and/or work on the streets of Brazil. Although the vast majority of street children are boys, the Brazilian government reckons that there are approximately 800,000 street girls in Brazil and about 500,000 girls aged 18 or younger working as prostitutes across the country (Barker, 1992).

Part of the problem in estimating the number of street children lies in the distinction between what are known as "children *on* the street" and "children *of* the street" (Campos, Raffaelli, et al., 1994; Lusk, 1989). Children *on* the street work in informal sector occupations to supplement the family income but return home at night to sleep. These children typically reside in households headed by impoverished single women and spend most of the day and night in the street selling candy or gum, guarding cars, shining shoes, or carrying groceries.

By contrast, children *of* the street have often completely severed ties with their families. Children *of* the street seemingly choose to leave homes where hunger, neglect, and exploitation are commonplace, making life on the street preferable. A very small number of children actually live full time in the streets, often engaging in illegal activities to survive. In fact, children *of* the street are more often associated with theft, drug sales, petty theft, prostitution, and gang activity. Younger children often begin their careers on the street by begging and rely increasingly on crime to support themselves as they age and become less successful at panhandling. Young street girls commonly use prostitution as a way of supporting themselves.

As indicated in Table 9.1, the United Nations Children's Fund (UNICEF; Barker, 1992) estimated that the number of "working children" (children *on* the street) and "street children" (children *of* the street) throughout Latin America may total as many as 40 million.

As the number of street children and their related criminal activity continue to grow, so does public opposition to their presence. Over the past 20 or so years, public opinion has shifted dramatically. Children who were once looked on as street urchins deserving of compassion and sympathy are now viewed at best as a nuisance, and at worst as a danger to public safety—future criminals who ought to be locked up. Although popular views characterize these children as delinquents and thieves, perhaps Scheper-Hughes and Hoffman (1994) most accurately described them as simply "poor children in the wrong place" (p. 22). Perhaps it was this sentiment that enabled the Brazilian National Congress to pass the Child and Adolescent Act in 1990. This statute was designed to reform the legal status of children

Table 9.1 Numbers of "Working Children" and "Street Children" in Selected Latin American and Caribbean Nations

Country	Working Children	Street Children
Argentina	2,350,000	20,000[a]
Bolivia	72,000	200
Brazil	7,400,000	8,000,000[b]
Costa Rica	53,000	5,300
Ecuador	1,000,000	4,000
El Salvador	231,000	10,000
Guatemala	1,620,000	1,000[c]
Haiti	120,000	10,000
Honduras	275,000	800
Mexico	10,000,000	250,000

SOURCE: Data from UNICEF, Regional Office for Latin America, Bogota, cited in Barker (1992, p. 7).
a. Includes Buenos Aires only.
b. May include children working, but not living, on the street.
c. Includes Guatemala City only.

in Brazil and to create councils that would act as children's rights advocates, with an eye toward integrating impoverished children into the larger society. However, negative attitudes toward street children by the Brazilian people prevail, and public resistance to such reforms continues to frustrate attempts to implement the statute.

The Children of the Favelas

Important to understanding the presence of large numbers of street children in Latin America in general and in Brazil in particular is a comprehension of the nature of "primate cities" and what life is like in the thousands of primate city shantytowns.

Most developing countries contain one or more primate cities, urban areas that grow in population and influence far beyond the other cities in the region or nation. In many Latin American countries, and elsewhere in the Developing World, the largest cities may have several times the combined populations of the next two or three urban areas and may also have a significant share of the national population. Mexico City's population of 16 million, for example, accounts for 20% of the nation's population, whereas other cities are considerably smaller: Guadalajara, 1.6 million; Monterrey, 1.1 million; and Puebla de Zaragoza, 1.1 million. Similarly, the populations of Brazil's two largest cities—São Paulo and Rio de Janeiro—combine to account for some 16% of the national population.

Primate cities typically are located on the coast or in other areas close to transportation routes because many were political and economic centers when under colonial rule. The orientation of such cities had been toward the developed nations that they supplied with raw materials and other goods rather than toward the urban areas and hinterlands of their own country.

Among the greatest difficulties experienced by these cities in Latin America are those of stimulating industrialization and providing employment. People who move into these urban locales do so not because of the employment opportunities the cities provide but because the living conditions in rural areas seem so much worse. Recent research has suggested that rural populations have been forced to relocate because of increasing agricultural density and the inability of the land to support its people (Firebaugh, 1979). Rural-urban migrants believe that the cities offer a better life and at least the hope for employment. Some do find work in small enterprises, but because of the lack of sophisticated technology and industrial production methods, the cities cannot provide for the large pool of unskilled labor to the extent that characterized the Western industrial revolution. As a result, the unemployment rates in the cities of many developing nations exceed 25% of the labor force.

Common features of the primate city landscape are the sections made up of shanties, shacks, and makeshift huts inhabited by those who have no other shelter. Known as *barriadas* (Peru), *ranchos* (Venezuela), *villas miserias* (Argentina), or *favelas* (Brazil), depending on the nation, these squatter settlements have been estimated to house as much as one third of the urban population (Butterworth & Chance, 1981, pp. 151-157). Mexico City has some 4 million squatters, Calcutta 2 million, and Rio de Janeiro over 1 million.

Favelas have been a feature of urban Brazil for generations (Freyre, 1986). *Favela* in Brazilian Portuguese means "slum." Yet it is a particular type of slum that takes its name from the hill near Rio de Janeiro where the first one appeared. In 1963, the noted journalist and biographer John Dos Passos commented:

In Rio—this was in 1948—there were said to be three hundred thousand people living in *favelas*. Today there are nearer a million. You come on *favelas* in the most unexpected places. In Copacabana a few minutes walk from the hotels and the splendid white apartment houses and the wellkept magnificent beaches you find a whole hillside of *favelas* overlooking the lake and the Jockey Club. In the center of Rio a few steps from the Avenida Rio Branco on the hill back of one of the most fashionable churches you come suddenly into a tropical jungletown. (Dos Passos, 1963, p. 31)

Similarly, in 1966, travel writer John Gunther described Rio's *favelas* as "vertical" in character—because they were situated on hillsides:

This came about partly because much of the land in Rio is too steep for normal building purposes and, when urbanization began on a serious scale, speculators let the hills alone. So the squatters swarmed to the cliffs, scraped off plots from jungle shrubbery, and built their miserable huts out of tin cans, hunks of stone, and cardboard, on the sharpest slopes. The irony is that they now have the best views in the city. But there are no amenities whatever, not even water or a postal service. Filth and flies are everywhere. Dogs howl, and children drip with slime. (Gunther, 1966, p. 72)

Gunther went on to note:

Nowhere in South America is the contrast between rich and poor more dramatic than in Rio, where slum dwellers live in such close proximity to the well-to-do. And nothing could have made this contrast more tragically pointed than a storm which smothered Rio in rain in January, 1966, and washed out thousands of shanty dwellings on the hillsides. Mud and rubble cascaded into the town almost directly on the heads of residents of glossily rich hotels and apartment buildings. About fifty thousand people became homeless; no fewer than four hundred were killed, some drowned in fetid mud. (Gunther, 1966, pp. 72-73)

The *favelas* began to appear on the hillsides of Rio de Janeiro at the end of the 19th century and spread rapidly after 1930 as shelters for newly arriving migrants (Burns, 1980, p. 569). Fleeing regions hard hit by drought and unemployment, rural Brazilians thronged to the *cidade maravilhosa*, the "marvelous city" of Rio de Janeiro, lured by its illusionary riches. There has been a steady stream even since, and at the close of the 1980s it was estimated that some 1,500 *favelados* were arriving each day (Archambault, 1989).

Little has changed since Dos Passos and Gunther made their observations three decades ago. In Rio de Janeiro, *favelas* have been estimated by Brazil's Municipal Planning Institute to number 545 and to house more than 1 million persons (Loveman, 1991). Clustered on the hill and mountainsides that overlook Rio's fashionable beaches and elegant shopping and high-rise centers, the *favelas* are slums in which only a small portion of households have electricity, running water, or sewage facilities. In the absence of public medical facilities and unemployment benefits for the more than 50% of the out-of-work *favelados,* disease and social problems multiply. There is prostitution and drug use, and a key feature of most *favelas* is cocaine trafficking (Guillermoprieto, 1990). Within such a setting, it is no wonder that so many children retreat from the *favelas* to the streets—to Copacabana, Ipanema, Leblon, Lapa, Leme, Botofogo, Tijuca, and other sections of the "asphalt city."

Drug Use and Sexual Activity

Anecdotal accounts of drug abuse among street youths in Brazil are commonplace. Numerous media stories have reported the widespread use of inhalants (such as glue, gasoline, lighter fluid, and *bim*—a mixture of ethyl alcohol, sugar, and benzene), marijuana, cocaine, and Valium among street children in Rio de Janeiro (Brookes, 1991; Larmer, 1992). Also common is the use of coca paste and Rohypnol.

Common not only in the drug-using communities of Brazil but also in those of Colombia, Bolivia, Venezuela, Ecuador, and Peru is the use of coca paste, known to most South Americans as *basuco, susuko, pasta basica de cocaina, pasta de coca,* or just simply *pasta* (Jeri, 1984). Perhaps best known as *basuco,* coca paste is one of the intermediate products in the processing of the coca leaf into cocaine. It is typically smoked straight or in cigarettes mixed with either tobacco or marijuana.

The smoking of coca paste became popular in South America beginning in the early 1970s. It was readily available and inexpensive, had a high cocaine content, and was absorbed quickly. As the phenomenon was studied, however, it was quickly realized that paste smoking was far more serious than any other form of cocaine use. In addition to cocaine, paste contains traces of all the chemicals used to process the coca leaves initially: kerosene, sulfuric acid, methanol, benzoic acid, and the oxidized products of these solvents, plus any number of other alkaloids that are present in the coca leaf (Almeida, 1978). One analysis undertaken in Colombia in 1986 found, in addition to all of these chemicals, traces of brick dust, leaded gasoline, ether, and various talcs.[2]

When the smoking of paste was first noted in South America, it seemed to be restricted to the coca-processing regions of Bolivia, Colombia, Ecuador, and Peru, appealing primarily to street children and low-income groups due to its cheap price when compared with that of refined cocaine (Jeri, Sanchez, & Del Pozo, 1976). By the early 1980s, however, it had spread to other South American nations, including Brazil, and to numerous segments of the social strata. Throughout the decade, paste smoking further expanded to became a major drug problem for much of South America.[3] Among Rio's street youth of the 1990s, the smoking of *pasta de coca* remains an enduring problem.

By contrast, Rohypnol is a legal drug, readily available in pharmacies in many parts of the world. Also known by its generic name *flunitrazepam,* Rohypnol is a benzodiazepine drug having anticonvulsant and sedative effects, slowing psychomotor performance, and inducing muscle relaxation and sleep. It is used for the short-term treatment of insomnia. However, its use can lead to the development of physical and psychic dependence, with the risk of addiction increasing with dose and duration of use.

Rohypnol is similar to Valium but 10 times as potent. It was first introduced in the 1970s and is legally available throughout Europe and Latin America. Since the 1980s, it has been used to counter some of the negative side effects of cocaine abuse. In addition, combining Rohypnol with alcohol, cocaine, or marijuana reportedly produces a fast hit followed by a mellow state that lasts for several hours.[4]

Many street youths in Rio de Janeiro see their use of inhalants, coca paste, marijuana, Rohypnol, and other drugs as an escape—a way to dull their hunger and facilitate acts of prostitution and other crimes (Barker, 1992; Vasconcelos, 1990). As one young female prostitute observed:

> When I was prostituting at the boarding house, my father would go there and want to pay me to have sex with him. I would never do it and every time he would leave, I would smoke a lot of marijuana to try and forget the things that he would say. (Vasconcelos, 1990, p. 27)

Indeed, it has been observed that drug use by street children is a nearly universal phenomenon because these youths are confronted with the harsh realities of street life on a daily basis (Lusk, 1989). Given that drug abuse among youths has emerged as a concomitant of life on the streets, the paucity of scientific studies that have examined this and other related topics among street children in Brazil is troubling.

Although previous research on drug use among street children is limited, existing studies have found rates of use to be high. A survey among 119 street children in Sao Paulo, for example, classified 45% as heavy drug users, indicating the use of up to three drugs a day (Dimenstein, 1991). In a study of street youths in Belo Horizonte, a city of 2 million people some 452 kilometers northeast of Rio de Janeiro, 84% of the children living full time in the street had histories of illegal drug use, 10.6% reported injection drug use, and 83.5% were sexually active (Campos, Raffaelli, et al., 1994). In addition, in an earlier study involving this same sample, 82.6% reported having had sex while under the influence of drugs and/or alcohol. In comparison, of the working but "home-based" children interviewed, only 25% had histories of illegal drug use and none reported the use of injection drugs (Campos et al., 1992). A similar study supported these findings by reporting higher rates of drug use among "street-based" youth than "home-based" youth, 76.9% versus 29.1%, and earlier onset of drug use—9.8 years versus 11.2 years (Pinto et al., 1992). Moreover, in a 1992 study of 98 street children in Rio de Janeiro, 90.8% of the children believed drug abuse to be a problem in the community, and 38.8% stated that drug use was a personal problem for them (Eisenstein & de Aquino, 1992). The most commonly used drugs among these children were glue (13.3%), marijuana (13.3%), alcohol/tobacco (12.2%), and cocaine (11.2%). Nearly 70% of this sample refused to respond to questions about injection drug use.

Regardless of whether they reported any use of illegal drugs, street children have frequently related engaging in risky sexual behaviors. Street studies in Rio de Janeiro have concluded that a "second shift" of children are visible on the streets at night. Unlike their daytime counterparts, these "second-shift" children tend to be older and are more likely to be female. Among them, prostitution by both boys and girls is frequent (Lusk, 1989). A 1992 study of 62 children found that 48.4% had engaged in sex, 60% with adult men, and that 16.6% reported sex for money exchanges but only 33.3% reported any use of condoms (Campos, Greco, et al., 1994).

In addition to solicitation for prostitution, many street children have reported incidents of rape. Scheper-Hughes and Hoffman (1994) observed that street girls and boys are frequently raped by police and others. Surprisingly, however, the perpetrators are not always male. Vasconcelos (1990) noted that older street girls will sometimes force younger girls to have sex with them, thereby continuing the cycle of violence of which they too have been victims. Of the 98 street children interviewed by Eisenstein and de Aquino (1992), 53.1% were sexually active and 44.9% reported being forced to have sex. Similarly, a survey of 52 HIV-seropositive street youths under age 16 in Rio de Janeiro found that 28% had had anal intercourse, presumably forced. Of those ages 7 to 12, 63% had had anal intercourse, and 57% had been forced to have anal intercourse by older street children (van Buuren & Bezerra, 1992).

Although this type of sexual violence appears to be common, it is not always necessary. Many street children use sex as a way to gain affection and attention (Scheper-Hughes & Hoffman, 1994). For this reason, younger girls at times voluntarily seek sexual contact with older girls (Vasconcelos, 1990). Sexual activity among boys is also relatively common. Some 21% of street boys interviewed in a 1991 study reported same-sex anal intercourse (Ude et al., 1991). Heterosexual anal intercourse was reported by 43% of these same respondents.

Despite high rates of sexual activity among street children, attitudes regarding condom use are for the most part negative, and usage rates are low. Various studies have reported the proportion of sexually active street children having ever used condoms to be in the range of 8.2% to 33.3% (Campos, Greco, et al., 1994; Eisenstein & de Aquino, 1992; Raffaelli et al., 1992; Ude et al., 1991).

Risk of exposure to HIV is rapidly becoming an area of concern because of the large number of street youths engaging in unprotected sexual acts, both renumerated and nonrenumerated. The World Health Organization reckons that there are between 50 and 100 HIV seropositive individuals for each diagnosed AIDS case, so there are probably between 50,000 and 100,000 HIV-positive children and adolescents in Brazil. Going further, it has also been estimated that between 1% and 2% of Brazil's population of 7 to 8 million street children, or between 70,000 and 110,000 individuals, are HIV-positive. A study in 1987 to 1988 at the FUNBEM Hospital in Rio de Janeiro found that among 3,389 street children, 50 (1.5%) were HIV-positive

(Eisenstein, 1993). However, a more recent study conducted between May 1991 and January 1994 found that of 126 street children interviewed and tested, 94% reported HIV risk behaviors and 6% were HIV-seropositive (Adams, Martins, Campos, & Paiva, 1994).

Violence Against Rio's Street Children

Street children in Rio de Janeiro and elsewhere in Latin America are viewed by many police groups, merchants, and other citizens as undesirable, pariah populations. And because of their drug use, predatory crimes, and general unacceptability on urban thoroughfares, street children have frequently been the targets of local vigilante groups, drug gangs, and police "death squads."

Perhaps most notorious have been the death squads, which initially appeared in Brazil in 1968, and principally in Rio de Janeiro, at first to avenge the terrorist murder of a well-known police officer. The death squads proliferated during the years of Brazil's military rule, which ended in 1985. As the killings spread, political and community leaders were often targeted, and the victims were easily recognized. Their hands were always tied behind their backs, their tongues were cut out, and a crudely drawn skull and crossbones was left on the corpse, with the initials "E.M."—"Esquadrão de Morte"—appended.

News reports have suggested that there are many such police assassination squads in Latin America (Barker, 1992). Guatemala had its La Mano Blanco (The White Hand), Argentina its Anti-Communist Alliance, the Dominican Republic its La Banda gang, and Brazil, Paraguay, Honduras, and El Salvador their Esquadrão de Morte or Esquadron de Muerte—"Death Squad." All were organized but unofficial police vigilante organizations established with the aim not only of preserving their respective political regimes through selective political murders but also of eliminating those viewed by the police as "undesirables"—trade unionists, drug dealers, thieves and other criminals, and, not surprisingly, street children.

Many of the death squads still exist, particularly in Brazil, and street children are common victims. Because they survive, in part, through prostitution and crime, they have become the targets of retributive violence by police death squads and merchants' vigilante groups (Martins, 1992). Store owners hire off-duty police officers or professional killers to eliminate the "disposable children" because they consider them to be bad for business. Moreover, there is considerable public support for the death squads as the result of perceptions that street children are dangerous criminals. Residents of the poorest communities are often the strongest supporters of violent solutions to local crime, perhaps because their neighborhoods are the least secure.

Street children are also the targets of drug gangs. Because Brazil's Protective Child Statute holds that children under 18 years of age may not be arrested unless caught committing a crime, to the drug gangs the youths' immunity makes them ideal couriers. But the children are often killed because they know too much, steal too much, or get caught in the crossfire (Michaels, 1993).

The *favela* drug trade is organized hierarchically, with children recruited into the lowest level, serving primarily as lookouts. They progress to running errands for the hillside dealers, and if they are successful, they begin delivering drugs to customers. Survivors from these operations may become armed "controllers" (security guards who protect the operation and proceeds of drug transactions). Finally, there are the corporate levels of the local drug business, but few children ever last that long. Most die while they are still at the low end of the hierarchy. When a hillside dealer is dissatisfied with a child's work or decides that he or she is dangerous as a witness, the child is simply killed (Raphael & Berkman, 1992).

It has been estimated that as many as five street children are murdered each day throughout Brazil, and two each day in Rio de Janeiro alone. Yet only rarely are their killers apprehended. One of the few exceptions occurred in Rio de Janeiro in 1993 after eight youths were gunned down while sleeping in front of the Candelaria Church, a Rio tourist attraction (Ellison, 1994). Five men were arrested and charged with the murders. Four of them were police officers.

Intervention Strategies

Although there appear to be many proposals and programs for addressing the problems of Brazilian street youth (Eisenstein, 1993, 1994; Kirsch, 1995), it would appear that only minimal progress has been achieved. At the most general level, programs appear to be of four types: correctional, rehabilitative, outreach, and preventive (Lusk, 1989).

The *correctional* approach views street children as the province of juvenile justice organizations. This correctional vision seems to dominate the thinking of many of the public and criminal justice authorities. The result is that thousands of street children are housed in institutions. In Brazil, the National Foundation for Child Welfare (FUNABEM) operates 20 treatment centers and "reform" schools for abandoned and delinquent youth. Conditions in these facilities have been described as both crowded and abusive (Lusk, 1989). However, some changes appear to be under way, involving the substitution of correctional initiatives with community-based treatment alternatives.

The *rehabilitative* approach has been gaining momentum throughout Latin America. This perspective holds that street children are not delinquents as much as they are victims of poverty, child abuse and neglect, and untenable living conditions. Because street children are seen as having been harmed by their environments, hundreds of church and voluntary programs have been organized in their behalf. These typically provide housing, drug detoxification, education, and/or work programs. But there is a difficulty. The programs benefit only a limited number of youths and are unable to address the needs of the millions of boys and girls who continue to call the streets their home.

Because the institutional capacities and resources of virtually all programs are limited and unable to accommodate the overwhelming majority of street children, services are also provided through a variety of *outreach* strategies. In São Paulo, for example, the Catholic Church supports young lay workers who provide educational, counseling, and advocacy services to children in a street setting. In addition to teaching basic hygiene, literacy, and business skills, the general program approach is to instill self-reliance and empowerment so that children will find solutions to their problems. However, it would appear that this street educator model is overly ideological and fails to deal with the immediate physical and safety needs of street children. Most recently, outreach strategies have been focusing on HIV prevention and risk reduction (Siqueira et al., 1992; Wiik, Filgueiras, & Castro, 1989). The effectiveness of these initiatives, however, is unclear.

The *preventive* approach attempts to address the fundamental and underlying problem of childhood poverty. In this regard, UNICEF is conducting educational campaigns to alert policy makers to the causes of children's moving to the streets. In addition to policy advocacy, UNICEF provides technical assistance and support for promising local efforts. Those receiving

UNICEF's focused attention are of two types: (a) programs that provide daytime activities, schooling, jobs, and other alternatives to street work for high-risk children, and (b) efforts focusing on the prevention of family disintegration—cooperative day care centers, family planning clinics, small business services, and community kitchens (Lusk, 1989).

The most comprehensive effort on behalf of Brazilian street youth is the National Movement for Street Children (Movimento Nacional de Meninos e Meninas de Rua/MNMMR), a nationwide coalition of street children and adult educators founded in 1985 (Raphael & Berkman, 1992). MNMMR initiatives focus on the decriminalization of the treatment of street children, the codification of the rights of children into law, and the structuring of innovative approaches for providing education and training for youths directly on the streets where they live. MNMMR projects are targeting an estimated 80,000 youths, the great majority of whom work on the streets and live in nearby *favelas,* with the remaining actually living on the streets.

Postscript

Street children in most Latin American cities are legion. Their actual numbers are difficult to estimate, however, and have often been exaggerated. In Rio de Janeiro, the figure of 1 million abandoned and runaway children living on the streets has been repeatedly quoted. Such an estimate is impossible, however, given that Rio has a population of just under 6 million people. The number of children working and/or living in the streets of Rio de Janeiro is more likely in the vicinity of 10,000 to 20,000, though this figure is itself still a major social problem. And as one observer put it, the children

> seem to be everywhere: begging in front of restaurants, peddling cigarettes in sidewalk cafes, shining shoes outside the train station, washing clothes in public fountains. Take a morning stroll on the elegant, black-and-white mosaic sidewalk that curves along Rio's Copacabana Beach and you'll smell them; dozens sleep under the palms there, and the beach serves as a toilet. (Brookes, 1991, p. 14)

For those who work the streets during the day, returning to their *favela* homes at night, life is harsh and unkind. For the rest who live in the streets day and night, life is mean and unusually short. And for the great majority of Rio's street children, it would appear that few changes are likely. Prostitution, drug use, infections, and illiteracy are common, yet there are few programs available to address the many needs of youths.

After his election in 1991, Brazilian President Collor de Mello announced a dramatic plan to build 5,000 model schools called Centros Integrados de Apoio a Criança/Integrated Support Centers for Children (CIACs) for indigent children and youth over a 4-year period. They were conceived to offer indigent youths comprehensive classroom instruction and after-school care, three meals a day, medical and psychological attention, shower facilities, sports and cultural activities, and a library. But by the time President Collor was removed from office on charges of fraud and embezzlement, only 20 centers had been built, and only a few of these had actually been opened. Not surprisingly, the future of the remaining schools continues to be in doubt. In the meantime, as poverty endures, the numbers of street children slowly increase, as does their involvement in drug use, prostitution, crime, and HIV risk behaviors.

Notes

1. Poverty and indigency lines are established by the World Health Organization (see Eisenstein, 1992).

2. See *El Tiempo* (Bogota, Colombia), June 19, 1986, p. 2-D.

3. See Ross (1989) and the following newspaper articles: *El Universal* (Caracas, Venezuela), October 4, 1985, pp. 4, 30; *Zeta* (Caracas), September 12-23, 1985, pp. 39-46; *Jornal do Comercio* (Manaus, Brazil), May 20, 1986, p. 16; *El Tiempo* (Bogota, Colombia), June 1, 1986, p. 3-A, and October 6, 1986, p. 7-A; *El Colombiano* (Medellin, Colombia), July 22, 1986, p. 16-A; *El Nacional* (Lima, Peru), November 14, 1986, p. 13; *Presencia* (La Paz, Bolivia), March 3, 1988, sec. 2, p. 1; *Folha de Sao Paulo* (São Paulo, Brazil), June 11, 1987, p. A-29; *La Prensa* (Buenos Aires, Argentina), June 20, 1987, p. 9; *O Estado de São Paulo* (São Paulo), March 8, 1988, p. 18, and June 18, 1989, p. 32; *El Espectador* (Bogota), April 2, 1988, pp. 1-A, 10-A; *El Diario* (La Paz), October 21, 1988, p. 3; *Los Tiempos* (Cochabamba, Bolivia), June 13, 1989, p. B5; *Manchete* (Rio de Janeiro, Brazil), October 28, 1989, pp. 20-29; *Philadelphia Inquirer,* September 21, 1986, p. 25-A.

4. Rohypnol is manufactured in Switzerland by Hoffmann-LaRoche and is not legally available in the United States. However, it first appeared in Florida in 1992, and by 1995 it was reportedly available in 13 states. According to officials at the Drug Enforcement Administration, Rohypnol is smuggled into the United States from Colombia and Mexico. The drug is particularly attractive to youths because of its low price and perceived safety. See *Drug Enforcement Report,* June 23, 1995, pp. 1, 5; *Substance Abuse Letter,* July 3, 1995, pp. 1, 6.

References

Adams, I., Martins, R., Campos, M., & Paiva, J. (1994, August). *The Ammor street kids cohort: Window on epidemiology in this population.* Paper presented at the 10th International Conference on AIDS, Yokohama.

Almeida, M. (1978). Contrabucion al Estudio de la Historia Natural de la Dependencia a la Pasta Basica de Cocaina. *Revista de Neuro-Psiquiatria, 41,* 44-45.

Archambault, C. (1989, April). Rio's shaky shantytowns. *IRDC Reports,* pp. 18-19.

Barker, G. (1992, January). More than a minor problem. *Institute of the Americas Hemisfile, 3,* 6-7.

Brookes, S. (1991, August 5). Life on Rio's mean streets. *Insight,* pp. 12-19.

Burns, E. B. (1980). *A history of Brazil.* New York: Columbia University Press.

Butterworth, D., & Chance, J. K. (1981). *Latin American urbanization.* Cambridge, UK: Cambridge University Press.

Campos, R., Antunes, C., Jeronymo, M., Raffaelli, M., Payne-Merritt, A., Halsey, N., & Greco, D. (1992, July). *Comparison of behavioral risks for HIV infection among sub-groups of Brazilian street youth.* Paper presented at the 8th International Conference on AIDS, Amsterdam.

Campos, R., Greco, M., Ude, W., Machado, A., Raffaelli, M., Campos, M., & Greco, D. (1994, August). *Female street youths: Social factors associated to behavioral risks for HIV infection.* Paper presented at the 10th International Conference on AIDS, Yokohama.

Campos, R., Raffaelli, M., Ude, W., Greco, M., Ruff, A., Rolf, J., Antunes, C., Halsey, N., & Greco, D. (1994). Social networks and daily activities of street youth in Belo Horizonte, Brazil. *Child Development, 65,* 319-330.

Dimenstein, G. (1991). *Brazil: War on children.* London: Latin American Bureau.

Dos Passos, J. (1963). *Brazil on the move.* New York: Paragon.

Eisenstein, E. (1992). *Street youth.* Mimeographed paper from the Nucleo de Estudos e Pesquisas em Atençao de Drogas, Rio de Janeiro.

Eisenstein, E. (1993). Street youth: Social imbalance and health risks. *Journal of Paediatrics and Child Health, 29*(Suppl.), S46-S49.

Eisenstein, E. (1994, April). *Access to health services specially [sic] in relation to street children and drugs.* Paper presented at the Conference on Street Children and Psychoactive Substances, Geneva.

Eisenstein, E., & de Aquino, M. T. (1992). *Street children and drugs.* Mimeographed paper from the Nucleo de Estudos e Pesquisas em Atençao de Drogas, Rio de Janeiro.

Ellison, K. (1994, July 28). Rio's tough street kids still live in fear. *Miami Herald,* p. 12A.

Firebaugh, G. (1979). Structural determinants of urbanization in Asia and Latin America. *American Sociological Review, 44,* 199-215.

Freyre, G. (1986). *The mansions and the shanties.* Berkeley: University of California Press.

Guillermoprieto, A. (1990). *Samba.* New York: Knopf.

Gunther, J. (1966). *Inside South America.* New York: Harper & Row.

International Child Resource Institute. (1994, Summer). *Brazil Street Children Bulletin,* pp. 1-3.

Jeri, F. R. (1984, April-June). Coca-paste smoking in some Latin American countries: A severe and unabated form of addiction. *Bulletin on Narcotics, 22,* 15-31.

Jeri, F. R., Sanchez, C., & Del Pozo, T. (1976). Consumo de drogas peligrosas por miembros familiares de la fuerza armada y fuerza policial Peruana. *Revista de la Sanidad de las Fuerzas Policiales, 37,* 104-112.

Kirsch, H. (Ed.). (1995). *Drug lessons and education programs in developing countries.* New Brunswick, NJ: Transaction.

Larmer, B. (1992, May 25). Dead end kids. *Newsweek,* p. 38-40.

Loveman, B. (1991, July). Latin America faces public enemy no. 1. *Institute of the Americas Hemisfile, 2,* 6-8.

Lusk, M. W. (1989). Street children programs in Latin America. *Journal of Sociology and Social Welfare, 16,* 55-77.

Martins, J. P. S. (1992, April 16). Brazilian police go after street children. *Latinamerica Press,* p. 7.

Martins, J. P. S. (1993, December 23). Children in Brazil victims through the ages. *Latinamerica Press,* p. 4.

Michaels, M. (1993, August 9). Rio's dead end kids. *Newsweek,* pp. 36-37.

Pinto, J. A., Ruff, A., Paiva, J. V., Antunes, C. M., Adams, I., Halsey, N., & Greco, D. (1992, July). *Comparative assessment of risk behavior and seroprevalence of HIV-1 among homeless and underprivileged youth in Belo Horizonte, Brazil.* Paper presented at the 8th International Conference on AIDS, Amsterdam.

Raffaelli, M., Merritt, P., Campos, R., Siqueira, E., Ude, W., Greco, M., Greco, D., & Halsey, N. (1992, July). *Correlates of condom use among street youth in Belo Horizonte, Brazil.* Paper presented at the 8th International Conference on AIDS, Amsterdam.

Raphael, A., & Berkman, J. (1992, September). Children without a future. *Brazil Network,* pp. 1-35.

Ross, T. (1989, September). Bolivian Paste Fuels Basuco Boom. *WorldAIDS,* p. 9.

Scheper-Hughes, N., & Hoffman, D. (1994, May/June). Kids out of place. *NACLA Report on the Americas, 27,* 16-23.

Siqueira, E., Merritt, P., Ude, W., Campos, R., Greco, M., Raffaelli, M., Halsey, N., & Greco, D. (1992, July). *HIV outreach communication intervention for Brazilian street youth.* Paper presented at the 8th International Conference on AIDS, Amsterdam.

Tilak, J. (1989). *Education and its relation to economic growth, poverty, and income distribution: Past evidence and further analysis* (World Bank Discussion Paper No. 46). Washington, DC: World Bank.

Ude, W., Payne, A., Antunes, C., Holt, E., Rafaelli, M., Ottone, Z., Rolf, J., Pinto, J., Paiva, J., Campos, R., Greco, M., Siqueira, E., Greco, D., Ruff, A., & Halsey, N. (1991, June). A comparison of three methods of obtaining information from street youths regarding HIV risk behaviors. Paper presented at the 7th International Conference on AIDS, Florence.

van Buuren, N., & Bezerra, C. A. (1992, July). *The need to open a discussion about a public secret.* Paper presented at the 8th International Conference on AIDS, Amsterdam.

Vasconcelos, A. (1990). *SOS Meninas.* Recife, Brazil: Casa de Passagem.

Wiik, F. B., Filgueiras, A., & Castro, M. L. (1989, June). *Street teenagers and an AIDS prevention program in Brazil.* Paper presented at the 5th International Conference on AIDS, Montreal.

10

Drug Use and HIV Among Youth in Manipur, India

Swarup Sarkar
Anindya Chatterjee
Clyde B. McCoy
Abu S. Adbul-Quader
Lisa R. Metsch
Robert S. Anwyl

Manipur, a north eastern state of India, literally means "the land of jewels." This "land of jewels," the home of traditional religious, family, and other strong Indian values, is now experiencing the plight of other communities throughout the world: Its youth are facing the consequences of injection drug use, particularly heroin. Although psychoactive substances like cannabis and alcohol have been used in India for centuries, recognition and escalation of drugs as a social problem has surfaced only during the past three decades. This recognition has been associated with the banning of traditional drugs like cannabis, and the illegal introduction of newer synthetic substances like methaqualone, heroin, buprenorphin as well as newer routes of admini-

---

AUTHORS' NOTE: The views expressed in this chapter do not necessarily represent those of the organizations/institutions at which we are currently employed.

stration such as injection drug use leading to the development of a newer drug culture and its consequences, namely HIV and AIDS among Indian youth.

The use of drugs, especially psychoactive drugs and alcohol, has had a particular role in India for hundreds of years. These practices, including the use of cannabis, are noted in ancient documents and even in the sacred text of the *Vedas,* composed thousands of years before the birth of Christ. Hindu religious practices and Indian culture still include consumption of cannabis. One form of cannabis, bhang, not only is used for the traditional festival of Holi but can be seen in use in Indian society throughout the year. Religious use of another form of cannabis, Ganja, is often socially accepted by some religious sects.

Following the introduction of the newer drugs into Indian society, the Indian government has taken the decisive action of appointing a National Committee on Drug Addiction, which recommended the implementation of a National Advisory Board of drug control. The information from these committees signaled a new sense of recognition that drug prevalence was shockingly high, especially among students and other youth, and constituted a national problem. Recognition of the problem led to the involvement of other governmental agencies and health service organizations, including the Ministry of Health and Family Welfare. To treat increasing drug problems, hospital and addiction centers were established in many cities.

This chapter focuses attention on one of the world's most shocking stories of the effects and deadly consequences of drug use. It is shocking because this story unfolds in a very unlikely community, considering its thousands of years of history and traditional values and its relative isolation in the world and from the rest of India. The story of drugs and HIV in Manipur, India, illustrates that no community, however strong and durable its traditional, protective values, should think that it is isolated from the potential devastation that follows widespread drug use by youth and the involvement in criminal activities that follows.

Drug Use in Manipur, India

Manipur is one of seven states nestled in the northeast region of India. Bordered by Myanmar (Burma) on the east, Manipur has become a marketplace for heroin and the drugs processed in and transported from the Golden

Triangle. Following the same pathway taken by the smugglers of gold, silver, precious stones, and expensive wood, opium and heroin enter India along the Indo-Myanmerese border through a 40-mile stretch of what at best could be called "no-man's land." Once these drugs pass the border, there is wide circulation of the drug in *puriyas* (the paper pouch in which the drug is placed in Manipur) to be used by individual drug users or a small group of drug users. The dislocations created by the war in Vietnam, political instability, unemployment, and poverty, all coupled with the flood of cheap opium and its derivatives, have resulted in a dramatic increase in injection drug use during the last decade.

While cannabis, opium, and alcohol have been used in Manipur for centuries, drug injection is a more recent phenomenon. Beginning in the 1980s with morphine and Pethidine, especially among the young, drug injection rose rapidly due to the importation of cheap heroin ($5–$10 per gram) from Myanmar (Burma) (McCoy & Inciardi, 1995; Sharma, 1984).

The first survey on drug use in Manipur was conducted in 1988 by the Indian Medical Association. This household study of the rural and urban districts of Manipur surveyed approximately 18,000 people in 45 cities, towns, and villages. Nearly 11% of those surveyed used drugs, ranging from cough syrup and tranquilizers to alcohol, cannabis, morphine, opium, and heroin. Nevertheless, inpatient detoxification facilities were not available until 1990, when concern for the AIDS virus began to take hold (Pal et al., 1990). This is yet a further indication that the consequences of HIV/AIDS have heightened awareness and spurred action against drugs and that HIV/AIDS has been more of an impetus to action than the drugs in and of themselves. Because of the association between injection practices and HIV/AIDS (McCoy & Inciardi, 1995), another survey was carried out in a district town of 33,000 to estimate the numbers of injectors. The results indicated that 1.2% of those surveyed were heroin injectors. These results, extrapolated to similar areas of Manipur with high availability of heroin, yielded an estimated number of 15,000 injecting drug users for the state (Sarkar, Mukherjee, & Roy, 1991). A later survey conducted in 1992 by the Manipur Voluntary Association estimated the number of injecting drug users to be 40,000 (Sehgal & Singh, 1992).

Injection drug use is a particularly serious problem among males, predominantly between the age of 15 and 30 (Pal et al., 1990; Sarkar et al., 1993). Studies conducted estimate that one in every eight males between the ages of 15 and 30 would be an injection drug user.

Drug-Using Behaviors

While hypodermic needles and syringes are available legally over the counter, usually at inflated prices, especially if illegal drug use is suspected by pharmacy personnel, use of improvised injection equipment, such as ink droppers fitted with syringes, is more common (Delhi Science Office, 1994; Sarkar et al., 1993). Such injection paraphernalia, or "works," is frequently shared among friends. Sarkar et al. (1993) found that groups of needle-sharing partners typically ranged in size from three to five members. Tellis (1995) reported that among the estimated 20,000 injecting drug users reported by the Medical Association in December of 1993, 96.8% shared injection equipment. Moreover, the cleaning of injection equipment is not at all practiced by 62% of injectors, and the majority of those who do so primarily use ordinary tap water. The use of bleach, common in the United States for disinfecting injection equipment, was unknown until mid-1991 in India, and bleach typically is unavailable as a household item (Sarkar et al., 1993).

Interdiction by the Excise Department coupled with more stringent law enforcement has reduced the heroin supply available to Manipuri youth. Heroin, which once sold for $15 to $20 per gram, can currently cost up to three and four times as much, effectively reducing the number of injectors using heroin exclusively. However, the availability of cheaper synthetic opiates and analgesics suggests that although the drug of choice may have changed, the behavior contributing to and inducing injection of drugs has not (Sarkar et al., 1993). Most important, perhaps, is the latest trend in Manipur, the increase in the use of alcohol. The increased sex drive associated with alcohol as compared with the sexually repressive characteristics of heroin bodes ill in a land where condom use is almost nonexistent (Sarkar, 1993).

Although drug use has been noted as a problem in India, there is little doubt that HIV/AIDS has brought worldwide attention, especially to Manipur. The impact of drug use—not only the injecting practices, but also the effect of drugs on unsafe sexual practices—has led to increasing risk of HIV transmission. It is, therefore, both important and informative to address HIV/AIDS in Manipur within the context of AIDS in the rest of India and the world.

The Ever-Widening Circle of HIV/AIDS:
India and the Case of Manipur

HIV/AIDS was late coming to India and the rest of Asia. In the mid-to late 1970s, epidemiological and laboratory data indicated the presence of the AIDS virus in human populations (Piot et al., 1988). By the mid-1980s, the virus had spread extensively throughout Africa south of the Sahara, Europe, the United States, Canada, and Oceana to several Caribbean and Latin American countries. Few cases of HIV/AIDS were noted in South and East Asian countries, leading to the speculation that the disease would not reach the epidemic proportions it had reached elsewhere. However, since the late 1980s, the eruption of AIDS in several Asian countries has shaken the complacency with which governmental and health officials have viewed the potentially devastating impact of the disease (Chin, 1995).

By 1994, the Global AIDS Policy Coalition estimated that of the worldwide 22.2 million people infected with the AIDS virus, some 14% resided in South and East Asian countries (Chin, 1995). Moreover, the epidemic has grown more rapidly here than in any other region of the world (Chin, 1995) and is expected to continue to grow until approximately the year 2010, when rates of infection are assumed to begin leveling off. Chin (1995) estimated that cumulative HIV infections in Asia will reach 10 million by the year 2000 and more than 18 million by the year 2010.

The impact of such estimates for AIDS cases is especially ominous for the nation of India: the most densely populated country in Asia, the second most populous country in the world with an estimated population of some 880 million in 1993, and a country expected to be more populous than even China by the beginning of the next century (Jain, John, & Keusch, 1994). By early 1992, an estimated 300,000 to 500,000 Indian men and women were HIV-positive (Thant, 1993). By mid-1994, the figures had risen to 1 million (Chin, 1995). The World Health Organization estimated in 1993 that over the past 8 years, 1.8 million people had become infected with the HIV virus (Burton et al., 1995). The common thread running throughout these different estimates is the rapid increase in the numbers of HIV positive individuals since the virus was first detected in Bombay in 1986 (Narain et al., 1994).

In the Western world, and the United States in particular, the onset and early transmission of the AIDS virus was associated with the homosexual community and, some time later, the injecting drug user community. In India, however, from the onset, the transmission of the virus has been heterosexual, with the exception of the northeastern part of the country, most notably the states of Manipur, Nagaland, and Misoram, where injection drug use has been the predominant mode of transmission.

Sexual Behavior and the HIV Virus

In 1986, the first cases of HIV infection reported in India were found among commercial sex workers (CSWs) in Madras (Bollinger, Tripathy, & Quinn, 1995). Certainly, CSWs are a major vector for the transmission of the virus, perhaps especially in the case of truck drivers who frequent CSWs, do not regularly use condoms, and spread the disease along their travel routes throughout the country (Amed, 1993). However, a more important vector may be presented by the sex partners of Manipuri injecting drug users. From 50% to 70% of Manipuri male injecting drug users have reported engaging in sexual intercourse (Sarkar et al., 1993). Forty percent reported having had multiple sex partners (Delhi Science Office, 1994), with three being the median number (Sarkar et al., 1993). However, only 3% to 5% of the injectors reported using a condom (Sarkar et al., 1993). A screening of the injectors' female sex partners in 1991 indicated that 6% were HIV positive. In addition, a study conducted by the Manipur Voluntary Health Association of India in 1992 found that over 30% of the married male and female injectors had engaged in extramarital sex. Less than 2% (1.7%) had used condoms.

Drugs and HIV, as noted above, are currently presenting dual epidemics in India. Indeed, India is an important crossroads for the international trafficking of narcotics. Located between the illegal-opium-producing Golden Crescent region to the west and the Golden Triangle region to the east, India itself produces legal opium for pharmaceutical use more so than any other nation in the world. The government regulated outlet for licensed opium addicts in cities has been abolished for the last two decades. Substitution treatment by methadone, morphine, or opium has not been initiated. The legal drive against traditional small scale production of opium and cannabis, the banning of alcohol in the states of Mizoram, Nagaland, and Manipur, coupled with the ready availability of cheap heroin has made it the drug of choice among youth.

More importantly, Manipur, in particular, serves as a conduit for the trafficking of drugs from Myanmar (Burma) to other northeastern states. Unlike other areas of India, where heroin base (or brown heroin) is most prevalent, in Manipur injection of pure heroin shipped in from Burma is practiced (INM, 1995).

HIV Seroprevalence in Manipur, India

India first introduced HIV testing in 1985, with serosurveillance beginning in Manipur in 1986. Three hundred and seventy-one people were tested for the HIV virus, with no seropositives found. It was not until October 1989, when 828 Manipuri underwent testing, that the initial case of seropositivity was documented. Manipur's first documented person with AIDS was a 39-year-old businessman engaged in smuggling who was both injecting drugs and sexually promiscuous (Pal et al., 1990). However, in June 1990, when 1,564 injecting drug users were tested, 853 (54.5%) were found to be HIV-positive (Pal et al., 1990). Since then, the HIV epidemic among injectors has exploded, with seropositivity rising to over 64% by 1993 (Jain et al., 1994) and 89% by 1994 (ICMR, 1995).

Through March 1994, 17,253 citizens had been screened, with 2,347 identified as seropositive. Although Manipur's population was less than 0.2% of India's population at the time, the state was responsible for 18% of India's total cases of HIV seropositives.

By June 30, 1994, 32,395 citizens had been screened, with 3,247 found to be HIV-positive, a seropositivity rate of 99.92 per 1000 (Delhi Science Office, 1994). On the basis of the June 30 data, of the 3,237 people found to be HIV-positive, 83% were injecting drug users, and the next largest percentage, 7.6%, were HIV-infected blood donors. Of those who tested positive, 68% were ages 21 to 30, with 21% between the ages of 11 and 20 and 10% between the ages of 31 and 40 (Delhi Science Office, 1994).

With the concomitant emergence of the drug and HIV epidemics have come reports indicating a very rapid onset of infection with quick progression to AIDS and to death (ICMR Unit for Research on AIDS, 1995). This is particularly evident among Manipuri youth, many of whom have died at an early age. Such a rapid progression from injection to infection to disease to mortality raises grave concerns and questions about the characteristics of the virus, susceptibility within the population, and the need to respond more quickly to the epidemic. These concerns may be illustrated by a case study of a 17-year-old Manipuri youth.

Sketch of a Drug User

This young man was among the first group of HIV-infected drug users found during the fourth year of HIV surveillance by state health officials. A drug abuser since he was 12, he began injecting at age 13. As an employee in the family transportation business, he traveled frequently throughout Manipur and neighboring states, sharing his injecting equipment with friends and other drug users along his routes. He married at 15 and became a father the same year. His injection equipment, the ever popular ink dropper fitted with a syringe, was never cleaned, never disinfected. Although, like many others, he knew about how the AIDS virus could be transmitted, he had never heard about the use of bleach as a disinfectant and was never visited or contacted by public health or medical officials until he was HIV-positive. After repeated difficulties because of his drug use, his wife left him and his parents had him arrested and put into prison, a quite common method for detoxification in the absence of public and private inpatient detoxification centers. Two years after his release, at the age of 17, he died from an overdose of heroin.

The case study demonstrates the inability of Manipuri society similar to other developing regions in the world to respond to drug abuse and its attendant problems in a timely manner. From the first discovery of HIV in 1989 through June 1994, 3,237 individuals, largely Manipuri drug-injecting youth between the ages of 21 and 30, have become HIV-positive. In light of these and other such statistics, Manipuri as well as other Indian medical and public health officials have undertaken a series of steps to combat the AIDS epidemic.

Societal Responses to Drug Use and HIV

The spread of drug use and the AIDS virus is linked inextricably to sociocultural and economic factors. Poverty, coupled with illiteracy and inaccessibility to education and health services, creates and perpetuates myths and misconceptions about the virus and the means to contain it.

Behavioral modifications, so difficult to institute and promote in developed nations, are even more difficult to implement in developing nations (Jain et al., 1994).

Through public education, the risks of drug use and the HIV virus are gradually being introduced throughout India. With a literacy rate estimated to be 50% to 60% of the population and low accessibility to mass media, particularly in rural areas, introduction to drug use and AIDS awareness is only slowly making progress. However, because of the rapid increase of HIV seropositivity among injecting drug users in the north eastern states, particularly Manipur, efforts to eradicate injection drug use and prevent the transmission of the virus through other vectors, most notably the sexual partners of injecting drug users, have been given accelerated attention.

As noted earlier in this chapter, the first community-based survey on drug use was conducted by the Indian Medical Association, Manipur Branch, in 1988. Others soon followed (Delhi Science Office, 1994; Pal et al., 1990; Sarkar et al., 1991; Sarkar et al., 1993). Data from these surveys produced not only startling figures on HIV prevalence but also a clearer understanding of factors contributing to injection drug use and a more detailed and accurate profile of injecting drug users. Such information is essential for the development of programs to educate injecting drug users to the dangers of high-risk behaviors that promote the AIDS epidemic.

Drug Use Among Youth

Drawn to drug use by pleasure, curiosity, and/or peer pressure (Delhi Science Office, 1994) coupled with a cheap, ready supply, Manipuri youth have supported their habits by employment and/or family resources. The Delhi Science Office (1994) reported that 53% of injecting drug users are employed—perhaps not a surprising figure given that 78.5% are able to read up to high school and college levels. Nevertheless, relentless efforts on the part of governmental agencies to reduce the flow of heroin have driven the price of drugs upward, forcing even employed addicts to switch to a cheaper drug or to rely extensively on family members as a source of drug money. Sehgal and Singh (1992), in a study of some 498 injectors, found that 81% relied on family members fully or in part for the money to buy drugs. Selling drugs, stealing, borrowing, and the like are also sources for financing drug habits.

When the economic and social pressures become too great for the family to bear, addicts are frequently sent to prison for "detox" because of the unavailability of in-house drug treatment centers (Sarkar et al., 1993). With only one 30-bed detoxification center and four psychiatrists to deal with the addiction problem and few nongovernmental detoxification centers, especially with scientific programs and trained staff, jails and prisons have become the alternative (Pal et al., 1990; Sarkar et al., 1993). One 1990 study found that half of the injecting drug users sampled had been in prison at least once and that at least half had been sent by family members (Sarkar et al., 1993). The central jail in Manipur is often filled to capacity by injecting drug users either sent by families or arrested by police (Pal et al., 1990).

The prescription for detoxification in jail and prison cells is complete abstinence from drugs (i.e., "cold turkey"). Addicts are expected to detox without the aid of methadone or other such help. Furthermore, counseling of good quality is nonexistent (Sarkar et al., 1993). Not surprisingly, perhaps, only 2% of the some 298 imprisoned drug users interviewed wished to refrain from further addiction because of their imprisonment (Sarkar et al, 1993).

Coupled with the use of virus-infected injection equipment in the spread of AIDS in Manipur are unsafe sexual practices, no doubt also stimulated by current drug use. Long the most important vector for the transmission of AIDS in India, heterosexual transmission of the virus due to the failure to use condoms has rapidly spread the disease to sex partners of injecting drug users and beyond, into the general population. Sarkar et al. (1991) found that of 450 HIV addicts, 237 had had sexual experiences, and that of these, 162 had had only one partner. In 1993, Sarkar et al. reported that 50% to 70% of injectors had had sexual experiences. During the previous 5 years, the median number of sexual partners had been three. Only 3% to 5% of injecting drug users reported ever using condoms, which are generally unpopular among the population.

The propensity for drug use and unprotected sex among Manipuri youth might be thought of as functions of a lack of formal education generally and a lack of AIDS awareness specifically. However, as stated previously, Manipuri youth are largely literate, with nearly 80% reading up to high school or preuniversity level (Sarkar et al., 1991).

Sarkar et al. (1993) found that of 450 injecting drug users, 366 (81%) knew the name of the disease (AIDS) and that out of these, 338 (75%) and 315 (70%) respectively knew that needle sharing and having multiple sex partners could transmit the disease. That injecting drug users are more knowledgeable about HIV/AIDS is underscored by the finding that in a control group of 110 college students from Imphal, the capital of Manipur, a test on knowledge about the disease yielded scores lower than those of injecting drug users (Sarkar et al., 1991). Furthermore, the Delhi Science Office (1994) reported that 93% of injecting drug users wished to stop sharing injection equipment and that 95% of addicts wanted to go off drugs.

Why, then, the alarming growth in injection drug use, especially when it appears that so many (93%) want to stop sharing injection equipment and (95%) stop drug injection all together? One clue may be provided by a Knowledge, Attitudes, and Practices (KAP) study conducted in 1992 (Sehgal & Singh, 1992). Of 500 injectors, only a few obtained counseling, and a follow-up study of nearly 100 injectors who received counseling revealed no behavior modification. Because rehabilitation facilities are lacking, because available counseling are ill equipped to deal with practices in which relapse is very high (drug addiction) or utilization very low (condom usage), because funding is scarce, and because sociocultural factors inhibit the transmission and utilization of risk reduction behaviors, support from the international community will be necessary for the establishment of community-based intervention programs.

Community-Based Intervention Programs

Despite the obstacles to reducing drug use and the transmission of HIV, community-based intervention projects must be made available, accessible, and acceptable to the general public as well as to injecting drug users. Whether or not injection drug use increases, AIDS will continue to spread through heterosexual relationships, particularly the sexual partners of injection drug users. Consequently community-based interventions must focus on a wide audience, providing information and education on risk-reducing behaviors and most notably educating injecting drug users to stop sharing injection equipment, drugs, and other paraphernalia and to use condoms when engaging in sex.

Funded by international agencies, community-based intervention programs have been recently established in Manipur in the cities of Imphal and Churachandpur. In Churachandpur, where intervention is based on the behavioral change model, former injecting drug users disseminate risk reduction messages and educational materials along with condoms and bleach kits.

Drop-in centers have also been established for injecting drug users and their sexual partners to visit and acquire information as well as bleach kits and condoms. Some 600 injectors regularly ask for bleach. Nevertheless, poor follow-up, inadequate support services, and absence of rehabilitation centers, along with virtually no linkages to the few available community-based intervention programs, make it a daunting challenge to counter the increasing spread of the intersecting epidemics of drug use, sexual activity, and HIV/AIDS in Manipur, India. How many other international communities will have to face these dire social and health conditions fueled by drug use before enduring resolve and appropriate resources are made available?

References

Amed, S. I. (1993, June). *Truck drivers as a vulnerable group in North East India.* Abstract (PO-CO8-27737) presented at the 9th International Conference on AIDS, Berlin, Germany, June 6-11.

Bollinger, R. C., Tripathy, S. P., & Quinn, T. C. (1995). The human immunodeficiency virus epidemic in India. *Medicine, 74*(2), 97-106.

Burton, A., Mertens, T., & Shiv, L. (1994). Estimation of adult HIV prevalence in India by the end of 1994. *Indian Journal of Public Health, 39*(3), 3-8.

Chin, J. (1995). *Scenarios for the AIDS epidemic in Asia.* Asia-Pacific Population Research Reports No. 2, East-West Centre Programme on Population Media, University of Hawaii, Hawaiian Islands.

Indian Council of Medical Research (ICMR) Unit for Research on AIDS for North Eastern States of India. (1995). *Project Report 1992-1995.* DL-172, Salt Lake, Calcutta-91, India.

INM Department of State. (1995). *India.* New Delhi: INCSR.

Jain, M. K., John, T. J., & Keusch, G. T. (1994). Epidemiology of HIV and AIDS in India. *AIDS, 8*(2), S61-S75.

McCoy, C. B., & Inciardi, J. A. (1995). *Sex, drugs, and the continuing spread of AIDS.* Los Angeles: Roxbury.

Narain, J. P., Jha, A., Shiv, L., & Subhash, S. (1994). Risk factors for HIV transmission in India. *AIDS, 8*(2), S77-S82.

Pal, S. C., Sarkar, S., Naik, T. N., Singh, P. K., Tushiao, S. I., Shiv, L., & Tripathy, S. P. (1990). *Explosive epidemic of HIV infection in North Eastern State of Manipur and Nagaland.* Center for AIDS Research, Indian Council of Medical Research, 3(3), 1-6.

Piot, P., Plummer, F. A., Mhalu, F. S., Lamboray, J., Chin, J., & Mann, J. M. (1988). AIDS: An international perspective. *Science, 239,* 573-579.

Sarkar, S., Das, N., Panda, S., Naik, T. N., Sarkar, K., Singh, B. C., Ralte, J. M., Aier, J. M., & Tripathy, S. P. (1993). Rapid spread of HIV among injecting drug users in north eastern states of India. *Bulletin on Narcotics, 45*(11), 91-105.

Sarkar, S., Mukherjee, P., & Roy, A. (1991). Descriptive epidemiology of intravenous heroin users: A new risk group for transmission of HIV in India. *Journal of Infection, 23,* 201-207.

Sehgal, S., & Singh, K. (1992). *Knowledge, attitudes, beliefs, and practices: KABP study related to AIDS in Manipur State, India and intervention strategies.* Manipur, India: Voluntary Health Association of India.

Sharma, S. G. (1984). *Analysis of 300 drug users at Manipur.* Paper presented at the Indian Psychiatric Society Annual Conference, Raneh, India, January 11-13.

Tellis, E. (1995, April). *Identification of potential areas for enhanced behavioral research in India.* Paper presented at the Indo-United States Workshop for Behavioral Research Priorities, Bombay, India.

Thant, M. (1993). The economic implications of AIDS in Southeast Asia: Equity considerations. In D. Bloom & J. V. Lyons (Eds.), *Economic implications of AIDS in Asia.* New Delhi, India: United Nations Development Programme.

Index

National Federation of Parents for
    Drug-Free Youth, 93
National Household Survey on Drug Abuse
    (NHSDA), 7-8, 11, 14
National Institute of Justice (NIJ), 134
National Institute on Drug Abuse (NIDA), 8,
    156
National Movement for Street Children, 187
National surveys of drug use:
    MTF (1975-1995), 8-12, 14-19
    NHSDA (1994), 7-8, 11, 14
    1960s-1970s, 4-5
National Youth Survey Delinquency Scale,
    140
Nation of Islam, 119
Native Americans, 159
Nebraska drug-free youth networks, 94
Needle sharing, 194, 198, 201
Needs assessment, 144-147
Neighborhood environment, 24
Newcomb, M. D., 126
NHSDA, 7-8, 11, 14
Norcross, J. C., 56

Observational learning, 54
Office of National Drug Control Policy
    (ONDCP), 103
Ohlin, L. E., xiii
O'Malley, P. M., 10
Opium, viii-x, xi, 196
Orlandi, M. A., 81-96
Outcome expectations, 54
Outputs, in preadult health decision-making
    model, 63, 66-67

Pain, repressed, 165
Pakistan, 25
Parental drug use, 25, 35, 160
Parental marital relationship, 25
Parental monitoring, 27, 36
Parent-child relationships, xii, 26-27, 29-30,
    32-34, 40
Parent groups, 92-94
Parents, DARE program popularity with,
    105-106
Parents' Movement, 92
Peer-directed individuals, 63

Peer influences, 28, 34, 47-48, 63
Peer leaders, as program facilitators, 86,
    89-91
Peer teaching, 90
Pentz, M. A., 95
Personal Experience Inventory (PEI), 140
Personality characteristics, 28-30, 32-34
    predispositions to drug use, xii
    protective factors, 36
    See also Psychosocial development
Personality theories, 49-51
Personal skills training, 87-88
Phoenix, River, 18
Pioneer Ranch, 160
Police officers, DARE program and, 102,
    105
Police vigilante organizations, 184
Political issues, 149-150
POSIT, 139-140
Pottieger, A. E., 3-21
Poverty line, 159
Preadult Health Decision-Making Model
    (PAHDM), 45-46, 61-70
    directedness component, 62-64
    empirical verification, 64, 67
    inputs, 63, 64-66, 70
    intervention planning, 67-70
    outputs, 63, 66-67
Preble, E., xiii
Predictive factors:
    health belief model, 55
    prior behavior, 37, 57-58
Pregnancy and drug/alcohol use, 35
Prevention and intervention, 81-96
    affective education, 83
    Ajzen-Fishbein model, 57
    Brazilian street children and, 185-187
    community-based approaches, 92-95,
        201-202
    corporate sponsors, 104
    DARE, 101-108
    demand reduction strategy, 18
    effectiveness of. See Effectiveness of
        interventions
    ethnicity/race considerations, 126
    etiologic findings and, 40-41
    fear-based approaches, 55, 59, 83, 84, 124
    information education, 20-21, 82, 84. See
        also Education

About the Authors

ABU S. ADBUL-QUADER is a social scientist with the World Health Organization (WHO) studying issues related to HIV/AIDS prevention among injecting drug users and their sexual partners in developing countries. He has been working in the field of HIV/AIDS prevention for more than 10 years. Before joining WHO in 1993, he worked in New York City conducting HIV/AIDS intervention research targeting injecting drug users and women. He received his doctorate in sociology from the Maxwell School of Citizenship and Public Affairs, Syracuse University, Syracuse, New York.

ROBERT S. ANWYL is Professor of Sociology and Peter Masiko Jr. Endowed Teaching Chair in the Department of Behavioral Studies at Miami Dade Community College (North Campus), Florida, and has an adjunct appointment with the Comprehensive Drug Research Center at the University of Miami School of Medicine. His research interests and many publications are in the areas of epidemiology of drug abuse, AIDS, and cancer. He completed his graduate work at Florida State University.

NAYA ARBITER is a Principal in Extensions LLC, a Tucson, Arizona-based management consulting organization providing support for social service organizations. She is the cofounder and Chair of the Amity Foundation of California. She has been an international leader in modifying treatment programs, particularly therapeutic communities, to provide appropriate therapeutic environments for women and for mothers with children. She has also written over 50 volumes of curriculum for therapeutic community programs. She was the keynote speaker recently at the Congress on Drug Abuse at the invitation of the President of Argentina.

DAVID W. BROOK is Professor of Community Medicine at the Mount Sinai School of Medicine. A graduate of the Yale University School of Medicine, he interned at the University of Chicago Hospitals and completed his residency in psychiatry at Mount Sinai. He is board certified in psychiatry. He has served as the Principal Investigator or Co-Principal Investigator on several grants funded by the National Institute on Drug Abuse in the areas of the epidemiology of AIDS and drug abuse. He is the author or coauthor of numerous professional publications, and he is on the Editorial Board of the *International Journal of Group Psychotherapy.*

JUDITH S. BROOK is Professor of Community Medicine at the Mount Sinai School of Medicine. She received the first Dean's Distinguished Research Award from New York Medical College in 1992. She is the recipient of a Research Scientist Award from the National Institute on Drug Abuse (NIDA). She is the Principal Investigator or Co-Principal Investigator on several grants supported by NIDA and the National Institute of Mental Health in the areas of epidemiology and prevention research. She has published over 100 research papers and is the coauthor of *The Psychology of Adolescence.*

ANNE CATTARELLO is Assistant Professor of Sociology in the Department of Sociology and Anthropology at the University of Wisconsin–Eau Claire. She served as the study director for the Lexington D.A.R.E. evaluation and has also conducted research in the areas of HIV prevention and neighborhood effects on delinquency and drug use. She received her Ph.D. in Sociology from the University of Kentucky.

ANINDYA CHATTERJEE, a medical psychiatrist, is the Senior Research Officer of the Indian Council of Medical Research under the Ministry of

Health of the Government of India. His work includes psychological and social behavioral aspects of drug abuse.

DALE D. CHITWOOD is Professor of Medical Sociology in the Department of Sociology, holds adjunct appointments in the Department of Psychiatry and the Department of Epidemiology and Public Health, and is a member of the Comprehensive Drug Research Center at the University of Miami, Florida. His research interests include the epidemiology of drug abuse, HIV/AIDS, evaluation, and health services research.

RICHARD R. CLAYTON is Professor of Sociology and Director of the Center for Prevention Research at the University of Kentucky. He has been involved in drug abuse research since the early 1970s and has published a number of books and articles on various aspects of the drug abuse phenomenon.

RICHARD DEMBO is a Professor of Criminology at the University of South Florida in Tampa. He has conducted extensive research on the relationship between drug use and delinquency; has published over 120 articles, books, book chapters, and reports in the fields of criminology, substance abuse, mental health, and program evaluation; and has guest-edited several special issues of journals addressing the problem of drug abuse. He is currently working on a 5-year experimental, longitudinal service delivery project, funded by the National Institute on Drug Abuse, that is designed to implement and test a family empowerment intervention involving high-risk youth and their families, and he is responsible for the research component of the Hillsborough County Juvenile Assessment Center in Tampa. He received his Ph.D. in sociology from New York University.

NANCY GRANT HARRINGTON is Assistant Professor in the Department of Communications and Deputy Scientific Director of the Center for Prevention Research, University of Kentucky. Her research interests include substance abuse prevention, pregnancy prevention, health promotion, and interpersonal and health communication in social influence processes. She is a member of the Society for Prevention Research and serves on the Board of Directors of the Kentucky Coalition on Teenage Pregnancy. She received her Ph.D. in communications from the University of Kentucky.

LANA D. HARRISON is the Associate Director and a Senior Scientist with the Center for Drug and Alcohol Studies at the University of Delaware. She is currently the Co-Principal Investigator of a study on the efficacy of female condoms for women at high risk of HIV and a Co-Principal Investigator on an ongoing study of treatment for high-risk drug users. Formerly, she was a researcher with the National Institute on Drug Abuse and the National Institute of Justice. She has worked on the three largest epidemiological drug surveys in the United States—the National Household Survey on Drug Abuse, the Monitoring the Future survey, and the Drug Use Forecasting study. Her research interests center on drug epidemiology, treatment alternatives, improving survey methodology, comparative international research, and drug policy. She has numerous publications and presentations in these areas. She received her Ph.D. from the University of Michigan.

JAMES A. INCIARDI is Director of the Center for Drug and Alcohol Studies at the University of Delaware, a Professor in the Department of Sociology and Criminal Justice at the University of Delaware, an Adjunct Professor in the Department of Epidemiology and Public Health at the University of Miami School of Medicine, a Distinguished Professor at the State University of Rio de Janeiro, and a member of the South Florida AIDS Research Consortium. He has done extensive research and consulting both nationally and internationally and has published more than 40 books and 200 articles and chapters in the areas of substance abuse, history, folklore, criminology, AIDS, public policy, medicine, and law.

LILLY M. LANGER is Associate Professor of Medical Sociology, Department of Sociology and Anthropology, Florida International University. She is the Principal Investigator of a grant funded through the National Institute of Alcohol Abuse and Alcoholism that focuses on adolescents, substance abuse, and AIDS. In addition, she is a member of the Comprehensive Drug Research Center at the University of Miami School of Medicine.

CARL G. LEUKEFELD is Professor of Psychiatry and Behavioral Science, the Director of the Drug and Alcohol Research Center, and an affiliate of the Center for Prevention Research at the University of Kentucky. He was a Commissioned Officer in the U.S. Public Health Service assigned to the National Institute on Drug Abuse in various clinical, management, and scientific capacities. He has given numerous presentations and published on treatment, criminal justice, prevention, and AIDS. He received his doctorate in social work from the Catholic University of America.

DUANE C. MCBRIDE is a Senior Investigator with over 20 years' experience in drug abuse research. He is currently Professor and Chair of the Behavioral Sciences Department at Andrews University in Berrien Springs, Michigan, and Director of Research at the Institute for the Prevention of Addictions. In addition, he is also an Adjunct Professor of Epidemiology and Public Health at the University of Miami School of Medicine in Miami, Florida. Most of his research has focused on drug use epidemiology, the correlates of HIV risk behavior and serostatus, drug treatment evaluation, and the drugs-crime relationship. He has authored over 60 articles, chapters, monographs, or books in these areas. His most recent publications have focused on treatment barriers for women, the crack-crime relationship, the courts and drug abuse treatment and the correlates of HIV risk behavior. He is currently involved in a number of National Institute on Drug Abuse research projects including serving as the Co-Principal Investigator of a Health Services Research Center at the University of Miami. He received his Ph.D. in sociology from the University of Kentucky.

CLYDE B. MCCOY is Director of the Comprehensive Drug Research Center and Health Services Research Center, a federally funded center designated by the National Institute on Drug Abuse. He is also Professor of Epidemiology and Public Health at the University of Miami School of Medicine. He has had continuous federal funding for his research for more than 20 years and has served as Principal Investigator or Co-Principal Investigator on numerous studies. He currently is conducting both national and international research projects. His research interests include epidemiology, drug abuse, demography, HIV/AIDS prevention among drug users, and cancer prevention. He has more than 200 publications in these areas. He is a graduate of the University of Cincinnati and a recipient of the distinguished alumni award.

LISA R. METSCH is Research Assistant Professor in the Department of Epidemiology and Public Health and Assistant Director of HIV Studies of the Comprehensive Drug Research Center at the University of Miami School of Medicine. She is Project Director of three studies that evaluate HIV risk reduction intervention programs and she is Principal Investigator on two evaluation studies on women and children in drug treatment. Her research interests center on HIV/AIDS prevention and intervention, women who use drugs, and the children of those women. She is a graduate of the University of Florida, Columbia University, and the List College of the Jewish Theological Seminary of America, where she currently serves as one of the youngest members of the Board of Overseers.

ROD MULLEN is the cofounder and President of the Amity Foundation of California, an organization for research on the root causes of substance abuse and other related behaviors, the development of demonstration projects, and the dissemination of results through training, curriculum development, and publications. In the past 28 years, he has focused on the development of interventions based on the therapeutic community model, including numerous innovative projects for addicted mothers, children of addicts, incarcerated substance abusers (both adolescents and adults), prostitutes, gang members, and those at high risk of HIV infection. In addition to providing support to organizations involved in behavioral change, he has written numerous articles and spoken nationally and internationally about the development of holistic interventions and intentional communities to combat social deterioration.

BRIDGET MURPHY has worked as a drug abuse treatment provider and program evaluator for the past 9 years. She worked as a Counselor Supervisor at the Amity Las Rosas program, a therapeutic community for drug-involved adolescent girls. In 1993, she became the Project Evaluator for all adolescent treatment services at Amity. Currently, she is the Evaluation Coordinator for the National Development Research Institute's Desert Willow program. Desert Willow is a research demonstration grant for drug-addicted women and their children funded by the Center for Substance Abuse Treatment.

PATRICIA B. MUTCH received her Ph.D. from the University of California, Davis. She has over 10 years' experience in substance abuse education, prevention, and research. She currently serves as Dean of the College of Arts and Sciences at Andrews University. Her previous position was Director of the Institute for the Prevention of Addictions at Andrews University. Her research interests and publications have focused on substance abuse among women, needs assessments, the prevention of substance abuse, and nutrition.

MARIO A. ORLANDI was trained in clinical psychology and public health at Duke University and Harvard University. Following an academic appointment at Harvard, he accepted his current position as Chief, Division of Health Promotion Research at the American Health Foundation. In this capacity, he has supervised the development and evaluation of a wide variety of health promotion innovations for all age groups and for settings ranging from schools and worksites to entire communities. He also holds an appointment at Columbia University Teachers College as an Adjunct Professor. He serves as technical advisor to many local, state, and federal health agencies and is active in a number of international collaborative studies. He is a contributing editor of a number of peer-reviewed professional journals and is Series Editor of the Center for Substance Abuse Prevention (CSAP) monograph series Cultural Competence in Program Evaluation.

ANNE E. POTTIEGER is Scientist with the Center for Drug and Alcohol Studies at the University of Delaware, where she is currently Principal Investigator and Project Director of a research study, funded by the National Institute on Drug Abuse, entitled "Barriers to Treatment for Cocaine-Dependent Women." She has done sociological research on substance abuse for over 20 years. Her publications are in the areas of drug-crime relationships, substance abuse patterns and problems, and criminological theory. She received her Ph.D. in sociology from the University of Delaware.

JAMES E. RIVERS is Deputy Director of the Comprehensive Drug Research Center and an Associate Professor in the Department of Epidemiology and Public Health at the University of Miami School of Medicine. His 21 years in the substance abuse field include experience in program evaluation, survey research, information systems, and community epidemiology. He also helped establish one of the first local "Drug Czar" offices (in Miami, Florida) and helped to form the Miami Coalition for a Drug Free Community. He is an innovator in the use of substance abuse indicator databases and geographic information systems in community sampling, services needs assessments, and program outcome evaluation applications. He received his Ph.D. in sociology from the University of Kentucky.

SWARUP SARKAR, a medical epidemiologist, is Assistant Director of the Indian Council of Medical Research under the Ministry of Health of the Government of India. His research concentrates on interests in drug-related HIV in India, epidemiology, program evaluation, molecular epidemiology, and behavioral changes among drug users.

SALLY J. STEVENS is Associate Research Professor at the University of Arizona, Southwest Institute for Research on Women. She has worked in the addictions field for 11 years as a clinician and a researcher. She has been the Principal Investigator of several federally funded research grants, including (a) HIV prevention for drug users and their sexual partners, (b) homelessness and substance abuse treatment, and (c) substance abuse treatment for addicted women and their children. She has published numerous articles in clinical and research journals on HIV prevention, drug use, and drug treatment for special populations, including those who are homeless or incarcerated, women with children, and adolescents.

HILARY L. SURRATT is Research Associate in the Comprehensive Drug Research Center at the University of Miami School of Medicine and is Project Director of an AIDS seroprevalence and prevention study in Rio De Janeiro, Brazil, funded by the National Institute on Drug Abuse. She received her M.A. from the University of Florida and has published in the areas of AIDS, substance abuse, and drug policy.